LRUZ

CIRCULATION

THE
ROOTES
BROTHERS

Patrick Stephens Limited, a member of the Haynes Publishing Group, has published authoritative, quality books for enthusiasts for more than 25 years. During that time the company has established a reputation as one of the world's leading publishers of books on aviation, maritime, military, model-making, motor cycling, motoring, motor racing, railway and railway modelling subjects. Readers or authors with suggestions for books they would like to see published are invited to write to The Editorial Director, Patrick Stephens Limited, Sparkford, Nr. Yeovil, Somerset BA22 7JJ.

THE
ROOTES
BROTHERS

STORY OF A MOTORING EMPIRE

JOHN BULLOCK

Patrick Stephens Limited

© John Bullock, 1993

First published in 1993

British Library Cataloguing-in-Publication Data:
A catalogue record for this book is available from the British Library

ISBN 1 85260 454 9

Library of Congress catalog card number 93 79168

Patrick Stephens Ltd is an imprint
of Haynes Publishing, Sparkford,
Nr Yeovil, Somerset BA22 7JJ.

Typeset by BPCC Techset Ltd, Exeter

Printed in Great Britain by Butler & Tanner Ltd of London and Frome.

Contents

Introduction

BILLY AND REGGIE Rootes were born at a time when the motor car was looked upon with suspicion and subjected to a 4 mph speed limit. A man with a red flag had to walk ahead to warn other road users of its approach. Even so, men of vision, including their father William Rootes, were already seeing the motor car as a means of revolutionizing travel and knew that the time would come when everyone would want one and the independence it would provide for whole families to travel freely. To them, the motor car represented a challenge and they were encouraged by the fact that although pioneer motorists in Britain were being persecuted by a short-sighted Government, on the Continent road races were already taking place. In America, before the turn of the century, a young engineer called Henry Ford had also built and sold his first car.

By 1904 William Rootes not only owned a car which he used to take his family motoring in the Kent countryside, but he also sold and repaired cars and had one of the country's first car hire businesses. Billy Rootes in particular was fascinated by the exciting noises and smells which came from the variety of machines that arrived at his father's workshop each week for delivery or repair. He was only 10 years old when he experienced the thrill of driving his father's New Orleans, which he had borrowed to take his brother for a spin. The journey ended in disaster but those few minutes behind the wheel only served to encourage him to want to know more about this revolutionary form of transport and the men who not only sold motor cars but also made them.

Billy, however, was a poor scholar and it was with some relief that his father was able to send him off to Coventry at the age of 15 to become a penny-an-hour apprentice with the Singer Motor Company. There the poor scholar became the star apprentice, able to take full advantage of the knowledge he had gained from his father's motor business. It was also a fortunate coincidence that the Singer company had just designed

Britain's first real light car, which would bring motoring within the reach of many thousands more families during the period leading up to the First World War.

He was still a teenager when he not only proved his ability to sell and a willingness to back his own judgement, but also showed an intense pride in Britain and her achievements which remained with him throughout his life. With war approaching, his first hand-written advertisement for the cars and commercial vehicles he was selling included the words, 'The task of us all is to keep the flag flying'. This display of patriotism and leadership enabled him to play a leading part in the development of the British motor industry during the next 50 years.

After serving in the Naval Air Service during the First World War, he formed Rootes Motors with his father and persuaded his brother Reggie to give up a promising career in the civil service to help create the most successful family partnership in the history of the motor industry. Reggie, the quiet and thoughtful administrator with the cool, calculating mind, was the perfect foil for Billy, the extrovert with unlimited energy and ideas. A man who always enjoyed a challenge and could never resist the chance of a deal, particularly if it involved selling British goods abroad, he once admitted: 'I don't mind what I sell, provided it is British'.

It was the Rootes brothers' remarkable partnership, with each brother providing essential attributes which the other lacked, that made them such a powerful force. Billy cheerfully agreed: 'I think up the ideas and then Reggie tells me whether they will work'. They were even the opposite in appearance. Reggie was tall, bespectacled and mild-mannered, while Billy, who was shorter and more rotund, had a bouncing stride made more distinguishable by a slight limp, a legacy from the time he spent racing motor cycles. Throughout the motor industry it was always acknowledged that Billy was the driving force while Reggie provided the brakes and steering. This combination made them the most respected voices in the British motor industry for nearly half a century.

Chapter 1

Early days

FEW PEOPLE BELIEVED Sir David Salomons, the pioneer motorist, when he predicted in 1895 that the motor car would revolutionize travel throughout the world, and that the time would come when England would become one of the chief centres of the motor industry. To support this claim he organized Britain's first motor show, on 15 October at the Agricultural Showground, Tunbridge Wells, in Kent. The show was only open for two hours in the afternoon, from three o'clock until five, and all the vehicles on view had been imported from the Continent. There wasn't one British-made car among them.

The reason for such public scepticism was easy to understand. Although the French and German Governments had been actively encouraging the development of the motor car, even to the extent of allowing road races to take place, the British Government was doing everything it could to discourage motoring by imposing speed limits and severe penalties on motorists who attempted to travel at more than the permitted 4 miles an hour. Many motorists felt that they were being treated like criminals in comparison with other road users, and the Government's insistence on every car having a crew of at least three people, one of whom had to walk 20 yards ahead carrying a red flag as a warning, in accordance with the Locomotive Act of 1865, made travelling by motor car even less pleasurable.

Support for Sir David's views came from a small band of enthusiasts, one of whom was William Rootes, a young man from the village of Goudhurst in Kent, where he had a successful general engineering and cycle business. He had cycled over to Tunbridge Wells to see the latest models from France and Germany and returned home determined to add a motor section to his own business as soon as possible.

The Rootes name was already well known in Kent, not only because of the bicycles they built and sold, at a time when cycling was all the rage, but also because of their remarkable musical ability. The Rootes Band, which William's father had formed in 1870, included his five sons

Edward, Jim, Caleb, Sam and William, and a number of the villagers from Goudhurst. It was looked upon as being one of the finest bands in the country.

Despite having lost the tips of some of his fingers in an accident with a chaff cutter, the youngest son William was an accomplished pianist, cornet player and composer. Another son, Caleb, was also well known for his hymns and sacred verse. After winning first prize at the music competition held at Eastwell Park near Ashford in 1872, the band was renamed the Royal Rootes Band when it received patronage from the Duke of Edinburgh. Later the same year the band achieved further publicity when it was chosen to perform before Queen Victoria on a visit to Aldershot to inspect her troops, who included the Weald of Kent Volunteers.

William Rootes had sufficient talent to have become a professional musician, but instead he chose to follow his father into the family cycle manufacturing and repair business at the age of 12, selling Penny Farthing cycles from their shop at Goudhurst. When he got married he opened his own cycle shop in the village with the £75 which he and his wife had saved and began building his own cycles in the small workshop at the rear of the premises.

The business flourished and he became an agent for many well-known makes, including Humber, the first bicycle fitted with the pneumatic tyres invented by Mr J. B. Dunlop. William's musical ability was still put to good use and he augmented the family's income by repairing musical instruments. His fame spread and a visitor walking into his cycle workshop could sometimes have been forgiven for thinking that his love of music was greater than his interest in cycles. The walls and work benches were usually littered with a variety of instruments in for repair and the bench drawers were stuffed with musical scores, many of them compositions which William was working on.

After his visit to the motor show at Tunbridge Wells, however, William Rootes became more interested in the development of the motor car and the growing number of different makes which were regular sights on the roads in Kent. When Mr H. J. Lawson organized a second motor show in 1896, this time in London at the Imperial Institute in South Kensington, William Rootes was there at the opening, along with Colonel J. A. Cole, chairman of the Humber Bicycle Company.

The show was given additional importance by a visit from the Prince of Wales, but the most encouraging development for the growing band of motoring enthusiasts was the British Government's decision that year to introduce a new Locomotion Act, which did away with the man with the red flag and raised the speed limit to 12 miles an hour. The relaxation of the speed limit was marked by an Emancipation Day Run from London to Brighton, an event which the Veteran Car Club still celebrates each year. There were 58 entries for the first run in 1896, but only 13 of them reached Brighton, an indication of the determination shown by pioneer motorists and the unreliability of those early vehicles. The new Act was, however, a considerable move forward and encouraged companies to invest money in designing and manufacturing motor cars, even though they were still regarded with the utmost suspicion by many members of the general public and motorists were continually being harrassed by fines and the general disapproval of the authorities.

One of the companies which decided to start building motor cars was the Humber Bicycle Company, later to be so closely involved with the fortunes of the Rootes family. After visiting the motor show at the Imperial Institute, the Humber chairman Colonel Cole became an enthusiastic motorist and was determined that his company should play an active part in the development of the British motor industry. He was a man of considerable energy and foresight and the discussions he had with William Rootes, who not only shared his views but was one of his company's most important customers, encouraged him to persuade the other members of the Humber board that they needed to produce a car of their own. Even so, it was three years before his fellow directors finally agreed and he was able to instruct his mechanics to start working on designs for the first Humber car. This was the $3\frac{1}{2}$ hp Humber Phaeton which eventually went on sale in 1900.

It was during this era of opportunity and change, when men of vision and determination were needed in Britain, that William's wife gave birth to two sons. Both were born at Goudhurst, William Edward Rootes on 17 August 1894 and his younger brother Reginald two years later on 20 October 1896. Both were educated at Cranbrook, then a minor public school in Kent, but whereas Reggie excelled at schoolwork and games, winning a scholarship and becoming head boy and captain of football, Billy was rather the opposite and a constant source of concern to his father and the headmaster. He was, however, very bright in other ways and shared his father's enthusiasm for motoring and saw the opportunities ahead.

The motor car appealed to Billy's strong sense of adventure and the constant challenge of the rather unreliable and noisy machinery only added to the excitement. The family's workshops seemed more like an Aladdin's cave. Exciting new vehicles were arriving there each week, either for delivery or repair. William Rootes had added a motor section to his successful general engineering works at Hawkhurst in 1897 and had become an agent for Napiers, Darracqs, de Dions, Panhards, Stars, Clements, Swifts, Argylls, Humbers, Vauxhalls, and the White Steam Car, all famous makes of the day. He was also running a successful car hire business, providing chauffeur-driven cars for 3 and 4 guineas a day, although 'driver's refreshments' were charged extra.

His workshop had been enlarged and fitted with an electric plant and lighting, to enable repairs to be dealt with more efficiently, and Rootes became the first business in Hawkhurst to have a telephone installed. William Rootes was very proud of his Hawkhurst 1 telephone number.

He was also keen to build a reputation for quality and reliability and every car leaving his workshop was overhauled and adjusted before being delivered. A competent mechanic was sent with each vehicle free of charge for one week in order to explain the workings of the car and to teach the new owner how to drive.

Although William Rootes wanted his first car to be a British-built Humber, he had been persuaded by his wife to buy the better-known single-cylinder, $2\frac{3}{4}$ hp New Orleans, which they had first seen in 1903 at the motor show held at Crystal Palace in London. This was the car which gave Billy and Reggie their first taste of motoring, when their father used it to take the family on weekend drives into the Kent countryside. It wasn't very reliable and the boys and their mother often spent several hours sitting by the roadside when it had broken down or the engine wouldn't start after a picnic. Punctures were a frequent problem and when the spare wheels which they carried with them had been used, William Rootes had to stuff the flat tyre with straw, which they got from a local farmer, to enable them to continue on to the nearest garage. The New Orleans did, however, provide Billy with his first experience behind the wheel when he was still a 10-year-old schoolboy.

William and his wife had gone to London by train, leaving the two boys in the charge of a maid. While she was upstairs dusting one of the bedrooms, Billy saw his opportunity. He persuaded his younger brother to help push the New Orleans out of the garage and into the drive, and while Reggie worked the throttle controls, Billy swung the starting handle in the way he had watched his father and the mechanics do on many occasions. When the engine eventually roared into life, he jumped up behind the wheel and, ignoring the shouts of the maid, drove off down the drive and along the lane.

Billy knew how to work the controls, having watched his father during their weekend runs into the country, and, opening up the throttle, he became thrilled by the sense of power the car gave him. He was far too excited to listen to his brother's pleas to slow down. As the lane began to go downhill, the car gathered speed, swaying from side to side until it was out of control. By the time Billy realized what had happened and tried to apply the brakes, it was too late. They mounted the grass verge in a vain attempt to negotiate the bend, both boys were thrown out and the car ended up in the ditch. Fortunately, little damage was done to the car and apart from some cuts and bruises the boys escaped injury. Some years later, when Billy and Reggie were creating their own motoring empire, their competitors often claimed that the incident with the New Orleans was the only occasion when the two Rootes brothers were seen to fall out together and when Billy failed to listen to his younger brother's sound advice.

Billy was certainly always the driving force, but he was quick to admit, 'It is Reggie who provides the essential steering and brakes'. It was, however, Billy's brilliance as an entrepreneur and a man of vision which made them such a remarkably successful team. They always remained close friends and decisions regarding the future of the companies under their control were always taken together. (Desmond and Leonard Rootes, two of William's five sons by his second wife, joined the company later.)

The early 1900s saw the development of motor cars from 'horseless carriages', aptly named because the first models were very similar in shape to horse-drawn carriages, to the stage when they began assuming identities of their own. Production began to increase and by the turn of the century a number of British companies were claiming to be building a minimum of six cars a week.

Chapter 2

The American influence

ACROSS THE ATLANTIC, the American motor industry was taking shape, and in Detroit it would not be long before Henry Ford established the Ford Motor Company, which was to have such a remarkable influence on car production and design throughout the world. For a long time, though, his 'gasoline buggy' was the first and only car in Detroit. It was considered something of a nuisance because the noises it made scared the horses.

Henry Ford was in constant trouble with the police, either through speeding or because of the traffic hold-ups he caused when crowds gathered round his car every time he parked. Whenever he left the car, he had to chain it to a lamp-post to prevent inquisitive bystanders from trying to start it up and drive it away. He was eventually awarded a special permit by the mayor which gave him the distinction of being the only licensed chauffeur in America.

He covered about 1,000 miles (1,609 km) in his gasoline buggy before selling it for $200 in 1896 to Charles Ainsley, another Detroit resident, and then he started work on a lighter version. Although the car had been built as an experiment, it provided him with his first sale. During the time that he was with the Detroit Edison Company, Henry Ford built three cars and also repurchased his original model from Charles Ainsley for $100. He left the Edison Company on 15 August 1899 after being offered the general superintendency of the company on condition that he 'stopped experimenting with petrol engines and devoted himself to doing something really useful'.

The American motor industry was rapidly developing into a business for speculators and when a group of investors formed the Detroit Automobile Company, with the intention of exploiting the motor car, they provided Henry Ford with a small amount of stock and appointed him chief engineer. The company produced a number of cars based on his earlier designs, but few were sold because the aim was always to get the highest possible price for each car, and there was no support for his suggestion that the company should start making cars which more members of the public could afford. After three years he realized that company policy was not going to change and on 2 March 1902 he resigned, determined never again to work for anyone else. The Detroit Automobile Company went on to become the Cadillac Car Company under the ownership of the Leland family.

During the period between building his first motor car and the formation of the Ford Motor Company, Henry Ford built 25 cars, 20 of which were made during his time with the Detroit Automobile Company. He started working on a new model in the little brick shed at the rear of 81 Park Place, which he and his wife had rented, and he had ample opportunity while they were there to develop his own ideas for mass production.

He needed financial help but the banks were only interested in the railroads. The public was only interested in speed and so in 1903, in order to gain recognition, with the help of Tom Cooper he designed and built two cars solely for speed. They were similar and both had large four-cylinder engines producing 80 hp, much more power than any previous engines had achieved. They were single-seaters and the roar of the engines was said to be quite frightening. When Henry drove the car they had named the '999' at full speed, he described the experience as being 'worse than going over Niagara Falls'. The other car, which was known as 'The Arrow', was no different.

They decided to employ Barney Oldfield, a professional racing cyclist, to drive the '999' in a race against Alexander Winton, who was the track champion of America and had challenged all comers to beat his Winton car. Although Barney Oldfield had never previously driven a car, he was known to be fearless and also had the strength needed for the two-handed tiller (steering wheels hadn't been invented and racing cars still had tiller controls).

The race took place at the Grosse Point track and when Barney Oldfield climbed into the seat, he cheerfully remarked: 'Well, this chariot may kill me, but they will say afterwards that I was going like hell when she took me over the bank'. He lived up to his promise by going flat out from start to finish and by the end of the race had a lead of nearly half a mile. Thanks to Oldfield's courage, the Ford '999' did what it was built to do—advertise the fact that Henry Ford was capable of building a winning car. Seven days later he formed the Ford Motor Company with a capital of $100 and within a few weeks the public had subscribed an additional $28,000.

Henry Ford realized, however, that he needed to have financial control if he was to achieve all his objectives and so by 1905 he had purchased enough shares from the money he earned to bring his own holdings up to 51 per cent. He continued to increase his percentage until he owned $58\frac{1}{2}$ per cent. When some of the minority shareholders disagreed with Henry's policies, in 1914 his son Edsel bought the remaining $41\frac{1}{2}$ per cent for $75 million.

The success of those early Ford cars depended on the provision of good service, but local repair men usually carried few stocks of spares and regarded car owners as essentially rich men who were there to be exploited. They were a major menace to a developing motor industry and Henry Ford played a large part in rectifying the situation.

His exploits didn't go unnoticed in Britain. William Rootes was impressed not only with the design of Henry's cars and his company's ability to increase production to meet demand, but also with their excellent after-sales service. The use of competitions to obtain valuable publicity was also very evident. The Rootes brothers' enthusiasm for American production and sales techniques when they started their own motor business, and their belief in the importance of good publicity, no doubt stemmed from the admiration they had for Henry Ford and the American influence.

Chapter 3

From chickens to cars

ALTHOUGH BILLY ROOTES had a dismal school record, he was very quick thinking and bright, and by his early teens was already showing a remarkable aptitude for business when he saw an opportunity to make money or to take advantage of a situation. The chicken farm which he started during the holidays, while he was still a schoolboy, was one of those occasions when he proved to his father that he was no slouch when it came to recognizing a good deal.

William Rootes complained one morning at breakfast about the increasing price of fresh eggs and Billy immediately offered to buy some hens and look after them if his father would pay for their food. William agreed. Looking after the hens would keep his mischievous son out of trouble and solve the fresh egg problem at what looked to him to be relatively little cost. The food for a few hens couldn't amount to much.

What he didn't realize was that his son planned to turn the deal into a business venture by renting the field alongside the house from the local farmer and starting a chicken farm. Billy spent all his savings on buying hens and because his father was paying for their food was soon able to sell eggs to other people in the village more cheaply than anyone else. While admiring his son's business acumen, William Rootes didn't appreciate being caught out by a 15-year-old schoolboy. There was little he could do about the situation, however, without having to go back on his word, and Billy was always quick to remind his father of the fact whenever he complained about the increasing food bills. By the end of the school holidays Billy had more than 100 hens and was making enough profit from the eggs to pay a man to look after them.

Some years later, Billy was to become a successful farmer and a world-famous breeder of Aberdeen Angus cattle and Hampshire Down sheep. It was those chickens, however, which gave him a start in the motor business and led to him becoming a millionaire by the time he was 30 and one of the most powerful men in the British motor industry.

By the time Billy had reached 16, his headmaster at Cranbrook

School suggested to William Rootes that Billy should be taken away from school as he was wasting his own time and that of the staff. Although the boy was always bright and cheerful, he didn't show any aptitude for schoolwork apart from arithmetic and geography and it seemed a waste of time and money trying to persevere with someone who was not interested in any other subjects. William Rootes agreed and was able to use his influence to persuade the directors of the Singer Motor Company to take Billy on as an apprentice at their Coventry factory. He hoped that after serving out his apprenticeship Billy might eventually become a useful member of the family motor business.

The Singer Company was acknowledged to be one of the most forward-thinking of the British motor manufacturers and the directors were not keen that someone with such a poor school record should join the company when there were hundreds of young men of outstanding ability keen to become apprentices at their Coventry factory. They only agreed for him to do so as a favour to William, so soon after his 16th birthday Billy moved into digs at Number 8, Priory Street, Coventry to start life in the motor industry as a penny-an-hour apprentice. In those days Coventry was only a relatively small country town with a population of 80,000 or less. Wolverhampton was probably better known for producing cars, but Coventry was developing more rapidly, thanks to Humber, Hillman and Singer.

In 1910 the Singer Company was already one of the most successful car manufacturers in Britain and their team of engineers and designers had instructions to produce a car which could satisfy the demands of a wider motoring public instead of just the very rich. The directors also understood the value of publicity and were not afraid to prove the ability of Singer products on the race track. It was just the right environment for an enthusiastic young apprentice and Billy was anxious to learn all he could about the motor industry and the problems of designing, making and selling cars in what was developing into a very competitive market.

Away from the confines of the schoolroom, Billy proved to be an outstanding pupil, and the knowledge he had gained from listening to his father and watching the mechanics at work in the family's workshop in Kent gave him an advantage over most of the other apprentices. From being bottom of the class at school he began to show an aptitude for learning and an enthusiasm to do well which delighted his father.

Unlike most other teenagers, he had a fetish for tidiness, almost to the point of obsession. His landlady remembered him as a cheerful but fastidious lodger whose room was always neat, with everything from hairbrushes to clothing always in the right place and carefully laid out ready for use. He always knew just where everything was when he needed it. This passion for tidiness and attention to detail became even more apparent when he set up in business. Rootes's offices and showrooms were always immaculate and his farms were also models of cleanliness and efficiency. Billy couldn't bear to see dirt and untidiness, or what he called 'sloppy housekeeping'.

Even as an apprentice, everything he did was carefully planned, and when he decided that he would like to race motor cycles in his spare time, his machine was always prepared with meticulous care and attention to detail. As a result he had many successes. He became friends with the great G. E. Stanley, who broke many world records riding Singer motor cycles and gave Billy advice about his own racing career. Stanley suggested that he should take his machine over to the Rover works in Coventry where Dudley Noble, another young motor cycle enthusiast, was tuning and testing motor cycles with Charles 'Bush' Newsome, who was a brilliant trials and hill climb rider of the day and a former pupil with the Daimler Company.

Harry Smith was the chairman of Rover and John Kemp 'J. K.' Starley was then the general manager. The popular foreman of the test shop, where Dudley Noble and the others worked, was Bob Whelan, who had a remarkable knack of putting out the fires which occurred frequently when engines were undergoing bench testing there. Dudley Noble was being paid five pence an hour to road test the motor cycles, so it was probably the only occasion when he earned five times as much as Billy Rootes.

Dudley Noble took an immediate liking to the young Singer apprentice and agreed to tune his machine. The two struck up a lifelong friendship and with Dudley Noble's help Billy became a successful racing motor cyclist, winning many trials and reliability tests including the race from Lands End to John O'Groats.

The 300-mile (483-km) London–Lands End run at Easter was particularly popular with all the competitors, particularly as the route through Cornwall took them past the garage owned by Donald Healey's father, and there were always cups of tea and fresh cakes laid out on tressle tables in front of the building. Donald Healey went on to become a successful driver and the sports cars which carried his name became world-famous. For a while he worked for Rootes in Coventry.

Some of the riders taking part in these events mistakenly thought that Billy Rootes was a bit naïve and tried to 'cook' his machine when he wasn't looking by inserting bits of paper in the contact-breaker of his engine. He took it all in good part, however, and his engaging personality and charm soon made him very popular. He never forgot the friends he made as a young motor cyclist and gave many of them jobs later at Rootes. The broken leg he suffered during one race left him with a slight limp and a characteristic roll to his walk which remained with him throughout his life.

Along with the other Singer apprentices, Billy worked his way through all the departments of the company, from the factory floor to the sales office and from the design office to the test shop. His enthusiasm for racing ensured he was one of those at Brooklands on the

Saturday in 1911 when a 15.9 hp Singer, with George Tysoe at the wheel, raised the 10-lap record to 81 mph (130 km/h), beating Louis Coatalen's record by 1.7 mph (2.7 km/h). The car, nicknamed 'Bunny III', also covered the half-mile at a speed of 90.04 mph (144.87 km/h), again beating Coatalen's previous record for the distance by 3.88 mph (6.24 km/h), and set new records for the flying kilometre and the flying mile. It was a remarkable performance for what was basically a standard car and 'Bunny III' went on to win many races at Saltburn and Brooklands with Gerald Herbert at the wheel.

Spectators at Brooklands who liked a flutter appreciated the reliability and performance of Singer cars like 'Bunny III' and were often able to get good odds from local bookmakers at the track, like the popular Long Tom, who was one of those who regularly took bets there.

These performances were further proof that Singer cars were among the best in the world, a fact which wasn't lost on young Billy, and it was fortuitous that his arrival in the test shop coincided with the test work being carried out on the revolutionary new Singer 10. It was the country's first real light car and was destined to become one of the most outstanding models of the decade. The new Singer had a new four-cylinder, 10 hp engine with a specially designed gearbox incorporated with the back axle. It was the first small car not to bear any resemblance to a motor cycle and its price and low petrol consumption of more than 40 miles to the gallon brought it within the reach of thousands of people who had previously longed to own a motor car but could not afford to do so.

Although he was enjoying himself at the Singer Motor Company, by the summer of 1913 Billy had served nearly three years of his apprenticeship and felt that time had come for him to put his knowledge and experience to good effect and start earning his own living. The new Singer 10 seemed to provide the ideal opportunity, particularly as he had the advantage of having worked on the car and been involved in the testing. This, he felt, would enable him to sell the model more effectively than other salesman who had not been so closely involved.

The company's sales manager had been very impressed with Billy's enthusiasm and ability when he had been working in the sales department, but the request that an 18-year-old apprentice should be given the agency to sell the new Singer 10 in Kent still came as a shock, even more so because Billy wanted to place an order for 50 of the new models. It couldn't be denied that a member of the well-known Rootes family selling Singers in Kent had some appeal, and Billy wasn't lacking in knowledge and enthusiasm but nobody had placed such a large order before. In the end the sales manager agreed to Billy becoming the company's agent in Kent and accepted the order for 50 of the new Singers, on condition that Billy also provided a £5 deposit with each order.

Billy was delighted and rushed home to tell his father the good news. Instead of being pleased, however, William Rootes flew into a rage and insisted that his son return immediately to Coventry in order to finish his apprenticeship. He refused point-blank to lend him the £250 needed for the deposits and wasn't interested in what he thought was a scatter-brained idea. He already employed some of the best salesmen in the country and knew that none of them was capable of selling 50 cars within the space of a few months; to expect an 18-year-old youth to do so was nothing short of insane.

Billy, however, was equally determined and insisted that, as he had already done a deal with the Singer sales manager, he couldn't go back on his word. If his father wasn't prepared to help, he would raise the money some other way. William Rootes's reaction was the same as always when faced with a difficult situation. He stormed off into his study, slammed the door and started playing one of the musical instruments which had been brought in for repair.

Although Billy had hoped for a better response from his father, he wasn't entirely surprised, and on the ride down from Coventry he had worked out an alternative plan if the approach to his father failed. As he rode off down the drive he could hear the music coming through the study window but knew that, although his father would calm down in time, it was unlikely that he would change his mind. Like his eldest son, William Rootes always stuck by a decision.

Billy put his second plan into action, and his approach to the next-door farmer met with a much more encouraging response. It didn't take long for him to sell his chickens and he was soon on his way back to Coventry with the £250 in his pocket. Billy Rootes the chicken farmer was about to become Billy Rootes the motor car salesman. The chickens had provided him with the capital he needed to set up on his own in the motor business and his 19th birthday was still some months away.

Chapter 4

War and peace

IN THE WEEKS that followed, Billy rode his motor cycle from one end of Kent to the other, visiting every motor trader and showing them the literature on the new Singer 10 which had been printed for him by Mr F. Williams of Hawkhurst. His enthusiasm was infectious and his undoubted knowledge of the potential and performance capabilities of the new car made him a persuasive salesman.

His task was made easier by the cars string of successes at the famous Brooklands circuit, where spectators were astonished to see the new Singer covering lap after lap at an average of 64 mph (103 km/h). It captured all the 1–9 hour records at Brooklands for a car in the under 1,100 cc class, and whenever it was due to appear the public flocked to watch.

The Singer directors had brilliantly anticipated the future trend in public demand and the designers had done their job well—so much so that by the end of 1914 the 10 hp model was taking up the bulk of the factory's production capacity. Within a few months Billy had taken orders for all 50 cars and had made a profit of more than £1,500. He had established himself as an astute salesman and, perhaps even more important, he had shown himself to be a man who stuck to a deal. When he took orders from dealers he had only been able to anticipate the factory price, but when the invoices arrived he realized that he could have charged more for each car. He stuck to the original deals, however, and every car was delivered to the dealers at the price they had agreed. Although in the short term he was worse off, he reaped the benefit in the long term because word quickly went round the motor trade that young Billy Rootes was a man they could trust.

The profit enabled him to take additional premises in Earl Street in Maidstone, but before long he joined forces with his father and they set up in business together and moved to Pudding Lane. William Rootes forgave his son for refusing to complete his apprenticeship and appreciated his undoubted business talents. He had wanted to move his business from Hawkhurst to Maidstone for some time but had been prevented from doing so by his wife's ill health. Despite having to run his own business from a small Kentish village, he had been selling more than 600 cars a year, a remarkable achievement for anyone in the motor trade, let alone someone based in a country village.

Soon after the opening of their business in Pudding Lane, the threat of war began to have a serious effect on the car trade and the period of boom quickly turned into a period of gloom. Even so, Billy refused to be downhearted and persuaded this father to agree to an advertising campaign calling on everyone's nationalistic pride and the need to 'fly the flag'. Teddy Williams, who worked for the local *Kent Messenger* newspaper for 43 years, was so impressed with the young businessman's advertisement that he kept the original copy which Billy brought into the office.

The advertisement was written in ink on the back of one of their sales pamphlets and emphasized 'The business of the moment is to keep the flag flying'. After listing the services Rootes could provide, it ended with the words, 'We shall be happy to show you how you can keep the trade flag flying'. There were several spelling mistakes, among them a reference to 'Commershall Vehicles'. Billy Rootes couldn't spell, but he certainly knew how to sell.

When war started he was anxious to join up. The hostilities were seriously retarding the growth of the fledgling British motor industry, allowing the ambitious manufacturers in Detroit to develop their own plans to supply the world with American cars. American manufacturers quickly achieved a virtual monopoly in overseas markets.

In Britain, the little Singer 10 with the 'go anywhere' reputation was also going into khaki and squadrons of them were ordered by the War Office for service in France. Instead of going into khaki, Billy Rootes chose the Navy and became Sub-Lieutenant William Rootes, RNVR, attached to the Naval Air Service, which was later merged with the Royal Air Force.

When he applied for a commission in November 1915 he took with him a reference from the Singer Company's sales manager which was a clear indication of the excellent reputation he had earned after only a comparatively short time in business. It stated: 'We are pleased to recommend Mr W. Rootes for any position in the motor business as a capital salesman who knows his work thoroughly. As a mechanic and driver Mr W. Rootes possesses exceptional capabilities and we feel sure he will discharge such duties with credit to himself and complete satisfaction to those whom he may have to serve. Mr Rootes left us entirely on his own initiative to commence business on his own account in Maidstone, which business we have reasons for knowing has been highly successful'.

Billy's former headmaster, Mr William Lee, having forgiven his earlier transgressions, wrote to him on 28 October 1915, expressing the hope that he would soon be Gazetted (commissioned). The formal reference enclosed with his letter declared: 'I have pleasure in stating that Mr W. E. Rootes was a pupil of mine at Cranbrook School some years ago and he bore a good character. I have seen him frequently since he left school and have no reason to change my opinion of him.' The last sentence could perhaps be interpreted in several ways but it was a generally helpful reference which wisely ignored Billy's poor school record.

Tilling-Stevens Limited was a company which Billy had been involved with before the war and which was later to become part of the Rootes Group. Percy Frost Smith, the joint managing director, when asked for a reference, wrote: 'During the past two years we have had business relations with Mr W. E. Rootes and, from our knowledge of that gentleman and the business he has conducted, are satisfied that he is a capable engineer. We have always been satisfied with any business he has done for us and we are certain that he is a gentleman who can satisfactorily discharge any duties in the automobile world put before him'.

Apart from his motor cycle racing activities, Billy had also shown a keen interest in flying and in 1912 had 'looped the loop' in an aeroplane piloted by Wingfield Smith. At the time he was only the second person to do so, but the Navy was more interested in Billy's engineering knowledge than in his enthusiasm for flying. He was sent to Clement Talbot Limited, another company which 20 years later became an important member of the Rootes Group. During the war, Clement Talbot was a contractor to the Navy involved with making aeroplane engines, but most of these had to be scrapped if they became damaged, instead of being repaired and used again.

Lieutenant Rootes was concerned about the tremendous waste of money and machinery which was taking place as a result of this system. By 1917 it became obvious that there was an urgent need for a change of policy and he persuaded the Admiralty, where his brother Reggie was working, to allow him to open up an engine repair factory. In September 1917 Rootes Maidstone was registered with a capital of £1,000 in £1 shares to 'carry on the business of aviation, automobile, agricultural and machine repairing experts'.

Billy took over the old tannery in Mill Street, Maidstone, and with the help of a £1,500 loan from his father turned it into a modern repair shop which he renamed the Lea Engineering Works. With his mechanics he worked late into the night making sure that demands were met, and before long a steady flow of reconditioned and repaired aeroplane engines was leaving the factory each week. Not everyone appreciated his efforts, particularly the other inhabitants of Mill Street, who complained about the continuous noise from the aeroplane engines under test. Fortunately for them, the war came to an end and so did the Navy's aero engine requirements.

Faced with having to pay the rent on a large building without the income from the aero engine business, Billy and his father decided to go ahead with the plans for developing their motor business which had been shelved because of the war. Billy had also become a family man, having married Nora Press in 1916. Their first son, Geoffrey, had been born at Loose, near Maidstone, on 14 June 1917, and their second son, Brian, was born two years later on 1 October 1919.

The Press family had been millers on the Norfolk and Suffolk borders for many generations and it was claimed, although probably apocryphally, that one of their ancestors was a Spanish sailor washed up on the Norfolk coast after his ship had been wrecked during the Spanish Armada. Nora's father, Horace Press, died of pneumonia as a comparatively young man after an evening's duck flighting, and when Geoffrey was born her mother Edith went to live with them and played a large part in bringing up Geoffrey and his brother Brian.

Shortly before Brian was born they all moved from Loose to The Cedars, a long, low, late-Georgian house at Aylesford, on the north bank of the River Medway. It was a good house in which to bring up young boys, being comfortable and roomy, and having a covered verandah at ground level along the whole southern frontage where they could play if the weather was bad. There were also well-kept lawns running down to the river.

When Geoffrey was four he was sent to St Christophers, a kindergarten on the outskirts of Maidstone, but Brian's schooling had to be postponed due to bad health. He had several convulsions soon after his birth which led to attacks of asthma, some serious, that were to trouble him for most of his life.

Reggie Rootes gave up what could well have been a distinguished civil service career and left the Admiralty after the war to join his father and brother at Maidstone. It was a courageous decision, because although there were rapid developments in the motor industry during the years immediately following the Armistice, the failure rate among motor manufacturers was still very high and some of the best companies only managed to survive after close encounters with the official receiver.

Even so, the Rootes brothers were brim-full of confidence and ideas. They now had the full support of their father , who was chairman of the company and able to provide sound business advice, as well as many useful contacts within the motor industry. But it was Billy who was the driving force, the extrovert, enthusiastic and energetic salesman, with his brother proving to be a sound administrator and organizer, with considerable financial and commercial flair. The two complemented one another and their close working relationship and respective qualities provided the basis for their success.

They learned about the downs as well as the ups of the motor trade during their first years in business together, and witnessed many examples of the retribution which so quickly followed any errors of policy, or foolish decisions. Their father's reputation and Billy's pre-war successes in the motor trade stood them in good stead when they decided to put all the capital they had into the development of the wholesale side of their business, becoming agents for a number of foreign makes.

They were also fortunate that Joe Chaldecott decided to join them in 1919. He went on to run the export division of the Rootes Group, becoming a successful and well-respected ambassador for the company throughout the world. He had been born at Woodford in Essex on 15 June 1895 and so was a year younger than Billy. After emigrating to Canada at the age of 17 to join one of his brothers who was farming in Nova Scotia, Joe volunteered as a gunner in the Royal Canadian Army at the outbreak of war and also became an army boxing champion. He was commissioned, served in France as a captain in the Canadian Artillery, was wounded, and came back to England to recuperate.

When war ended he not only joined Rootes, but also became a member of the Rootes family when he married Reggie's first wife, Joyce. Their son John worked for the Rootes's export division and went on to run a number of the Group's overseas companies with considerable success.

In the days following the First World War, when entertaining was an essential part of many deals, Joe Chaldecott's remarkable capacity for being able to drink alcohol without showing any ill effects was used to considerable advantage. Entertaining clients was a side of the business which Billy and Reggie were happy to leave in his capable hands, as they both hated long drinking sessions. The tremendous amount of entertaining which Joe did on behalf of Rootes for more than 40 years, in many parts of the world, did not seem to affect his health, and he outlived Billy, being well into his 70s when he died.

Joe Chaldecott's arrival on the scene, however, helped to strengthen an already formidable team, and Rootes Limited began showing good profits. A status report on the company which Messrs C. Lindley, a London firm of steel stockists and engineering merchants, received from their accountants on 9 July 1919 stated: 'There is nothing registered against them. Payments so far as we can trace are in order and your credit is looked upon as an average trade risk, on definite terms'.

Chapter 5

Horses and horsepower

THE START OF the 1920s was an exciting period for young men and women with a thirst for adventure. Billy Rootes had followed the successful flight of Alcock and Brown across the Atlantic from Newfoundland to Ireland in 1919 with particular interest. Although the crossing had taken more than 16 hours, with their frail aircraft flying at times only 10 ft above the waves, Billy knew that the time was not far off when businessmen would be crossing the Atlantic by air and a whole new market would be opened up for British companies. Brown had served in the Naval Air Service with him during the war and had often spoken of his plans for flying the Atlantic when war ended. Billy in turn had outlined his plans for building a world-famous motoring empire. Both men showed determination and courage and neither doubted the other's ability to achieve their objectives.

In 1920 the only way for a businessman to cross the Atlantic, however, was by boat, so, taking letters of introduction to all the major American motor manufacturers with him, Billy set off on what was to be the first of many hundreds of visits to America. There was a growing demand for cars in Britain but not enough new models being built to satisfy that demand. As a result, the price of second-hand cars began to soar. In addition to their other agencies, Rootes entered into an agreement with Nouvelle Société Anonyme des Automobiles Martini of St Blaise, Neuchatel, in Switzerland, to sell 75 per cent of the total production of their Martini cars in Britain and several overseas countries, but even so Billy and Reggie Rootes were still unable to get enough new cars to satisfy the demand they were creating. They were keen to take advantage of the very large number of different models being produced in America and were determined to secure an agency for one of the larger American companies, which they felt would provide them with the cars they badly needed. It was a period when fortunes were being made and audacity and ability reaped ready rewards.

A month later Billy sailed for England with the General Motors

Agency safely in his pocket and full of enthusiasm for the way in which American manufacturers were increasing efficiency and reducing production costs, as well as their ability to make quick decisions. The impressions he gained on that first visit had an important bearing on his own business philosophy and the development of the Rootes Group.

For someone so relatively young and inexperienced in world trade, his clear, forward-thinking views were remarkable. In a letter to *The Times* he warned British industrialists:

'Even if our home market is smaller than the American market, it is inexcusable for us not to boost it. We must not neglect the overseas markets, which offer such unbounded possibilities for any British manufacturer whose vision is great enough and who has the necessary energy and determination.

We must not lose sight of the fact that if British industrialists would only take up a fresh attitude in business direction, leaving behind the conservative and out-of-date methods of their forefathers, and start a new and modern era in organisation, their influence would be such as to carry the impetus from chief executive to office boy.

Many will say that such ambitions cannot be achieved on account of the strikes and labour conditions experienced in England. I do not believe this, and am of the opinion that it is the chiefs of our industry who are mainly to blame for the state of affairs which exists in this country. Had our industrialists been more progressive and introduced modern methods into their factories, both in machinery and organisation, the working man in turn would have been educated in more modern conditions.

He would have realised as a matter of course that progress would mean more money for him and increased pleasures. Owing to the resulting lower cost of articles, because of a vastly increased production, he could then afford a better home, a cheaper motor car and other things, all bought with the earnings from the greater general volume which he had helped to produce.'

They were true but brave words from a young British businessman in the 1920s. Unfortunately, it was to be many years before the majority of his colleagues were prepared to follow his advice.

The deal with General Motors provided Rootes with the impetus the company needed and helped the brothers to become the largest and most successful motor distributors in Britain. Although they were still only distributors and were not yet motor manufacturers, their visits to America had shown them the importance of publicity and the power of the media. As a result they decided to hold regular motor shows at their Maidstone showrooms, putting on display their latest imports.

They made sure that the Rootes motor shows always coincided with the local hunt point-to-point races. Chauffeur-driven cars were sent to

London to collect the country's leading motor writers, and after they had been shown all the new models and been given test drives, the guests were given lunch at one of the Maidstone hotels before being taken for an entertaining and usually profitable day at the races. As soon as they got there, Reggie took over as host and tipster. He was an accomplished horseman who hunted regularly with the West Kent Foxhounds and knew the form of all the horses and their jockeys. While out hunting he was always quick to note a potential winner and this information enabled their guests from the motoring press to return home after a good dinner with their wallets stuffed with pound notes.

The older members of the motor trade disliked the brothers' unorthodox methods, but the friendships Billy and Reggie forged with influential writers like Harold Pemberton, Thornton Rutter, Claude Wallis, Dudley Maddox, Bob Paul and Armstrong James Percy proved invaluable, and by the time the brothers decided to move to London from Kent their names were already well known throughout Britain.

By the mid 1920s, customers were able to choose any car they wanted from an almost bewildering variety of makes. Good salesmanship was becoming more important, along with the need for an excellent after-sales service, and that is what the two brothers were prepared to offer. Their old Alldays and Onions breakdown van was replaced by a smart fleet of service vehicles all bearing the Rootes livery, and when their Maidstone and Rochester premises became too small, the lure of London's West End led to them renting larger offices and showrooms in Long Acre, although they decided to retain their properties in Kent.

Chapter 6

The world's largest car and truck distributors

THE MOVE TO London was followed by another period of rapid expansion, during which Rootes took additional premises at 141 New Bond Street and gained control of a number of important dealerships, including Tom Garner in Manchester, Robins & Day in Rochester and the Medway towns, and the Canterbury Motor Company. In September 1923 the news that George Heath Limited of Birmingham, one of the pioneer motor car companies in the Midlands, was in serious financial difficulties provided Billy and Reggie with the opportunity they had been waiting for and which would establish them as the largest motor distributors in Britain.

George Heath was a friend of theirs and they had been watching his progress with interest. In only three years he had built up a chain of 20 main dealerships and about the same number of retail outlets, selling a wide variety of makes and models. They ranged from the humble but extremely successful Austin Seven to the luxurious Rolls-Royce limousines, and included such famous names as Alvis, Ariel, Armstrong, Bean, Berliet, Buick, BSA, Calcott, Crossley, Chevrolet, Daimler, de Dion, Durant, Essex, Fiat, Ford, Hubmobile, Hudson, Humber, Maxwell, Morris, Overland, Rover, Rode, Rour, Standard, Star, Swift, Vauxhall, Vulcan and Wolseley.

Although there was hardly a well-known make of car which George Heath and his dealers didn't sell, it was his company's premises in Birmingham, at John Bright Street and Lower Temple Street, and his 40 other sales outlets in the wealthy Midlands towns which the Rootes brothers wanted to have under their control.

George Heath Limited was recognized as the leading wholesale car distributors in the Midlands, but the company had run into financial difficulties because of bad management and a lack of sales expertise. Both had become far more important following the halcyon days immediately after the war, because cars were no longer in short supply and models now had to be sold to a public spoilt for choice. Like so many other companies in the motor trade which had mushroomed during the post-war period, George Heath had failed to keep up with the changing demand.

The company's financial problems unfortunately came at a time when the Rootes brothers were themselves short of cash. The move to London had proved expensive and had left little money for takeovers, particularly any involving a company the size of George Heath. To try and find a way round the problem a series of meetings were held at London's Savoy Hotel and at the Brooklands motor racing circuit between the Rootes brothers, George Heath and Charles Hyde, a wealthy Birmingham businessman who lived at Acocks Green. He was a friend of George Heath who offered to put up a substantial part of the purchase price provided he was given a seat on the Rootes board and that what he described as 'an important situation' was found for his son.

Neither suggestion appealed to Billy and Reggie and Charles Hyde pulled out of the deal because, as he pointed out, 'the first object I had in mind when considering putting money into the concern has vanished'. As a result, the brothers had to look elsewhere for financial support.

Bracher Son and Miskin, the Rootes solicitors in Maidstone, produced an ingenious scheme whereby George Heath employees would help finance the deal themselves and share in the profits. It would have been one of the earliest forms of employee participation, and was referred to as the 'George Heath Limited Employees' Deposit Account Scheme'. The proposal was that employees should make deposits of not less than £10, to be repaid at six months' notice, and would also receive a basic interest of 5 per cent per annum and an additional 1 per cent for every 5 per cent per annum which George Heath paid on the company's ordinary shares. It sounded like a good idea, but the scheme was eventually turned down because of the difficulties involved when employees wanted to leave.

Despite the problems in finding the necessary finance, George Heath refused to consider any deal involving shares and insisted on a cash payment. He wanted Rootes to settle the £18,000 outstanding on the company's stock and pay £20,000 for the goodwill and the leases for the Birmingham premises and a further £2,000 for the fixtures and fittings. The brothers realized that the only way to make him change his mind was to buy the company from a liquidator.

W. R. Lane, the well-known Birmingham firm of chartered accountants, was brought in during the early part of December and Stanley Lane, the senior partner, was appointed liquidator. Billy persuaded him to agree to their suggestion that Rootes would form a new company with the title of George Heath (1924) Limited, and as soon as the liquidation had been completed the figures 1924 could then be dropped from the title.

Stanley Lane then put pressure to bear on George Heath, who finally agreed to an offer of £20,000 of preferential shares in the new company and a seat on the board, instead of the £20,000 in cash which he originally demanded. The new company would also pay for the outstanding stock and take over the various leases. As a result, Billy and Reggie Rootes not only got their way, but also brought off a deal which gave them control of the largest car and truck distribution organization in the Midlands, for only a small injection of cash. Everything was completed in time for the start of the 1924 selling season.

Although the deal meant that Rootes had become by far the largest and most important car and truck dealers in Britain, Billy was still keen to take advantage of the growing export market for British cars. Overseas sales opportunities were being largely ignored by British car manufacturers when Rootes decided to open a depot on the River Thames above Chiswick, specifically for exports. They coined the slogan 'Cars packed, shipped and delivered to all parts of the world' and set out to persuade motor manufacturers to let them handle all of their export business.

As most car manufacturers had little knowledge of overseas markets, they were pleased for Rootes to do so, and the Rootes export business began to flourish. Every car arriving at their new depot was given an extensive road test and then submitted to a further detailed inspection prior to being packed. The crates were loaded into lighters for the journey down-river to Tilbury, or one of the other docks, before being transferred to one of the large ocean-going vessels.

The first order dispatched from Chiswick was for His Highness Prince Hamidullah Khan, later to become the Newab of Bhopal, and included a special-bodied Bentley with headlamps designed to be used for big game hunting at night. The hold of the Rawalpindi was filled with other Rootes' crates containing a selection of Rolls-Royce, Sunbeam, Austin, Clyno and Hillman models.

Later that year, at the request of the Wolverhampton-based Clyno Company, Billy undertook an extensive overseas tour to explore the possibility of exporting more Clyno cars. The company had given Rootes worldwide distribution rights for all their models, but Billy ended the agreement after taking a closer look at their overseas potential and the management refused to update their models to cater for modern demands. The latest Clyno model had been described by R. W. Luckett, a leading motoring writer of the day, as 'an elderly character car' and was hardly the sort of vehicle the brothers were prepared to spend time and money on trying to sell. Clyno went out of business soon afterwards, after turning down Rootes' offer to buy the company.

During 1925 and 1926 more than 3,000 cars passed through the Rootes packaging and shipping department for delivery abroad, and crates bearing the Rootes name became familiar sights in many parts of the world. The methods the brothers adopted proved so successful that more British motor manufacturers took advantage of their knowledge and experience of export markets, even to the extent of relying on them entirely for all their overseas distribution and sales. A steady stream of senior Rootes executives left England to set up new distribution and service outlets abroad, until Rootes had a complete network of sales and service companies throughout the world.

Billy realized the importance of taking the British models they were selling for overseas buyers to try in their own countries and Rootes was the only British company to exhibit at the 1926 Berlin Motor Show. The show enabled them to increase their European sales and service facilities still further and encouraged them to exhibit more widely.

The motor exhibition in Columbo was their next overseas show. Rowlands Garage was the Rootes distributor there and Hillman and Rolls-Royce cars were shipped from Chiswick to be displayed on the Rowlands' stand. The show was so successful that Rootes went on to take one of the largest stands in the most prestigious position at the Paris Automobile Salon. They invited all the British motor manufacturers to display their cars on the Rootes stand and the experiment proved a great success.

The company's export business developed so rapidly that the Chiswick depot had to be extended, enabling more than 6,000 cars to be shipped from there during 1927. A new publication was launched called *The Rootes Overseas Message*, and the first issue, published in January 1927, contained messages from leading political and automotive figures of the day, including a number from overseas. All wrote in glowing terms about the Rootes brothers' export achievements and Billy and Reggie published a policy statement setting out their business philosophy and explaining why they had stopped being distributors for American and other foreign makes and were now concentrating all their efforts on selling British. The statement declared: 'We saw the future of the British car a long time ago and now we see it more clearly still. At the present time we administer the largest car distribution business in the British Isles, with headquarters in the finest building in London and with a chain of depots throughout the country.'

The building they referred to was the new Rootes headquarters at Devonshire House in Piccadilly, which in 1926 became the nerve centre for their worldwide business empire. They took a 99-year lease on Devonshire House, the large imposing new building opposite the famous Ritz Hotel, which had been built on the site of the magnificent former home of the Grosvenor family. It covered the whole area bordered by Piccadilly, Berkeley Street, Mayfair Place and Stratton Street. The ground floor provided the most prestigious car showrooms in London and the large basement was turned into a special reception area for overseas customers, staffed by salesmen who were linguists and who also had specialized knowledge of the intricacies of shipping cars and trucks abroad.

During that period of uncertainty, when Britain was still suffering form the serious effects of a general strike, it was a move which took not only courage, but also a voracity for success which few young business tycoons of the time possessed. The annual rent of £10,000 was considered very high for any company in the depressed motor business. Elder statesmen in the motor trade shook their heads in disbelief and predicted that this time the young Rootes brothers had really overstepped the mark. They prophesied that it would only be a matter of time before the magnificent new headquarters would become a white elephant and a millstone around their necks. How wrong they were.

Billy's creative brain produced a wealth of new ideas which enabled new sales records to be created, despite the difficult economic climate. A second-hand department at Devonshire House was set up to serve all the Rootes depots, with a central register of cars for sale. This move to increase used car sales at a time when every sale was of vital importance gave Rootes a considerable edge on their competitors. Even though the motor industry was going through a troubled period, Rootes retail salesmen earned regular commission payments. As a salesman, Billy knew how important it was to motivate all the sales staff and the depots had to pay the second-hand department five shillings for every car its salesmen sold on their behalf, encouraging everyone to work more closely together as a team.

He insisted that the company's advertising should be 'made more snappy and less stereotyped than their competitors'. The same applied to the company's sales literature. The export department at Devonshire House introduced a repurchase scheme for overseas visitors coming to Britain, which was far and away the most adventurous the motor industry had ever tried before, and it worked. No other organization was able to offer customers similar facilities. Every company involved with Rootes's export activities took part in the scheme, so that all their customers were able to have a new car waiting for them the moment they arrived in England. When the visit was over they could either resell the car at a previously guaranteed price, or have it shipped home.

Deferred payment and other hire purchase schemes were also available, but the repurchase scheme proved the most popular, because buying a car that way was far less expensive than hiring one. It also provided the company's newly formed second-hand department with a steady flow of low-mileage used cars to sell through Devonshire House and Rootes depots. There was an additional benefit. Billy knew that anyone buying a good second-hand car would probably want to purchase a new one later, and his salesmen were able to keep in close touch with these customers and make another sale as soon as the time was right.

Rootes's entrepreneurial methods of doing business certainly had the approval of their customers, who bought cars from them in increasing numbers, and proved to British motor manufacturers that they were the driving force the industry needed to sell their products. During the 1920s they took so much of the Austin factory's output that the brothers came close to dominating the manufacturing and sales policies of the company. Rootes sold more Austin Seven cars than any other company in the world and in 1927 earned a profit of more than £1$\frac{1}{2}$ million, a tremendous achievement at that time.

When the Austin company ran into financial difficulties despite the success of the remarkable Austin Seven, the Government tried to persuade Herbert Austin to join forces with Rootes. Negotiations broke down, however, due to a clash of temperaments between the rather traditional Herbert Austin and the dynamic Billy Rootes, the super salesman who wanted stylish new models that he could sell abroad. Despite their failure to agree either on an amalgamation, or for the Austin Company to be taken over by Rootes, the brothers helped to form a consortium which provided Austin with the necessary finance and they continued to sell Austin cars until the early 1930s.

Although many of the larger Austin models were rather outdated, the Austin Twelve and Sixteen retained their popularity remarkably well and so did the Gordon 2/3-seater, all-weather fabric coupé. Built on an Austin chassis, it was sold as 'a dignified business car', but passengers were expected to face the elements in a 'comfy dickey seat to carry two people' which could carry luggage when not in use. Even so, the Gordon Coupé was all the rage at the time. Billy recalled later: 'I can well remember we were all very enthusiastic over that particular vehicle. At the time when it was dreamed up it seemed the only model that mattered.'

As the 1920s drew to a close, big changes were under way, not only in motor car design, but also in the manner in which they were manufactured and sold. On his return from America in June 1926, after spending some time with Chevrolet and Chrysler, Reggie Rootes put forward ideas for merchandizing new cars and commercial vehicles involving exclusive dealer representation, which had never been tried in Britain. There was also, he felt, an urgent need for the British Government to follow the example being set in America and provide manufacturers with detailed sales figures so that more accurate sales and production forecasts could be made. He told the Rootes board: 'The American motor manufacturer knows every day exactly what his competitors are selling in each territory, and this is of the greatest service in enabling him to gauge the market accurately. It also goes far in stimulating selling and production effort.'

The system of trade discounts being used in Britain today are very similar to those which Rootes urged other manufacturers, including Austin and Morris, to use following Reggie's trip to America. Talks were held, but it took some years before his recommendations were accepted. Changes to the original system needed to be made, however, because the profits motor traders were making from the sale of cars during the late 1920s were frequently not sufficient for them to survive and certainly not high enough to justify the investment needed to improve sales and service methods. In America, where competition was still intense, price-cutting existed only between motor manufacturers and not between motor traders, which was the situation in Britain. It is clear that the Rootes brothers' proposals were ahead of their time and their vision for change was too far advanced for other British motor manufacturers to accept until some years later.

Chapter 7

The challenge of speed

ALTHOUGH IN 1929 Britain had built an aeroplane which could fly faster than any other, the speed records on land and sea were still held by America. A great deal of time and money was being spent on trying to achieve new speed records and the Rootes brothers were fully aware of their importance at a time when nations were vying strongly with each other for world markets. The success of a country's cars frequently depended on performances on the race track, or record-breaking attempts.

The wealthy British businessman and racing enthusiast Sir Charles Wakefield, of C. C. Wakefield & Company Ltd, the makers of Castrol oil, presented the Wakefield Trophy in 1927 to be awarded to the holder of the world land speed record, irrespective of nationality. He had been encouraged by the success of another Englishman, Malcolm Campbell, who had been the first person to travel on land at 200 mph (321.8 km/h), a speed which had previously been thought to be beyond human powers of endurance and engineering ability.

Because they appreciated the value of solving the innumerable scientific and technical problems involved, the Americans set about constructing a still faster car, becoming the holders of the Wakefield Trophy in 1928 when Ray Keech set a new land speed record of 207 mph (333 km/h) at Daytona Beach in Florida. His speed, however, was only 1 mph (1.6 km/h) faster than the record set by Malcolm Campbell in February of that year, and represented a saving of only a fraction of a second over the measured mile, which was the distance used for the land speed record.

As the magical 200 mph barrier had been broken twice in only a few months, the next real milestone was obviously going to be a speed of 240 mph (386 km/h), or 4 miles a minute (6.4 km/min) and it was with this speed in view that a group of British companies, including Rootes, got together in 1928 to build the 'Golden Arrow'. Soon after their move to London, Billy and Reggie had acquired one of the most famous body-building companies of the time, Thrupp & Maberley, and it was that company which was chosen to build the special streamlined body for the new car.

Fourteen other companies were involved, with the Napier Company of Acton providing the engine, Marles Limited the steering units, John Thompson of Wolverhampton the chassis frame, T. B. Andre Limited of London the shock absorbers, Ransome & Marles Limited the ball-bearings, Hardy Spicer Limited of Birmingham the cardan shafts, Gillett & Stephens Limited of Bookham the gearbox, and Clayton Dewandre Limited of Lincoln the brake operating gear. The Gloucester Aircraft Company built the special radiators and the complete car was to be assembled and finished by the Robinhood Engineering Works of Newlands, Putney Vale. Specially compounded dope fuel would be supplied by the British Petroleum Company Limited and the oil was to be provided by London-based C. C. Wakefield & Company Limited.

Although the record-breaking attempt certainly caught the imagination of the Rootes brothers, it was mainly financed by three well-known British sportsmen of the time, Sir Charles Wakefield, Mr O. J. S. Piper and Major H. O. D. Segrave, who was also to be the driver. Billy Rootes had first met Henry Segrave during the war, and in the early 1920s they had frequently travelled together on business trips to Europe and America. He admired Segrave's ability as a driver, but was also impressed by the development work he was doing on the new 3-litre Sunbeam car, particularly as Rootes were hoping to buy the Sunbeam company when they felt the price was right.

Responsibility for the design of the aptly-named 'Golden Arrow' was left to Captain J. S. Irving, an outstanding engineer who had many years' experience of experimental and research work and probably knew more about the design and construction of racing cars than anyone else in Britain. He was given an entirely free hand and a drawing office was provided for him at 150 New Bond Street, only a short distance away from the Rootes headquarters at Devonshire House.

Before the 'Golden Arrow' left for America, Billy achieved considerable publicity for Rootes by arranging for the car to be exhibited at the company's main showroom at Devonshire House. The public flocked there to see the remarkable machine, which one motoring writer described as 'looking like an infuriated giant charging head down upon an enemy'.

On 11 March 1929 at Daytona Beach, Major Henry Segrave succeeded in covering a mile in 15 seconds, breaking the previous record by nearly 24 mph (38.6 km/h) and recording the amazing speed of 231 mph (372 km/h). Many of those who watched the car make four runs backwards and forwards over the course claimed afterwards that the 'Golden Arrow' had been travelling so fast that it was some way ahead of the extraordinary roar created by its Napier Lion engine, a power unit similar to the one used in the Supermarine Schneider Trophy seaplane.

Billy Rootes was there to congratulate his friend Henry Segrave and to use all his undoubted public relations and marketing skills to make sure that the world media, who had gathered at Daytona Beach, received all the information and facilities they required, and that Britain gained maximum publicity from such an outstanding feat.

Apart from the world speed record, Major Segrave also had his sights set on the motor boat speed record which had become almost exclusively the property of America. The record was held by *Miss America VII* driven by Garfield Wood, and an entirely new boat, aptly named *Miss England*, had been built for Major Segrave by Hubert Scott-Paine. Billy went on from Daytona to Miami to lend his support to this second British record-breaking attempt. The race between *Miss England* and *Miss America* was the culmination of the biggest regatta ever organized in the United States and was run over a 25-mile course just off the coast of Miami. Both races, run over two days, took place in heavy seas and under terrible conditions, with the British boat running out an easy winner.

With the world land speed record and the motor boat championship of the world both going to Britain within the space of a few weeks, Major Segrave's successes were celebrated in London with a luncheon at the Connaught Rooms given by Sir Charles Cheer Wakefield. Henry Segrave was the guest of honour and the occasion was well supported by important figures from commerce, politics and the media. The British Imperial Orchestra, under its conductor Arthur Crudge, played a selection from 'Merrie England' and everyone bristled with national pride. Companies looked forward to taking full advantage of the tremendous boost to international prestige which the two records had achieved, and Billy and Reggie Rootes planned to use the situation as a timely springboard into the 1930s. None were more enthusiastic about the future of the British motor industry. They felt that the 1930s would prove to be a new era of opportunity and they were right.

Henry Segrave was knighted for his achievements, but his death the following year was a sad loss to Britain, robbing Billy of a close personal friend. He wrote:

'No British subject has ever been more determined to establish the superiority of this country in the realms of speed than Sir Henry and his exploits have placed us all under an obligation which will be impossible to discharge. There is not a country in the world which has not thrilled at his marvellous performances and the value of the prestige they have conferred upon British industry cannot be overestimated. Not only was he a magnificent all-round sportsman, he was also without question a great ambassador.'

It was a tribute which expressed not only his admiration for a courageous and talented friend, but also confirmed once again his great pride in Britain and her achievements.

Chapter 8

The Prudential
to the rescue

BY 1929 ROOTES had created a worldwide market for the cars and trucks they were selling and had established export agencies and distribution outlets as far afield as India, Australia, New Zealand and the Far East. Their problem was finding enough cars to satisfy the demand they had created and it was becoming increasingly obvious that many of the models they were selling were outdated and were also rarely being delivered on time. It was a period of considerable change and uncertainty in the motor industry, when the producers of mass-produced light cars were forcing many of the established specialist firms out of business.

To make matters worse as far as Rootes was concerned, they had the worldwide export rights for Humber and Hillman cars and Commer commercial vehicles, but Humber and Hillman and their lorry-making subsidiary Commer Cars of Luton had got into serious financial difficulties. Many of their models were also uncompetitive, particularly in export markets where the motoring public was more knowledgeable and spoilt for choice. Ford in particular, with their mass production methods, had been biting into the traditional market for hand-built cars, and the bicycle repairer turned car manufacturer William Morris was also planning further mass production at his Oxford factory. He was already producing cars there at a rate of more than 65,000 a year.

Billy and Reggie Rootes knew that if the distribution business they had steadily been building up was not going to suffer, they would have to become motor manufacturers themselves, and have control over the design, quality and production of the cars they were selling. They would then no longer have to rely on the ability of other companies to satisfy their needs. They realised that their successful export business had given them a unique knowledge of the type of cars the public wanted, but their efforts to influence the design and quality of the models being produced by the British car manufacturers whose products they relied on had not been successful.

Their inability to influence Clyno had led to them giving up that company's distribution rights and Clyno had gone into liquidation shortly after the directors had turned down Rootes's offer to purchase the equity. With Humber, Hillman and Commer also in trouble, something had to be done quickly to prevent the situation from deteriorating further. Billy and Reggie went straight to Sir George Hay, later Lord Hay, the chairman of the highly successful Prudential Assurance Company, and Sir George and his fellow directors had no hesitation in backing their bid to buy all three companies. With The Prudential behind them, the young entrepreneurs were sure that their offer would be successful. The Humber chairman, Colonel Cole, had also been a friend of the Rootes family for many years, from the days when William Rootes was one of the company's major customers in Kent and had encouraged Colonel Cole and his colleagues to start making cars in the late 1890s.

The Humber Company had bought the assets of Commer Cars Limited when it ran into a number of serious financial difficulties during the slump and was wound up. The Commer Company had been started in London in 1905 to make gears for the motor industry, and it had pioneered the easy-change gearbox. It had moved to Luton later the same year. The company's Lindley gear was fitted to the first Commer truck and was looked upon as being a major innovation at the time.

Humber and Hillman, who had adjoining factories in Coventry, were merged in 1928, but the move didn't overcome their financial problems and the Rootes offer provided an immediate way out of their difficulties, which they could hardly turn down. The Humber–Hillman–Commer combine reported a loss of £67,158 for the 11 months ending 31 July, following similar heavy losses during the previous 12 months, and this was one of the reasons why their Coventry factories lacked modern equipment and there were no new models in the pipeline. Even so, with the purchase of Humber, Hillman and Commer the Rootes brothers now had control of three of the most distinguished companies in the British motor industry and their immediate task was to turn them as quickly as possible into well-equipped, modern companies, whose products would be competitive worldwide.

Humber had always been keen to sell their products abroad, but they lacked the necessary knowledge until the Rootes brothers came on the scene. Indeed their first attempt at exporting, in 1900, when they shipped a car to India, proved a complete fiasco and the car had to be returned to England because there was no petrol in India on which to run it properly.

In the summer of 1900, however, when the Rawalpindi docked at Rangoon, the large crate in the ship's hold contained not only the first Humber car to be exported, but also the first car to be imported into the continent of India. Humber bicycles were very popular there and when a leading Rangoon businessman read about the Humber Company's first motor car he persuaded George Blackstock, who was head of the firm of

importers Rome & Company Limited, to place an order for him. It
seemed a good idea at the time, but they had overlooked the fact that
the car would need fuel and there was neither petrol nor any suitable oil
in India. As a result, when it was removed from its crate on the docks,
to the interest and amusement of the crowds of spectators who had
gathered to watch, it had to be pushed to the Rome & Company
premises in Fytche Square.

The model was the two-seater Humber Phaeton, which had a $3\frac{1}{2}$ hp
air-cooled engine, a coil and dry battery ignition, direct steering, two
speeds and the carburetter, ignition and speed-change levers all fitted
on the steering column under the steering wheel. Although it was relatively simple to drive, it couldn't be delivered because the owner refused
to take delivery without a demonstration and test drive, and without
any petrol that proved impossible. In desperation, George Blackstock
appealed to Andrew Campbell, the works manager of the Burma Oil
Company, for help and he agreed to try and refine some petrol. After
some weeks of experimentation he managed to produce a fluid which
looked rather like petrol, but even so the only lubricating oil available
was of the type used for steam engines.

A Bengali engineer from Calcutta called Luck Coon was brought in
to try and get the engine started, but swinging the starting handle in
accordance with the instructions in the handbook had little effect and,
after every effort had failed, it was reluctantly decided to send the car
back to England. Before it was put back in its crate, however, someone
suggested that the Humber should be put into gear and pushed, in a
final attempt to get the engine going. The following Saturday afternoon
the tank was filled with Andrew Campbell's petrol concoction and,
with the owner at the wheel, Luck Coon was invited on board as passenger, handed the horn and told to 'blow it like hell' if the car started.

With everyone helping to push, the Humber steadily gathered
momentum until the engine suddenly roared into life. Luck Coon, grin-
ning happily, sounded the horn for all he was worth as they turned into
Merchant Street, which was then one of the busiest thoroughfares in
Rangoon. As usual on a Saturday afternoon it was crowded with Ticca
gharries and bullock carts, most of whose drivers were half asleep, and a
teeming mass of Burmese, Chinese and native pedestrians, who seemed
to throng every street in India.

Although he had never driven a car before, or received any proper
instruction, the driver did his best to keep control as the Humber
reached its top speed of 23 mph and then began zig-zagging from one
side of the street to the other. This was partly due to the car's sensitive
steering, but it was also because of the driver's frantic efforts to miss the
other vehicles and terrified pedestrians who were scattering in all directions.

Merchant Street was in an uproar. The Burma ponies attached to the
gharries and the bullocks pulling the carts bolted with fright at the sight

of the car speeding towards them, engine racing and with Luck Coon still frantically blowing his horn. The driver was too busy trying to steer to think about applying the brakes, but he managed to avoid most of the pedestrians and the bullock carts as he negotiated Phayre Street and Montgomery Street on his way to the comparative safety of Fytche Square. After several circuits of the square the car's engine seized, probably due to the heat and the poor quality of the engine oil, and the car shuddered to a halt.

The driver turned to congratulate Luck Coon on performing so well with the horn, but his terrified passenger dropped the instrument, leapt from the vehicle and bolted, never to return. Leaving the car where it stood in Fytche Square, the exhausted owner-driver made for the bar of the Strand Hotel, where he had to sink several large whiskies before he was able to stop shaking. When he arrived at his office on the following Monday he found a letter waiting for him from the Rangoon Commissioner of Police, who wanted to see him immediately. The meeting was far from harmonious, although the commissioner did concede that if anyone had been walking in front of the car with a red flag, as required by law in England, he would almost certainly have been killed and manslaughter might then have been added to all the other charges. After some argument it was agreed that all the charges would be dropped if 'generous compensation' was paid for the damage done to all the Ticca gharries and bullock carts and for the animals which had either been killed or injured in the mayhem caused by India's first motor car. The other stipulation was that the Humber should be shipped back to England, where there were no gharries and bullock carts, on the next available boat.

India was also involved some nine years later with the first and only aeroplane designed by the Humber Company. Despite Colonel Cole's protest that Humber should be concentrating on making bicycles and motor cars, his fellow directors insisted in 1909 that the company should design and build an aeroplane, which was then taken for its inaugural flight to a large meadow near the factory in Coventry. Captain Dawes, one of the most experienced pilots of the day, had agreed to fly it, but on seeing the weird-looking contraption for the first time, departed to a local inn and drank several glasses of brandy before he could be persuaded to return and sit behind the controls.

He made several attempts to get the machine into the air, but did eventually do so and circled the field once before landing. Despite repeated requests from Colonel Cole and the other directors to take it up once more, Captain Dawes climbed out of the aircraft visibly shaken and, as the effect of the brandy was wearing off, refused to go near the aircraft again. 'I have got down safely and that is all I intend to do,' was all he would say as he got into his car and drove away. Colonel Cole, who witnessed the whole proceedings with rather mixed feelings, told his wife later, 'I don't think it was petrol that got that aeroplane into the air today—it was much more likely to have been the brandy!'

Despite such a precarious inaugural flight, the aircraft went on show at the Aeronautical Exhibition in London and for a brief period was used to carry mail in India. It remained the first and only aeroplane designed by the Humber Company, although they did produce some air-craft during the First World War which had been designed by other companies.

Chapter 9

William Hillman and his six lovely daughters

LIKE THE HUMBER Company, Hillman had been involved with the cycle industry and the growth of the two companies during the early years was closely entwined. William Hillman, who was an Essex shoemaker's son, was born at Stratford in 1849. Like his contemporary, George Singer, he worked initially for the Penn Engineering Company in London, where James Starley, who went on to develop the Rover Company, was also an employee. Hillman and Starley joined forces for a brief period and in 1875 Starley built and patented the first Penny Farthing bicycle, with Hillman's assistance. They were only together for a short time, however, and Hillman went on to join William Herbert, the elder brother of Alfred, who later became world-famous for his machine tools.

Much of the Herbert family's fortune came from farming and building interests in Leicestershire, but Automachinery, the company which William Herbert formed with William Hillman, was initially concerned with the manufacture of cycle components, sewing machines and roller skates. When a further partner, George Beverley Cooper, joined the firm, he provided the additional finance needed to expand and start making complete bicycles. The cycle side was separated in 1896, but continued trading successfully as the New Premier Cycle Company.

William Hillman's business interests developed, and by the turn of the century he was a millionaire, living in Abingdon House, an impressive mansion at Stoke Aldermoor on the outskirts of Coventry. The Humber factory was close by and when, in 1905, he started to nurse ambitions to become a motor manufacturer, he recruited Louis Herve Coatalen, a 26-year-old Breton designer who was working for Humber. The young Frenchman had already gained valuable experience of motor car design through working in the drawing offices of the three French motor manufacturers, Panhard et Levassor, de Dion-Bouton and Clement, who were leading the way in Europe. This was followed by a short spell in Germany before he moved to England at the age of 21 to work for the Crowden Motor Car Company in Leamington Spa. He left there after only a few months to become chief engineer at Humber, working under the company's manager at the time, Walter Phillips. Coatalen was responsible for the success of the 8/10 and 10/12 hp cars but, like so many other good men who left the Humber Company during that period, he was disenchanted with management policy. He joined Hillman in 1906.

His first task at Hillman was to design a car for the 1907 Isle of Man Tourist Trophy race. This had a 25 hp, four-cylinder engine and was built in a small factory constructed in the grounds of Abingdon House. With Coatalen at the wheel, this first Hillman–Coatalen model had a ding-dong battle for the lead with the Beeston–Humber and during the first circuit averaged a remarkable $37\frac{1}{2}$ mph (60 km/h). The pace was too fast to last and the car had to be retired, after losing a tyre and breaking a rear spring. Its performance did create enough public interest to encourage William Hillman to go into production with the 25 hp model and to produce an enlarged, six-cylinder, 40 hp model in November 1907.

The two cars entered for the 1908 TT were based on this latest 40 hp version. Coatalen and Kenelm Lee Guiness, who later became well known through his KLG sparking plugs, were the drivers, but the cars had little success in the race. Although Coatalen was married to one of William Hillman's daughters, he left the Hillman company to join Sunbeam at Wolverhampton, where he did achieve considerable success until the late 1920s.

Production of Hillman cars was transferred to a building on the nearby Pinley Estate and in 1908 work commenced on a smaller 12/15 hp model which was ready for the 1909 season. Until 1913, Hillman production rarely exceeded 50 cars a year. Coatalen had sold his shares in the company back to his father-in-law in 1910 and the name was changed from the Hillman–Coatalen Motor Car Company to the Hillman Motor Car Company. The change reflected Coatalen's final break with Hillman, although the company continued to use some of his designs for the next three years.

The Hillman company's fortunes fluctuated considerably until William's death in 1921 at the age of 72. In 1913 a new designer, A. J. Dawson, had been brought in and William Hillman increased the capital he had invested from £2,000 to £20,000 in order to develop the Dawson-designed Hillman 9 hp model. This probably saved the company and enabled production to be increased from a modest 65 in 1913 to a more healthy 244 in 1915, when Hillman switched to war work. Dawson left in 1918 to start the Dawson Car Company in Coventry and manufactured a light car under his own name from 1919 until 1921. Only about 65 found customers, however, and the factory was eventually bought by Triumph when that company started car production in 1923.

Dawson's place at Hillman was taken by John Black who, like

Coatalen, had married one of William Hillman's six daughters. He had left the army with the rank of captain and showed good, if autocratic, management skills. The company's Hillman 11 hp model, which was a bored-out version of the successful 9 hp car, faced strong competition, made more serious by the post-war slump in the early 1920s.

A 10 hp Super Sports version, with its distinguishing pointed radiator, had a number of competition successes, mainly because of its reliability. The cars raced at Brooklands, where George Bedford, the head tester, was usually on hand to give advice to the growing number of Hillman owners who were keen to compete, but it was the 11 hp car, with a variety of open and saloon bodies, which remained the main model until 1925. Local coachbuilders were used to produce the bodies, but by 1927 the company had started making their own and the factory was enlarged to cater for further models, including the Hillman 14, which was intended to compete with the Austin 12/4. Another of William Hillman's sons-in-law, Spencer Wilks, who had trained as a barrister, joined the company in 1919 to share control with John Black. He was also a former army captain and it was due to the management skills of the two men that Hillman was able to weather the storms of the 1920s.

Having given up the Clyno distributorship, Rootes became sole British and overseas distributors for Hillman cars in Britain and abroad in 1927, and again in 1928, when Hillman merged with Humber and Commer. When Rootes purchased all three companies in 1929, John Black and Spencer Wilks were so annoyed that they left. Black, who later became Sir John Black, moved to the Standard Motor Company and Spencer Wilks went to Rover.

That didn't worry Billy and Reggie. They knew that, with the help of the 'Pru', they would soon have Hillman in a position to compete on level terms with other major manufacturers, and the lights in Devonshire House burned late into the night as they worked on an urgent programme of reorganization, aimed at centralizing control and reducing costs. The works director in charge of the Coventry factories was Harold Heath, a man the Rootes brothers felt they could trust and who was the son of their friend George Heath, whose distribution company in the Midlands they had bought in 1924. He, along with other senior Rootes executives and staff from the Coventry factories, was frequently called at short notice to meetings at Devonshire House, in order to provide the brothers with information, or to be updated on the latest developments. Those who lacked the necessary drive and enthusiasm demanded by the exuberant and seemingly tireless young millionaires were quickly sent packing, or found other jobs more suited to their ability and temperament, but Billy's physical energy and ebullient nature were matched by a warmth of human understanding which made him popular with his employees. It is a tribute to the loyalty and enthusiasm he was able to instil into those executives at that time that many of them remained with Rootes until the time came for them to retire.

Billy made the same demands on everyone, including other members of his family, insisting on their loyalty and total dedication to the task of making Rootes the most efficient and successful manufacturing and sales organization in the motor industry. This led to one humorous situation.

When he found that his half-brother, Desmond Rootes, was not achieving the targets which had been set, Billy decided that, regrettable though it might be, Desmond would have to go, and the task of firing him would have to be done by himself personally. He invited Desmond to lunch at the Ritz and, after a few softening dry Martinis, was about to suggest that he might be better off working for another company when Desmond announced that he had been offered a job with the Austin motor company, which was better than the one he had at Rootes and which he felt he should accept.

Billy nearly exploded with rage. 'What!' he roared, to the surprise of other diners at nearby tables. 'You want to leave and join a rival company? I won't have such disloyalty from an important member of my team, and a member of the family as well.' Desmond Rootes continued working for Rootes for the next 20 years, but in a capacity more suited to his capabilities.

Throughout his career Billy always had the ability to generate loyalty among his senior staff and few left him, although many could undoubtedly have earned higher salaries elsewhere. As I know from my own experience (on one occasion he doubled my salary in order to persuade me not to leave), he was sometimes prepared to go to extreme lengths to ensure that people he needed remained with Rootes.

The same was true if he saw someone working elsewhere whom he felt had exceptional ability and who could prove a valuable asset to the company. Rupert Hammond was a typical example. He was a brilliant accountant working for The Prudential Assurance Company. Billy and Reggie Rootes were so impressed with the way he handled the negotiations for the Rootes loan that they persuaded The Prudential to allow him to become their financial director and replace H. A. Holmes, who left Rootes in October 1931 to join the board of the India Tyre and Rubber Company.

It was a wise choice. Rupert Hammond remained with Rootes for nearly 40 years and played an important part in the development of the Group. His keen analytical brain was behind many of the financial deals which the Rootes brothers negotiated and he enabled them to clinch a series of successful acquisitions.

Chapter 10

The battle for Pressed Steel

ALTHOUGH THE ROOTES brothers had gained control of three important manufacturing companies, they continued to sell Austin cars in order to ease their cash flow problems. It was probably because of their reliance on Austin that Billy and Reggie had helped to arrange finance for the company earlier, when it ran into serious financial trouble. In 1929 they still had to face the problem that neither Hillman nor Humber had any new models in the pipeline and, like Commer, their factories were badly equipped and using out-of-date production methods, even by European standards. American automobile manufacturers were much more advanced, so Rootes looked to Detroit for help and advice.

Reggie paid a number of visits to America, studying production methods and buying the latest machine tools and equipment needed to modernize the Luton and Coventry factories. He had talks with Ford and Chrysler and it was at their suggestion that Billy spent some time in Philadelphia, where the Edward G. Budd Manufacturing Company had their headquarters. Edward Budd was a brilliant designer and production engineer and his company was making all-steel car bodies for a number of American companies. Budd also had a substantial financial interest in the Pressed Steel Company at Cowley, near Oxford, whose other shareholders were Schroders & Baring, a well-known British financial institution with a fine name in the city, and William Morris of Morris Motors. Pressed Steel used a number of Budd patents.

The Rootes brothers were interested in Edward Budd for two reasons. They had persuaded Captain Irving, the successful designer of the record-breaking 'Golden Arrow', to join them as chief engineer and they wanted Budd's co-operation and advice with the new Hillman which Irving was designing, because it was to have an all-steel body. They had also heard that William Morris wanted to sell his shares in the Pressed Steel Company, and Billy in particular wanted control of the body-building plant at Cowley, which he knew other manufacturers would need for their future models. Pressed Steel was to play a major role in the Rootes brothers' arrival on the motor manufacturing scene and they had to ensure that the company had a financially secure and lasting future. Since their purchase of Humber, Hillman and Commer, Rootes and Morris had become rivals and it was unlikely that William Morris would be willing to sell his shares in Pressed Steel to Rootes, except perhaps at a greatly inflated price. By using Edward Budd as a front man, Billy thought he might be able to get hold of the shares without William Morris knowing.

Edward Budd had taken a liking to Billy and his rumbustious way of doing business. Both men were frustrated by the old-fashioned opinions and business methods found in many British companies and he was impressed that such a relatively young man, with little or no manufacturing experience, had succeeded in persuading The Prudential Assurance Company to place £1 million at his company's disposal. Billy was the sort of Englishman he wanted to do business with and he felt at the time that there might be benefits to be gained by supporting his plans.

Billy suggested that Budd should purchase William Morris's shares and sell them to Rootes, but the plan backfired when William Morris agreed to sell, but only on condition that none of the shares went to his competitors. Billy's behind-the-scenes dealings with Budd over the future of the Pressed Steel Company led to animosity between Morris and Rootes which lasted until Morris died. It prevented a closer relationship in later years that could have been beneficial to both companies and to the British motor industry.

Although Billy realized that he could no longer gain control of Pressed Steel, he was anxious that the company should remain in British hands and enlisted the help of the Lord Privy Seal and Sir Horace Wilson at the Treasury. Budd had taken an option on the Morris shares which would give his company financial control, with the remaining 5,000 preference shares and 19,000 ordinary shares still being held by J. Henry Schroder & Company.

Billy urged the British Government to impress upon Budd that considerable benefits would accrue to his company if British car manufacturers could be persuaded to use the Cowley plant, but to emphasize that they would only use their influence in this direction if the control of Pressed Steel was in British hands. Pressed Steel had never been particularly profitable, which was one of the reasons William Morris had wanted to sell his shares, but that was a situation which could quickly change if more British manufacturers could be persuaded to give the company their business.

The problems were still unresolved when Billy returned to London in January 1930 after spending the Christmas holidays in St Moritz. He wanted the negotiations kept alive because Pressed Steel was a major factor in Rootes' production plans for future Humber, Hillman and

Commer models. After Christmas, Budd began to get rather worried about the situation and wrote to Baron Schroder Tiarks, asking him to talk to Billy, because he had become increasingly concerned at his insistence that William Morris should be kept in the dark. He also realized the effect Billy's attitude might have on Ford, as well as Morris, who were both still important customers. William Morris had been a friend for some years and Budd didn't want his company to suffer because of Billy's scheme.

Thanks to Billy's behind-the-scenes activities, however, Budd received confirmation from the British Government that if the Pressed Steel Company was sufficiently British-controlled, with Henry Schroder becoming the majority shareholder, the Government would call a meeting with Sir William Morris, Sir Herbert Austin and Sir Percival Perry of the Ford Motor Company, to remind them of the need for greater rationalization between motor manufacturers in order to help solve the unemployment problem. They would point out that there were now no obstacles to prevent them from fully utilizing the Pressed Steel Company's plant at Cowley.

Budd appreciated the benefits, but was concerned about his company losing control of Pressed Steel. He wrote to Billy explaining that, while he had every trust in Schroder, he still didn't want to turn the control of Pressed Steel over to them. He asked him if he thought the British Government would be satisfied with an assurance that the majority of the board would be British citizens of standing, to be selected by the Budd Manufacturing Company in consultation with the Government.

Billy discussed the suggestion with Sir Horace Wilson and told Joe Chaldecott, who was leaving for New York on the liner *Berengaria* to attend the New York Motor Show, to try to persuade Budd to come to England, so that the difficulties could be solved without further delay. He asked Chaldecott to emphasize to Budd that he fully understood the importance of Morris to his company and wouldn't do anything to hinder the negotiations.

On 27 February, Billy cabled Budd:

'After attending many long conferences with the Minister and his chief consultant to define means of increasing the output of the motor industry in Britain, and with your interest always before me, I am convinced that the government can, and will, help your company materially. But it is essential that the Minister is put into an impregnable position so that, in the event of any questions arising, he cannot be embarrassed in Parliament.

Although the control would technically be on this side, provision could be made so that your position and benefits are safeguarded. The majority of the earnings going to a British group is not necessary, and nor does the majority of the board being British materially help, as everyone has the utmost confidence in your administration, and realises that the majority of the benefits must go to you.'

Budd agreed to visit England in March to speed up negotiations, but soon after arriving in London was taken ill and had to be moved from the Carlton Hotel to the Alfred House private nursing home. The negotiations were taken over by Paul Pleiss, his company's foreign director, which meant that a final decision could not be reached until the end of April, when Budd left the nursing home. It was eventually agreed that, with various safeguards, voting control of Pressed Steel should remain in British hands. The Schroder Group would hold more than 50 per cent of the 42,500 ordinary voting shares and the rest would remain with the Budd Manufacturing Company, who would also hold the balance of the 17,500 non-voting shares. The other stipulation was that the terms were agreeable to Morris, Austin and Ford, as well as Rootes, as all four companies were important Budd customers.

Although Billy had failed in his attempt to gain control of Pressed Steel, he was pleased with the outcome, because it meant that the Pressed Steel Company would remain in British hands and the company on which they were depending now had the strength of Government support. It was also essential to his plans that Pressed Steel should be profitable and in a strong position to trade efficiently, because the all-steel bodies for Rootes's new cars were to be made there.

While the negotiations had been taking place, the Rootes brothers had gone ahead with plans for their first new model since becoming motor manufacturers. When Captain Irving discussed his ideas with Edward Budd, he suggested that they should produce a car similar in size to the small Dodge, but with a 13–15 hp, six-cylinder engine, under 2,500 lb (1,134 kg) in weight and selling for £165. But his suggestion that the engine and transmission should be supplied by the Continental Car Company of America, and the axles produced by the Timken Company, did not meet with Billy's approval. He told Budd

'I have given a great deal of thought to your suggestions that we should consider obtaining our engines from Continental, especially as the manufacturing resources and the experience gained by Continental in the manufacture of cheap car units would be at our disposal. Unfortunately in England we have to deal with a rather peculiar temperament and a scheme of this nature, although showing us in the first instance reduced manufacturing costs, might materially affect our sales if the public really thought our car was of American manufacture. I do not mean that they would think it inferior because if was of American manufacture, but there is a growing feeling of patriotism in Britain that everyone should buy a British-made vehicle. A rumour that Morris had been obtaining engines from Detroit seriously affected the company's business until it was flatly denied by William Morris himself.'

The rumours had probably been believed, because when William Morris was hardly known in the motoring world, the Morris Cowley which he had shown at the Olympia Motor Show in 1913 was built mostly of American parts. He was then being financed by a wealthy aristocrat, the Earl of Macclesfield, who had placed an order for several thousand engines with the Continental Car Company in Detroit. Because of the war, many of the engines were never delivered and when peace came William Morris sent Lord Macclesfield a cheque for £25,000 to clear his indebtedness and to stop him from interfering in the development of his motor business.

Lord Macclesfield was not at all pleased when Morris Motors (1926) was formed as a public company and he realised that his £25,000 loaned to William Morris could have been worth many times that amount. The Morris Company expanded considerably in 1927 when William Morris also bought Wolseley from the official receiver.

Billy Rootes discussed the possibility of Timken establishing a factory in England, but the idea was turned down on account of the cost. As a result, Rootes laid down a new axle gear and transmission unit at their Coventry Humber factory, which operated successfully and produced units at very competitive prices.

Although Billy and Reggie planned to use the latest American methods to produce their new models as efficiently as possible, and had asked Edward Budd to find them a top American production engineer and time and motion expert, they were determined that their cars should be British throughout, even if that meant a possible cost penalty.

Chapter 11

A Wizard launch

WITH THE PROBLEM of Pressed Steel behind them, their assembly lines ready at Coventry, and all the new equipment installed, the Rootes brothers turned their attention to creating maximum impact for their first new car, the Hillman Wizard. They wanted a professional publicist to ensure that it achieved major press exposure throughout the world, and the man they chose was Billy's old friend from motor cycle racing days, Dudley Noble. American car manufacturers had employed professionals to promote their new products for some years, in the same way the Hollywood film studios had press agents to create publicity for their stars, and Billy wanted to do the same.

Since returning to Rover after the war, Dudley Noble had been in charge of the company's publicity department. When Spencer Wilks left Hillman in 1929 to become managing director of Rover, he was determined to make the Rootes brothers sit up and take notice. He told Dudley Noble to devise a plan which would put the new Rover Six on the front page of all the national daily newspapers. 'I want something which will really make people talk and steal a march on our competitors,' he explained.

As a result, Noble thought up the most adventurous publicity stunt attempted by any British car maker and one which caught the imagination of the media and the motoring public. He planned to race the famous Blue Train, which took the wealthy away from the cold winters in England to the sunnier climate of the French and Italian Rivieras in a little over 24 hours. The train was the epitome of gracious travel, with its luxurious blue-painted coaches and restaurant cars. Passengers from Britain usually caught the 11 a.m. from Victoria to Dover, which connected with the high-speed cross-Channel mail boat, and boarded the Blue Train at Calais before it departed for the Riviera at 2.30 p.m. The train was said to average a mile a minute, or 60 mph (96.5 km/h), as it travelled across Europe to its terminus at Ventimiglia, across the Italian border from Menton, but Dudley Noble calculated that the average

speed was nearer 40 mph (64 km/h), which he felt was within the capa-
bility of the new Rover.

He persuaded Harold Pemberton of the *Daily Express*, the most outstanding motoring correspondent of the day, to join him, along with a
tester from the Rover factory called Bennett. Beverley Baxter, the celebrated editor of the *Daily Express*, promised his paper's full support and
so did the general manager, Robbie Robertson, and the advertising
director, Bill Needham. Dudley Noble and his crew crossed the Channel
on the evening of 20 January 1930 and stayed the night in Calais. After
a leisurely lunch the next day, they stationed the Rover alongside the
Blue Train's locomotive, on the side of the level crossing which enabled
them to get through the town and onto the main route south to
Boulogne, Abbeville and Beauvais the moment it moved off. As 2.30
approached they started the engine and engaged first gear, and as the
first tell-tale puff of smoke emerged from the locomotive, the Rover
sped out of the dock area on its way to Ventimiglia.

Despite all the careful planning, they soon ran into difficulties.
Pemberton was knocked unconscious when Bennett misjudged a sharp
bend in heavy rain and the Rover careered over the edge of a mountain,
coming to a stop in a small gulley. Passers-by helped to manhandle it
back onto the road, but further bad weather and fog gave them no
chance of beating the train. They had better luck, however, on the
return journey, and when the Blue Train steamed into Calais, the Rover,
plastered with mud, was parked alongside the platform, its three-man
crew red-eyed and unshaven enjoying a well-deserved celebratory bottle
of champagne. They had beaten the Blue Train by 20 minutes, to the
delight of the Rover company and their dealers, but there were protests
to the Royal Automobile Club by the French authorities, who warned
that action would be taken against any future offenders who broke
international competition rules.

Details of the Rover's remarkable achievement were blazoned across
the front pages and Billy Rootes wondered how he could induce Dudley
Noble to leave Rover and help him with the launch of the Hillman
Wizard. The opportunity came about five months later when they met
by chance at the Queens Hotel in Birmingham, where Dudley and Ted
Sherren of the *Daily Mail* had been having dinner together. Billy invited
Dudley to come and see him at Devonshire House and on 30 June he
accepted the invitation to become Rootes's first publicity manager.

Dudley's first task was to think of a way of showing that the new
Hillman Wizard was an ideal car for world markets and able to cope
with all types of climate and road conditions. His main problem was
that details of the car had to be kept secret until it was unveiled to the
public in April 1931, because the company's competitors wanted
advance information about the Wizard and Austin and Morris in particular were anxious to know about Rootes's marketing plans. Everyone
expected a great deal from the company's link-up with The Prudential

and other companies began planning more aggressive sales programmes for their own models and increased production at their factories.

The new Hillman Wizard was certainly different from previous models. It featured alternative engine sizes, with a 15.72 hp unit for the home market, where cars were being taxed according to their RAC horsepower ratings, and a larger 20.9 hp version for export markets, where there were no such penalties. The all-steel bodies were the same for both versions and their four-speed gearboxes had a silent third gear ratio known as the 'traffic top'. Edward Budd had provided Rootes with information about the latest technical developments used by American manufacturers, as well as confidential details of component prices for the smaller of the Dodge models, which they were able to use as a yardstick for their dealings with the British companies supplying equipment for the Wizard. This meant that the Hillman Wizard had a number of important new concepts and was also very competitively priced, thanks to the help received from Budd.

Billy agreed that Dudley Noble should take Harold Pemberton into his confidence and discuss with him the best way of demonstrating the Wizard's ability to deal with conditions in world markets. Pemberton suggested that they should drive the car from the heat and sands of the North African desert to the mid-winter cold and snow of the Alps. This was agreed, but due to supply problems with the bodies from Pressed Steel and the need for strict security, the Wizard wasn't able to leave Britain until the last week of December 1930.

On Boxing Day afternoon it left Southampton for Le Havre on the first stage of the journey to North Africa. Apart from Dudley Noble and Harold Pemberton, the third member of the crew was George Bedford, who had been given the title of technician, in case referring to him as a mechanic might have given the impression that they were expecting trouble. Bedford was no stranger to competitive challenges, having been successful in several speed events with a Hillman before Rootes bought the company. A Hillman Vortic accompanied the Wizard as a tender car and to provide transport for a news agency photographer who had a cine camera, in addition to a stills camera, so that a publicity film could be made of the journey.

Everyone was working to a tight schedule, because they had to be back in England by 20 January to allow time for the photographs and film to be developed and edited, ready for the launch. Press releases also had to be prepared and Harold Pemberton had to have the story of their journey ready so that serialization could start in the *Daily Express* and finish on the day of the announcement, when the name of the car would be revealed.

Until the final article, however, the car was to be referred to as the Cosmo, a new British car making an overland journey across Africa and the Alps. The Rootes' monthly magazine *Modern Motoring* was also to carry the full story of the trip. The magazine's new editor was Tom

Mulcaster, who had been editing *Motor Owner*, a glossy publication owned by Captain de Normanville, which had been forced to close because of the depression.

The Wizard withstood the demands of the journey well, despite the extremes of weather and road conditions it had to face, ranging from the intense heat and desert tracks of Morocco, the fierce storms and spring-breaking problems in Algeria, to the fast roads and hairpin bends of the Alps and weather which included snow, ice, fog, frost and rain. They even had to cope with an avalanche. It was an impressive performance by a new car and just the test of its ruggedness and reliability which was needed.

Not everyone appreciated the enthusiasm with which Billy Rootes tackled the task of ensuring that there were enough of the new models available for the launch. Hillman workers often worked late at night because of the late arrival of supplies, while other firms in Coventry were having to lay off workers. Some other manufacturers thought Rootes was cutting costs by making people work overtime instead of taking on additional labour, and complaints were made to the local Home Office Factory Inspector.

This was an unfair accusation, because they were only working overtime to cope with hold-ups in material supplies and the irregular arrival of some of the components for the new Wizard. They could only work on the new car after the deliveries had been made, but even so the company received 10 summons involving the Factories Act and overtime regulations, following a visit to the trim shop by a local factory inspector. Despite a fine, Rootes won a moral victory in court for what had been described as a technical offence, and the Mayor praised the company for bringing fresh employment to Coventry at a time when there was considerable unemployment elsewhere, and on investing heavily in new models and machinery which would ensure the future of two of the main car companies in the area.

Billy Rootes hired the Albert Hall in the centre of London for the Wizard's launch, which he planned would be the most spectacular send-off given to any new car outside America. Since its opening in 1851, the Albert Hall had been used mainly for exhibitions, although Ford had held a motor show there, but it had never been used for the sort of function Billy was planning, which involved a luncheon for more than 1,000 people.

As with everything they had done so far, the Rootes brothers launched their new car in style and tackled every problem in characteristic fashion. Billy insisted that each detail should be carefully minuted and checked time and again so that everyone involved knew exactly what to do. Members of the staff were even instructed about leading the applause. 'You should try and encourage applause, particularly when slides of the car are being shown,' Billy informed them, 'but if the applause after the film is loud enough, let it continue as long as possible until there is a signal from the toastmaster.'

Catering for so many presented a number of problems. To enable everyone to be seated for lunch, alternative rows of seats were removed and replaced by specially designed long-legged tables. The Albert Hall didn't have any suitable kitchens and so food had to be prepared and brought in. The guest list was impressive and included members of the British Government, foreign dignitaries, executives from all the main motor companies, personalities from motor racing and aviation, officials from the Society of Motor Manufacturers and Traders and other motoring organizations, representatives from all three services and the War Office, members of Parliament, and the mayors and local government officials from all the areas where Rootes had factories or offices.

As with every major function which Billy Rootes arranged during his business career, he insisted on doing the table plan himself. A large board was made showing the location of all the tables, and cards with everyone's name and title were pinned to it. These were changed round repeatedly until he was sure that everyone was being seated according to their status, but also that the people they were sitting next to had similar interests and would be likely to enjoy their company.

The completed list and table placings looked more like a *Who's Who?* of the motor industry and international trade. Members of the press were also there in force and it was perhaps typical of the brothers that they broke with convention and invited the chairmen and chief executives of all the other motor manufacturing companies who were now their competitors. The car had been a closely guarded secret, but now that it was ready to be launched they wanted everyone to know that the Rootes brothers were going to be a force to be reckoned with as motor manufacturers, as well as distributors.

Despite all the careful planning and attention to detail, there was bound to be a last-minute hitch. When the expensive programmes arrived on the eve of the launch, with their thick red covers and gold lettering and containing a congratulatory message from the Prince of Wales as well as a list of all the guests and the full seating plan, they had a mistake in them. Lord Waleran had been personal assistant to the Governor General of New Zealand before becoming Billy Rootes's personal assistant, and he knew the name and correct title of all the important dignatories on the guest list and their decorations. He noticed that the Rt Hon Austen Chamberlain's name had been spelt with an 'i' instead of an 'e'. Although it was by then 10 pm, Billy insisted that all the programmes must be reprinted before the guests arrived at noon the following day. Dudley Noble came to the rescue and contacted the director of a printing firm at Letchworth who had done some business for him in the past, and he agreed that key personnel should be brought in to work through the night. They reset the guest list and table plan, stripped the plush covers from the original programmes and rebound them to include the new pages, by 9 am the following day. The driver who had been dispatched from London to Letchworth with a corrected copy of the programme had instructions to remain at the printers and make regular progress reports until the work had been completed. He was then to deliver the new programmes to the Albert Hall by 12 noon. There were only minutes to spare when he arrived, but Billy was relaxed and obviously enjoying the occasion as he received the first of his guests. Reggie was unable to be present because he had been visiting some of the Rootes overseas distribution companies in readiness for the arrival of the new Hillman Wizard and was now attending the British Exhibition in Argentina, which was being opened by the Prince of Wales. The Prince had cabled his good wishes for the success of the Wizard launch and his regret at not being able to be present, and Billy was able to read out the cable during the luncheon. Reggie Rootes was so impressed with the potential he found during his visit to the exhibition that he arranged for Rootes Argentina to be formed later that year.

The Wizard launch was certainly a lavish party. The guests consumed 278 bottles of champagne, 199 bottles of hock, 104 bottles of sherry and 30 bottles of spirits, and smoked a total of 2,000 cigarettes and 2,000 cigars. Unfortunately, not all the guests were well behaved. One was seen with a full bottle of champagne, which exploded in his pocket, while others helped themselves 'very liberally' to the cigarettes and cigars. But Billy didn't mind and the overall cost of the reception was still only about two shillings a head!

When the guests sat down to lunch they looked down on seven large boxes with covers over them on which were written tantalizing questions about the Wizard and its performance. During the meal, cables which had arrived from all parts of the world expressing interest in the car and its potential as a world-beater were flashed onto large screens at one end of the hall. Colonel Cole made a speech of welcome which was followed by a response from the Rt Hon J. H. Thomas, PC, MP, the Minister who had been involved with Billy Rootes in the recent successful takeover of the Pressed Steel Company.

According to one American guest, Mr Thomas was in great form. 'No old-time Fourth of July orator in America was ever more wrapped up in his subject and made more of it,' he later told Edward Budd, who had been prevented from coming, adding, 'He lost more "aitches" and gave a greater number of new phonetic expressions to common words in the English language than I have ever heard before in so short a period of time. Nevertheless his speech and his frequent reference to the new 'illman Wizard and to the Rootes organization in general was very effective.'

After the speeches, the lights were dimmed and Mr Wilson, the organist, who had been playing a selection of popular musical numbers, broke into 'more bright and snappy topical music of a fairly loud nature'. The curtains at one end opened to reveal a full-size cinema screen in readiness for the guests to watch the 20-minute film of the Hillman

Wizard taken during its successful journey across North Africa and the Alps. While it was being shown, the stage hands from the Drury Lane Theatre, who had been brought in specially to ensure that the unveiling went smoothly, silently removed the boxes and their covers to reveal seven gleaming new Hillman Wizards. As the film ended, the spotlight fell on Billy Rootes who, to loud applause and with Mr Wilson this time 'crashing out some popular music of an appropriate nature', invited the thousand guests to go down and inspect the new cars.

The launch was undoubtedly a huge success. More than 400 Wizards had already been delivered to the main British dealers, and overseas distributors were particularly enthusiastic as a result of all the carefully planned publicity. The company's advertising campaign with the theme 'the car of the moderns' brought in a large volume of orders, and Billy and Reggie proved that they were going to provide a serious challenge to all the other British car makers, particularly Austin, Standard, Rover and Morris.

Unfortunately, the Wizard had a number of design faults which prevented it from becoming the world-beater Rootes had hoped. The sports Coupé with a Mulliner body proved very disappointing and the model was dropped soon after the launch, as well as the touring car version, which did not attract many sales.

Chapter 12

The remarkable Minx

HILLMAN WAS THE linchpin of the Rootes brothers' plan to make their newly acquired manufacturing companies profitable, and the majority of their investment from 1929 until 1932 went into the revival of the Hillman marque through the launch of the Wizard, closely followed by the Minx. The first new Humber model did not arrive on the scene until 1933. At the time of the merger with Humber in 1928, Hillman had a poor range of cars. The 14 hp model had been on sale for too long and could no longer compete with the more exciting models being produced by other companies. Their new Straight-Eight was also a failure. It had a stodgy engine, was badly engineered and still struggled for sales even after being renamed the Vortic in 1931. The Vortic was an unimaginative name for a very unimaginative model which Billy and Reggie wanted to get rid of as soon as possible.

They had hoped that the Wizard would start them off on the right foot, but it unfortunately proved to be little more successful than the Vortic. What they now needed was a popular family car which could be produced in volume and provide the cash flow required to finance their investment. Although they had inherited the Vortic with all its faults, the Wizard was different. It was their first all-new model and its lack of success was beginning to tarnish the image which the young entrepreneurs had built up during the 1920s. Fortunately for them, the Hillman Minx, which went on sale in 1931 and was seen that year at the Paris Salon, was an immediate hit and became a firm favourite among families worldwide for nearly 40 years. It ensured Rootes a secure place among Britain's big six motor manufacturers and became the greatest commercial success of all their models.

The fact that it was a success from the start was a tribute to Billy Rootes's attention to detail and his insistence on supervising all the overseas testing of the prototype himself. He knew that their new model would have to sell in large enough numbers to put Rootes into the big manufacturers' league, and to do so it would also have to sell well abroad and appeal to the mass overseas market. It was cheaper than any previous Hillman and was new from end to end. For that reason he felt it necessary to give the prototype a thorough testing over some of the worst terrain in Europe.

The Minx had been conceived by Captain Irving and A. H. Wilde, who was responsible for the successful Standard 9 launched in 1928. Wilde had a high reputation as a small car designer and was noted for his simple but sturdy designs. The Minx proved no exception and had a channel section frame, front and rear half-elliptic springs and Bendix cable brakes. The early models were fitted with a three-speed gearbox, which did not have synchromesh in order to keep down costs, and the rugged little cast-iron, side-valve engine proved to be so popular that it was used in some form or another for the next 25 years.

Billy Rootes, accompanied by his chauffeur, George Vallet, a former Olympic runner, took the prototype Minx across to Europe in May 1931. For part of the trip his wife Nora also accompanied them, because he was anxious to get her view of the car's suitability for the whole family. Each evening he telephoned his brother with news of its performance and sent lengthy cables giving details of the modifications he wanted made before it went into production. The body leaked, the steering wheel position was not acceptable, there was not enough room for the driver's feet and the pedals needed to be repositioned. He was also not satisfied with the suspension and steering and the ride for the rear passengers was an important feature which his wife felt should be improved. Billy was also unhappy with the performance and fuel consumption of the side-valve engine and insisted that improvements would have to be made, even if the launch had to be postponed. The engineering department was left in no doubt about the importance of the changes he wanted, and worked overtime to ensure that the modifications were made in time.

Sporting their French berets, Billy and George Vallet could have been mistaken for Basque peasants. Vallet's unflappable nature was frequently stretched to the limit as Billy insisted on checking each day's performance figures over and over again, recording everything in careful detail to send back to the engineering and design team in Coventry. Vallet's remarkable ability to cope with Billy's rumbustious manner was no doubt helped by that three weeks they spent together testing the Minx in France, Germany, Switzerland and Italy, and he remained Billy's personal chauffeur for the next 40 years until Billy's death. During that period he was frequently loaned to members of the Royal Family to drive them on important overseas tours—always, of course, in a Rootes Humber.

Billy inspired great loyalty in all his personal staff and none ever left him, including Miss Linda Drury, his personal secretary for nearly 40 years, who was privy to many of his personal and business affairs, and the ubiquitous Charles Morris, who was his travelling secretary and valet from the early 1930s. Morris had been employed by the Maharajah of Alwar until he had been deposed by order of the Viceroy. Apart from regularly exercising his *droit de seigneur* over numerous Indian girls, the Maharajah had been misruling his state and misappropriating its funds for some years, and might have continued to get away with these malpractices had he not set fire to his polo pony after his team had lost an important match. That was too much for the British Raj and was his final undoing, leaving Morris free to return to England and work for Billy.

Morris proved to be a very efficient secretary as well as a good valet. In the days before fax machines Billy had a portable typewriter fitted to the front passenger compartment of his Humber Pullman, and on the way home from important meetings they would stop alongside a post box, so that Morris could type important letters or reports and post them in time to catch the last collection of the day. The other people at the meetings could never work out how there was always a letter or report from Billy waiting for them the next morning, even if the meeting had gone on until late into the afternoon. It was just one of the ways in which he kept his competition on their toes. Morris was often called upon to take dictation while they were travelling across Europe together, or flying the Atlantic, and even, on occasions when Billy was in his bath or on the lavatory, an idiosyncrasy he probably picked up from his friends Winston Churchill and Lord Beaverbrook, who were also both inclined to dictate during their ablutions.

Apart from being a competent secretary and valet, Morris's real forte was organizing of all Billy's travel arrangements and hotel accommodation all over the world. He did have some faults and was not always at his best after he had decided to have a night out on the town. On those occasions he would sometimes arrive at a restaurant or night club with a pretty girl on his arm, having booked a table in Billy's name to make sure they received the best service. He would also sneak any whisky or brandy which was not locked away or was left unattended, and he was sometimes guilty of watering his employer's gin, so that any he had taken wouldn't be noticed. He always marked the bottles, however, to prevent the watered gin from being used in a martini, where its strength, or lack of it, would probably be noticed. Whenever I was at Billy's London home and was invited to help myself to a favourite dry martini, Morris always rushed forward to help if he was there, in case I picked up the wrong gin bottle.

Those of us who worked closely with Billy lost count of the number of occasions he fired Morris, only to take him back again the next day. There was no doubt that he really rather liked him, in spite of his faults, and knew that he wouldn't be able to find anyone more loyal or efficient, or willing to work such long hours, or put up with his outbursts. On one occasion, during a meeting we were having at Devonshire House, Billy asked Morris why the Duke of Norfolk had been complaining again about a problem with his car. Morris started to say, 'I think we made a mistake by not replacing it', when Billy let out a roar. 'What's that, Morris? What's all this "we" made a mistake? I pay you to make the mistakes. I never make a mistake!' Morris knew that Billy was really annoyed with himself for not making sure that the Duke of Norfolk's complaint was dealt with properly.

Like Morris, George Vallet was devoted to Billy and could always be relied upon to do the right thing. When they arrived back in England with the prototype Minx, Billy sent Vallet up to Coventry with the car, with instructions to go carefully over their reports with the design team and make sure that every fault was being dealt with. Although they might have resented the fact that Vallet was only Billy's chauffeur, they soon realized that he knew exactly what was wrong with the car and was really the best person to help them deal with the problems. Billy also knew this and felt able to concentrate on the other urgent matters awaiting him in London.

Apart from the problems they had found with the all-steel, four-door saloon body being produced for the Minx at the Pressed Steel factory at Cowley, he was annoyed to find that an almost identical body was being sold by the company for a new BSA model. The main reason for this was the high tooling costs for the new body. Pressed Steel felt that, as Rootes had struck such a hard bargain and expected them to pay for most of the tooling, they had the right to maximize their own investment and sell the basic body to other people. Rootes couldn't afford to fall out with Pressed Steel with such an important model launch only a few weeks away, particularly as they urgently needed as many bodies as possible to ensure that enough cars were in dealers' hands by the announcement day. What could have developed into a long and expensive legal battle was eventually dealt with to his satisfaction by Billy, with the help of his old friend Edward Budd, but from then on he refused to trust the English management of Pressed Steel and was determined not to be caught out by them again.

Billy chose to show the Minx at the 1931 Paris Salon to emphasize its international appeal and the fact that it wasn't just intended for the British market. Much was made of the way in which the car had been tested so rigorously in Europe and the photographs which Billy had arranged to be taken during the testing were released to the press. The Minx was an instant success, with overseas orders leading to levels of production which put Rootes firmly into the mass production market. All the careful testing which he and Vallet had done had paid off and, unlike the Wizard, the Minx proved to be exceptionally reliable. It was Reggie who chose the name Minx. There was talk of calling it Merlin, and also the Witch, but both names were fortunately dropped when Reggie suggested the name Minx.

A wide choice of saloon, tourer and drop-head coupé bodies was available, all with a 7 ft 8 in wheelbase and using the four-cylinder, side-valve in-line 1,185 cc engine, mounted at the front and driving the rear wheels. The unladen weight was approximately 1,680 lb, (762 kg), which was within the limits suggested by Edward Budd when the model was being planned and enabled the Minx to achieve a top speed of nearly 60 mph (96.5 km/h) and a fuel consumption of 35 mpg. The basic price was £159.

The Minx boasted one feature which was to become a standard fitment on practically every four-cylinder car, large or small. Rootes called it 'cushion power', which was achieved by mounting the car's engine on rubber cushions instead of the normal procedure of bolting it rigidly onto the chassis frame. The three-bearing crankshaft was further evidence of the forward-thinking approach brought to the Minx. Until then, two-bearing crankshafts had been considered sufficient for all engines of less than 1 litre in capacity. The 'cushion power' idea was probably based on the 'floating power' featured on Chrysler models. This allowed the engines to rock, with the amount of movement being controlled by a leaf spring. Cushion power certainly smoothed out the roughness in the average four-cylinder model and probably accounted for the increased popularity of four-cylinder engines over the larger and more expensive six-cylinder units.

In 1933 a four-speed gearbox with a freewheel became available at a cost of an additional two pounds ten shillings; the following year the freewheel was dispensed with, and a four-speed, all-synchromesh gearbox was fitted. The Minx was given a facelift in 1934, consisting of a swept-forward grille and changes to the rear shape, to distinguish it from the earlier model. Semaphore direction indicators were also fitted. This continued until the Minx Magnificent series was launched in 1935.

In the meanwhile, within a few months of the first Minx models going into production, the stylish little Aero Minx was announced and soon caught the imagination of the more sporting members of the car-buying public. It had the same track, wheelbase, suspension and basic running gear as the Minx saloon, but there were changes to the frame, and the four-cylinder engine was given a high-compression cylinder head. There was also a remote control gear change. It was particularly attractive, with its swept-forward radiator grille and streamlined fastback coupé body. It carried three, with the rear seat passenger sitting crosswise. Priced at £245, it was a lot more expensive than the standard saloon, and although it didn't sell in large numbers, its rakish, low-slung appearance helped to give the name Minx more style. The Aero Minx also had more performance, with a top speed of 72 mph (116 km/h) and an acceleration from 0 to 50 mph in 31 seconds, but fuel consumption was still in the region of 30 mpg.

In 1933 a four-seat open tourer and a close-coupled foursome saloon were both added to the range, and in 1934, when the all-synchromesh four-speed gearbox was brought in as standard on all Minx models, there was also a streamlined, open two-seater sports version. Perhaps the most attractive of all the models was the two-seater Cresta Sports which went on sale in 1935. An excellent example of this can be seen at the National Motor Museum at Beaulieu, where many of the early Rootes models are on view. The Aero Minx went out of production at the end of 1935 with the announcement of the Talbot 10 hp. During the four years the Aero Minx was in production, a total of 649 cars were built at the Rootes Humber Road factory. Many owners were sad to see it go. Although it was sometimes described as a Minx in a party frock, it was more than that and created its own band of enthusiastic followers.

The Hillman Minx saloon was completely rebodied in the autumn of 1935 and the model was relaunched as the Minx Magnificent. It was a larger and heavier model than the original 1931 Minx, providing more accommodation, but the engine, transmission and suspension were much the same and, quite remarkably, so was the price. There was a choice of bodies, but the basic saloon was still available for £159. By January 1936, 10,000 Minx Magnificent models had been built at Humber Road and more than 80,000 more would be produced there before it was replaced by the Phase 1 monocoque Minx in 1939, shortly before the start of the Second World War. Many of these cars later did excellent service as army staff cars. During the first five years that the Minx in its various forms was in production, more than 100,000 were sold worldwide, earning a considerable amount of foreign currency for Britain and playing a leading role in establishing the Rootes Group in the forefront of British motor manufacturers.

Although they sold well, the other Hillman models did not create anything like the same impact. Between 1933 and 1935 Billy and his publicity team, led by Dudley Noble, used all their marketing skills in an attempt to popularize the Hillman 16 hp and the 20–70 range of models, but the public still looked upon them as being updated Wizards and sales suffered as a result. They offered the familiar choice of 2,100 cc or 2,810 cc side-valve engines and were available in saloon, tourer, drop-head coupé and limousine versions. Their Pressed Steel bodies bore a family resemblance to the Minx models of the same period, but in 1935, after some 4,000 of them had been built, all the large models were dropped and replaced by a new range of Hillmans with improved six-cylinder engines and new, independent front suspension.

William Haynes and Alec Issigonis, who later became famous as the designer of the Mini, were involved in the new chassis design. Its independent front suspension, which was given the trade name of Evenkeel, had a transverse leaf spring with upper wishbones and radius arms to keep the wheels going in the right direction. The rest of the chassis layout was quite conventional. They were spacious cars, but their 2,576 cc and 3,181 cc engines were really longer stroke, enlarged and updated versions of the original iron-headed Wizard power units. The more powerful versions were quite popular with company directors and government departments, but they had to compete with Rootes's own Humber models, which had the Humber reputation and name.

It was a rationalization programme which tried to provide Hillman and Humber dealers with a wider range of products, but it did not really succeed. The Hillman advertising and sales literature were both excellent, but the larger Hillmans never lived up to expectations and in 1937 the Hillman 16 hp and Hawk models were replaced with a far more attractive-looking Hillman 14 hp model, though the older, more conventional Hillman 80 did continue until 1938.

Although Rootes tried to separate the two makes, with Humber providing the larger models of 16 hp and above, the Hillman 14 hp still drew some components from the Humber 12 hp it replaced, as well as the now-obsolete Hillman 16 hp. The 1,944 cc side-valve, four-cylinder engine was a bored-out version of the Humber 12 hp unit and the car used the all-synchromesh gearbox from the Hillman Minx. The Hillman 14 hp was only sold as a saloon, with the bodies still being made by Pressed Steel. It was a model which was excellent value for money, with the de luxe model selling for only £268. Although it was discontinued after only two years, because of the outbreak of war, a total of 3,984 were built and the Hillman 14 hp was revamped and relaunched in 1945 as the Humber Hawk.

Chapter 13

Luxury and performance

THE NEED FOR models which would sell in large enough numbers to put Rootes in the big league of car manufacturers as quickly as possible meant that the majority of the company's investment went into the Hillman range of cars and the Wizard and Minx in particular, but in 1933 the new Humber 12 hp appeared. It was the third of the new Rootes cars to be launched in the early 1930s and fitted neatly into the gap left when the little Humber 9/28 was dropped in 1930. It gave Humber dealers a smaller and cheaper model to sell, to go with the larger Humber which had been launched in 1929.

Although the Humber 12 hp was conventional in design and its Pressed Steel body was similar to the one used on the medium range Hillman models, it had a number of very attractive derivatives, including the Humber Vogue and some smart open top versions. The 1,669 cc engine was an entirely new four-cylinder side-valve unit, which continued in one form or another until the end of the 1970s. It was fitted with a Hillman Minx gearbox for the Humber 12 hp but, unlike the larger Humbers, the car was never given independent front suspension. Big price reductions in 1936, due to falling sales, failed to save the model from going out of production in 1937, when it was decided to let Hillman cater for the lower end of the market, leaving Humber free to concentrate on producing luxury cars.

The Humber 16/60 and Snipe 80/Pullman were produced at Coventry from 1932 until 1935, during which time nearly 8,000 were sold. They were similar to the large Hillmans being built at that time, but in 1935 Rootes introduced the Humber 18 hp and Snipe models, which had completely new body styles. Although there was technically still a considerable overlap between some of the larger Hillman and Humber models, it was the start of the move to give the Humber marque a reputation for quality and luxury which would give it special appeal at the top end of the market.

Their six-cylinder, side-valve, in-line engines still bore some resemblance to the Wizard power units, with the 18 hp model having a 2,731 cc version and the Snipe a larger, 4,086 cc unit. The difference in power gave the Snipe a maximum speed of 83 mph (133.5 km/h) against the 18 hp's 67 mph (108 km/h), but there was relatively little difference in fuel consumption between the two models. The larger Humber Pullman, which was also produced in 1935, looked similar to the Snipe and used the same 4,086 cc engine, but the body was longer, more spacious and more expensive. The additional size and specifications reduced the top speed to 76 mph (122 km/h), but again the fuel consumption remained constant at about 15 mpg. People able to afford the Pullman, however, usually had little concern for economy or running costs.

Billy and Reggie wanted to establish the Pullman, with its 11 ft wheelbase and various Thrupp & Maberly limousine body styles, at the top end of the company's luxury range. It was a successful business and mayoral car, and saw service with government ministries and at British and overseas embassies as well, until it was finally made obsolete in 1939 and replaced by a new version in 1945.

Towards the end of 1937 Rootes made several alterations to their range of larger-bodied models, introducing a Humber 16 hp with a 2,576 cc engine and a new Humber Snipe with a 3,181 cc power unit. There was also the Snipe Imperial and the Super Snipe, which came onto the scene in 1938. Both models had 4,086 cc engines, giving maximum speeds in excess of 80 mph (129 km/h), and the Snipe Imperial was available with a range of special body styles, including as a Thrupp & Maberly bodied limousine. The 4.1 litre 'Blue Riband' six-cylinder engines used for the first time in the Snipe Imperial and in Super Snipe models were used in many later versions and always provided fast travel.

In 1939 the Humber Super Snipe went into battle dress and was made famous during the war by Field Marshal Montgomery, with his 'Old Faithful' and 'Victory' cars. 'Old Faithful' in particular had Thrupp & Maberly coachwork and was used by the Field Marshal throughout his North African and Sicilian campaigns. When peace came, Monty gave the cars to Billy Rootes to thank him for the reliable service they had given throughout the hostilities.

The Hillman Minx gave Rootes a strong entry into the mass production market and the latest Humbers now ensured that the company was firmly established in the luxury market. What was missing was a sporting image, and in 1935, with the help of The Prudential, they purchased two of the most famous names in motor sport with the acquisition of Clement Talbot and the Sunbeam Motor Company. To add to their manufacturing capabilities, they also bought British Light Steel Pressings Limited in 1937.

Billy and Reggie decided that they would capitalize on the name Sunbeam, but before they could do so a considerable amount of reorganization was necessary. At the time of the takeover the Sunbeam factory at Wolverhampton was turning out a variety of models which were not selling well. The 1.6 litre, four-cylinder Sunbeam Dawn was too expensive at £425 and rather slow, and the larger, six-cylinder models were old-fashioned, with designs which had first been produced in the late 1920s.

The Sunbeam company was losing money and as there weren't any new Sunbeam products in the pipeline, they decided to make a fresh start. The production lines were cleared and all existing stocks were sold off, even though it meant that in 1935, for the first time for many years, there wasn't a Sunbeam model on display at the Olympia Motor Show. The brothers were looking ahead to 1936, when they planned to have a brand new Sunbeam with a top speed of 100 mph (161 km/h) to show to the public. They gave the task of designing the car to Georges Roesch of Talbot and invited him to design a new engine and a new coachbuilt body, making use of the large Humber chassis with its Evenkeel independent front suspension. Thrupp & Maberly would be available to do the bodywork and he could also make use of another leading body-builder of the day, H. J. Mulliner.

There was another reason why the new Sunbeam was important which was not disclosed. Billy Rootes had been a friend of the Prince of Wales for many years and, as one of his most intimate associates, was trusted with the knowledge of the Prince's close friendship with Mrs Simpson and their intention to marry long before their relationship became generally known. Billy hoped that when the Prince of Wales became King Edward VIII he would continue to use Rootes-built cars, and he felt that the new Sunbeam Thirty, designed by Georges Roesch, would be more likely to appeal to the new king's sporting nature than the more staid Humber models. Billy and the Prince of Wales frequently shot together, usually at Billy's estate at Hungerford, and he was able to keep the Prince well informed on the progress of the new Sunbeam. Billy was also very close to Freda Dudley Ward, a glamorous socialite who had been a lady friend of the Prince before Mrs Simpson came on the scene, and had become involved with her in a number of activities 'by royal request'.

It was a request which he carried out with considerable enthusiasm and pleasure, for Freda Ward, who later became Freda Casa Maury, was one of the outstanding beauties of the day. She founded the famous Feathers Clubs to help deprived people. It was named after the emblem of the Prince of Wales and he became its first patron with Billy Rootes its first honorary treasurer. The first Feathers Club was opened in a particularly depressed area of London in North Kensington. Within the space of a few months, thanks to Billy's enthusiastic support, there were six similar clubs providing subsidized meals and social amenities for some of the poorest families in London.

Unfortunately, there were problems with the new Sunbeam which Georges Roesch did his best to overcome within the limits of the brief he had been given. If it was to have a top speed of 100 mph (161 km/h), a car of that size would need an engine capable of producing at least 150 bhp and he took the Talbot 3,377 cc six-cylinder engine and converted it into a straight-eight of 4,503 cc, matching it to the existing Humber four-speed gearbox and back axle. It was a sleek and beautifully engineered unit which fitted perfectly into the large Humber chassis.

The overstressed Humber frame gave serious problems. It had been stretched still further to take wheelbases of up to 11 ft 4 in and gave way during a test run when Billy was taking one of the prototypes to the Continent but, as planned, the model was still shown at the Olympia Motor Show in 1936. Also there was a Thrupp & Maberly saloon and an H. J. Mulliner Sedanca de Ville, along with the modified Humber chassis with its 4,503 cc engine. The Sunbeam Thirty never went into production, however, and the two prototypes were broken up. The official reason given for this decision was the involvement of Rootes in the Government's shadow factory scheme, but Billy and Reggie knew that the abdication of King Edward VIII in December 1936 made it less likely that the car would become the hoped-for royal flagship for the company.

The acquisition of the Talbot company by Rootes also saw the end of the vintage Talbots and a progressive increase in the use of chassis, engines and car bodies which were common to some of the other Rootes models being produced in Coventry. Although this was a move which the traditionalists were bound to deplore, it made good commercial sense and was the only way of saving a company which, like many others, was unable to compete with those using modern production methods, and was in serious financial difficulties. The era of the mass-produced car had arrived and British car manufacturers were having to follow the American lead and design new models with all-steel bodies and which offered the innumerable benefits which the public was demanding. This new method of construction involved expensive tooling, which companies like Talbot could not afford, and there was also a much longer design and development period. A larger skilled technical staff was needed to deal with all the additional requirements.

One of the first policy decisions Rootes made was to drop the Talbot 65 from the lower end of the range and replace it with the Talbot 10, based on the Aero Minx. This gave Talbot a serious contender in the less expensive category and the model became one of the stars of the 1936 Motor Show. There were three other new Talbot models at the show, the 75 and 105 saloons and the 75 Sports, and the public was still able to buy some of the cars which had been designed before the Rootes takeover. These included the Limousine, the 105 and 3½ litre Drop-Head Coupé, the 105 and 3½ litre Tourer, and the 105 Speed Air Line and Sports Saloon.

Although the chassis for the new Talbot 10 had been inspired by the Aero Minx, it had been redesigned and retooled. It had a 7 ft 9 in wheelbase and used the 1,185 cc Aero Minx power unit fitted with an aluminium head. The design team, led by Ted White, who was to be responsible for so many successful post-war Rootes models, did their job well and, by using the traditional Talbot radiator shell and grille, managed to make it clear that the new car was still a Talbot, with the tradition of quality and performance the name still meant to the public. They gave the radiator a modest slope and mounted the headlamps on tie bars going out to the pear-drop-shaped wings. The saloon body was a two-door pillarless 'fastback' without draught vents. It had clean panels without reveals or mouldings. Stepboards with rubber stripes, which were attached to the rear end of the front wings, and knock-off wire wheels completed the picture of a sporty saloon in a price bracket many more people could afford.

The drop-head foursome coupé version was notch-backed but, due to the need to seat four people, the folding quarter was rather heavy. It did, however, have hood irons which actually worked! The sports tourer had the traditional Talbot features of cut-away sides, a fold flat windscreen and an all-over tonneau cover.

The need to produce some new models quickly, to deal with sagging sales, meant that the Talbot 10 bodies were still wood-framed, steel-plated and panelled and were to a large extent handmade. With the amalgamation of Talbot with Sunbeam, styling work on the new range of Sunbeam Talbot 10 and 2 litre saloon, drop-head coupé and sports tourer models started in 1936. For security reasons they were still known in the company as Talbots until a few months before the announcement date, when they were given their new name of Sunbeam Talbot. It was a range of cars which, due to the intervention of the Second World War, was to continue in production until 1948.

Billy and Reggie decided that the sports saloon replacement for the Talbot 10 should have four doors, without increasing the wheelbase. This posed a considerable problem for the design team, particularly the entry into the rear passenger area, and the final result was only just workable. Ted White decided that the time had come to break away from fastback designs and a notched-back silhouette was planned. The aim was to minimize the length of the passenger compartment, provide maximum bonnet length and put plenty of 'beef' into the wings, to give the car a powerful sporty look. The result was one of the most successful designs White produced, in a career spanning nearly half a century.

The new Sunbeam Talbot models certainly appealed to the more sporty members of the motoring public and contained features copied later by almost every manufacturer. The front and bonnet differed little from the previous Talbot 10; the rear had corner bumpers, separate spare wheel door, a horizontal folding trunk lid and a reasonable luggage capacity. A novel feature was the sliding roof, which had only side channels and slid back in view. The head lining was stuck direct to the roof over the heads of the rear passengers, in order to provide sufficient headroom, but these innovations gave a considerable amount of trouble to begin with, due to water leaks and the frequency with which the head lining came away in hot countries. The 2 litre model, which did not appear until after the war, had a longer wheelbase and bonnet but was otherwise similar to the Sunbeam Talbot 10.

The rapid increase in tooling and development costs made it impossible for Sunbeam Talbot to sustain the multiplicity of models being produced in their London factory, and by the late 1930s the chassis and engine design work was already being carried out at Coventry. It was decided that more models would have to be derived from Coventry-designed and tooled bodies, but before that happened three other new models were built with the help of an outside coachbuilder. These were the drop-head foursome coupé, so popular with women owners, the sports two-seater and the sports tourer.

The first Coventry body shell to be adopted for a Sunbeam Talbot model was the Hillman–Humber Snipe, a fastback, all-steel, four-door body, which was used for the new 3 litre saloon. Fortunately, provision had been made in the original tooling for inserts, which enabled some of the reveals and waist mouldings to have a changed appearance.

Making use of this modified body being produced for the new Sunbeam Talbot 3 litre saloon in Coventry, Ted White and his team of stylists and body engineers were faced in 1938 with the task of achieving the maximum originality for their new model. They felt that the Hillman 14 and Super Snipe models seemed rather overbodied and so they adopted the same policy as they had done with the Sunbeam Talbot 10. The traditional front was used, along with a scaled-up version of the Sunbeam Talbot 10's wings and running boards. The interior was then given individual treatment, with the instrument panel and steering wheel being specially styled. The final result was a car which was the best-looking of all the pre-war models which made use of Coventry-made bodies. The longer bonnet and stronger wing treatment, along with the new interior gave it a much more powerful and sporting character, which was what the stylists wanted to achieve. It was a lesson on how to correct the balance of a car by the accentuation of some of its weaker components.

The 3 litre sports saloon had a largely wood-framed, London-made body, and was the last of a line of 'notch-back' sports saloons produced by the company. Like the saloon, it was also available with a 4 litre Coventry-built Super Snipe engine. Despite being mounted on the same chassis as the sports saloon and using the same radiator, bonnet and wings, the Sunbeam Talbot 3 litre and 4 litre drop-head coupé model was probably the least attractive. In providing seating accommodation for four or five people, the folding head became very heavy-looking and an overbodied effect was the result.

Sales of open sports tourers began to fall and the 3 litre and 4 litre sports tourers were the last of a long line of these models to be produced. The 3 litre and 4 litre touring saloon and the limousine models were styled and manufactured by Thrupp & Maberly. Both had quite attractive 'semi-razor edge' styles, with the limousine differing from the saloon by a division between the front and rear compartments.

Although most of these models ceased production in 1939, they were produced again in 1945 and continued until 1948 when they were replaced by the Sunbeam Talbot 80 and 90 models, which were influenced in their appearance by the aircraft designs the company worked on during the war.

Chapter 14

Hungerford and Hitler

BILLY AND HIS brother had each amassed considerable personal fortunes while they were both still young men but, while Reggie showed a rather more cautious approach with his property deals, Billy had taken the plunge and become a farmer and landowner in 1931 when he purchased the Stype Estate near Hungerford from the Hon. Ronald Whiteley, who was the son of Lord Marchamley. He had become very fond of shooting and along with some friends had rented a grouse moor belonging to Sir Watkin Williams-Wynn at Ruabon Mountain, near Llangollen. There were a lot of grouse in North Wales at the time, with the result that there was never any shortage of well-known and influential people willing to avail themselves of Billy's hospitality.

He wanted his own estate, however, with its own private fishing and shooting, and when Stype came on the market he had no hesitation in clinching the deal. At the time it was a comparatively small estate of about 650 acres, but it did have very good shooting and fishing. By the time he sold it to Sir Charles Clore, some 20 years later, he had acquired a considerable amount of adjacent land and the estate covered more than 3,000 acres.

When Billy purchased the estate there was no main house, as Stype Grange had recently burned down. The fire had occurred while Ronnie Whiteley and his wife were on a long trip to South Africa and had left their butler in charge. He was on the quay to meet them when their ship docked at Southampton to tell them that Stype Grange had been burned to the ground the previous night. He gave a graphic description of how he and his wife and child had only escaped death by the skin of their teeth and that, despite all their efforts, nothing had been saved.

The Whiteleys were naturally very upset. Apart from being very fond of the house, they had also spent a considerable amount of money on the estate, which included a nine-hole golf course and an indoor swimming pool and squash court. The golf course had been cleverly designed by the famous golfer Abe Mitchell and was played off four greens, making it very compact. Even so, it was far from being a chip-and-putt course and the longest hole was nearly 500 yds.

They accepted the butler's story and decided to move into one of the cottages until the main house could be rebuilt. A few weeks later, however, one of their friends saw a piece of furniture in an antique shop and recognized it as having been at Stype when he had stayed there as a guest. The police were informed and they traced the piece of furniture back to the butler. Further enquiries were made and a number of other items of furniture from Stype were found and again traced back to the butler. It appeared that during the months the Whiteleys had been away in South Africa, the butler had sold many of the antiques from the house and then to cover the thefts had set the house on fire when he learned that his employers were returning to England. Although there was insufficient evidence to convict him of the much more serious crime of arson, he was found guilty of theft and spent several years in prison.

The Whiteleys were so distressed by the whole affair, particularly as they had placed so much trust in their butler and his wife, that they decided to move away from Stype and sell the estate to Billy Rootes, who was more interested in the sporting features than the house itself. The original grange overlooked a beautiful garden with lovely lawns and shrubs and an attractive lake but, rather than spending money on having it rebuilt at a time when he was so heavily committed to his new business ventures, Billy joined up what had been the chauffeur's and butler's cottages and built additional rooms onto them to make a modest, but still very comfortable, family home.

The new house was large enough for Billy and his wife to be able to entertain on a lavish scale, and invitations to their house parties and shooting parties were always very popular. Their guests included members of the Royal Family, Government ministers, well-known actors and actresses, writers and leaders of industry. Regular visitors included the Prince of Wales, when he was friendly with Freda Dudley Ward, Freddie Lonsdale, Brenden Bracken (who was loaned a house on the estate called Folly Farm), and Poots and Humphrey Butler, who was equerry to Prince George, Duke of Kent, later to be tragically killed in an air crash during the war. Humphrey Butler and his wife were with the Prince of Wales and Mrs Simpson on the trip round the Adriatic which first drew attention to their romance.

Other close friends were Garrett Moore and his wife Joan, the brilliant concert pianist. He became Viscount Moore and later the Earl of Drogheda, and was managing director of the *Financial Times*, chairman of the Royal Opera House, Covent Garden, and a Knight of the Garter.

Billy's son Geoffrey recalled a visit which he paid to the Berlin Motor Show in 1939 with his father, accompanied by Garrett and Joan Moore and Freda Dudley Ward. It was soon after Hitler's meeting with Chamberlain at Munich and he had expressed a wish to visit the Rootes stand at the show. Hitler was accompanied by Goering and Goebbels and spent some time discussing car production with Billy, who was keen to find out more about Hitler's famous Volkswagen, or People's Car, which was called the 'Strength through Joy Car'.

Along with other British motor manufacturers, the Rootes brothers were very concerned at Germany's trade policy at that time and the way in which Hitler was subsidizing the country's motor industry. By paying a large subsidy to companies like Opel, German imports into Britain had increased considerably during the previous three years. In 1935 only 386 cars had been imported, or 2.8 per cent of Britain's total car imports, but German imports had risen in 1937 to 5,181 cars, or 28 per cent of the total. During the first quarter of 1938 the figure had increased still further and practically half of Britain's imports of cars came from Germany. Within four years, imports of German cars had risen from just over three cars a month to 1,000 cars a month.

One look at the import price of the 11.3 hp Opel Cadet was enough to see why this should be. At £135 the Cadet was £50 cheaper than the Austin 10 hp and the Morris 10 hp, £34 cheaper than the Hillman Minx and £22 less even than the Ford 10 hp. Billy and his colleagues had worked out that when dealers' discounts, handling charges, advertising and other normal costs were taken into account, along with the import duty and freight charges, Opel cars were being sold to dealers in Britain for a basic price of between £50 and £60.

The German Government was paying a subsidy of up to 43 per cent on the cars being imported into Britain and as much as 60 per cent in countries like Holland. The subsidy was being operated by the Automobilindustrie Verband (Federation of the Motor Industry), which had far-reaching powers over the German motor industry. It completely controlled the prices of all new and second-hand cars sold in Germany and abroad and price changes could not be made without the Federation's approval. German exporters were forbidden, under threat of imprisonment, to divulge the amount of subsidy they received.

The British Government was particularly concerned because of the effect the subsidy was having on employment in Britain, and estimated that about 4,600 jobs had been lost in British car factories during 1938. Before the German subsidy, British car manufacturers had had a very good home market for their smaller models, but at least 90 per cent of the German imports were now in the small car class of between 11 hp and 12 hp and they were making substantial inroads into British car sales.

Billy Rootes was also concerned at the effect German trade policy was having on exports. British manufacturers were losing out to Germany in practically every one of Britain's principal export markets. In countries like Norway, Sweden, Denmark and Belgium, sales of German cars had risen by as much as 500 per cent in only three years. Production of the Volkswagen at the new factory at Fallersleben was looking even more menacing, because the company had been given the powers to purchase its raw materials and other supplies from the producers at cost price, based on the cost of labour, materials and floating overheads, but without any allowance for fixed overheads. The cost of each Volkswagen would consequently be far lower than any of the models being produced in even the most efficient American plant. Hitler had ordered that at least 60 per cent of the Volkswagen production must be exported.

Billy's wife summed up the feelings of the British people when he rang home to tell her that he had been talking to Hitler when he visited the Rootes stand at the Berlin show. 'I hope you punched him on the nose!' was her immediate reply. It was assumed that all the telephone lines at the Adlon Hotel, where Billy and the other British manufacturers were staying, would be tapped, but there were no repercussions.

It was, perhaps, fortunate for the British motor industry that war started before Volkswagens began to make further inroads into car sales in Britain and export markets. It was, however, fortuitous that in 1945 the British Government invited Billy to take a close look at the Volkswagen project and decide whether the car should be built in Britain. His verdict was that the German People's Car was too outdated and too basic to be competitive and there was no point in the British Government going ahead with the idea.

It was a decision he was to regret many times over during the next 25 years, for the Volkswagen Beetle became one of the best-selling models of all time. It might not have been, however, if it had been a victim of the strikes which plagued the British motor industry in the 1960s and 70s. Billy and the Rootes engineers may also have been influenced by the military version of the Volkswagen which had been captured in the Western Desert and sent to them during the war for extensive testing and the production of a detailed report on its capabilities. The version they tested was very basic in design compared with similar British models.

Billy Rootes was not alone in his feelings about the Volkswagen. Henry Ford also came to a similar conclusion.

Chapter 15

From adolescence to manhood

BECAUSE OF HIS bad attacks of asthma, Billy Rootes's younger son Brian had been forced to leave Harrow and finish his schooling in Switzerland, where had had the advantage of being able to study languages in ideal surroundings. His elder son, Geoffrey, who later became the second Lord Rootes, had a more formal education, spending five years at Harrow before going up to Oxford in October 1936. In the months between leaving Harrow and going up to Oxford, Geoffrey gained his first experience of world travel when his father decided to turn his high-spirited elder son into a man of the world and prepare him for the role it was hoped he would play in the future development of the Rootes Group. It was to be a six-month transition from adolescence into manhood, but there was also a second objective. Billy was keen to broaden Geoffrey's experience of life, but at the same time he wanted him to see something of the world of industry and commerce, particularly in the export markets which were becoming so important to the Rootes Group.

In any event, he was determined that it would be a trip of a lifetime for Geoffrey and before they left sent him off to his tailor to be fitted for all the clothes he might need during their world tour, which was to last for six months, starting in Europe and ending in America. He arranged for Geoffrey to have three or four new lounge suits, several tropical suits, a morning coat, white waistcoat, evening tails, dinner jacket and all the necessary shirts and accessories. The detailed travel arrangements were made by Charles Morris and, leaving Reggie in charge, the three of them set sail for the Continent, travelling by train across France to Marseilles to board the old P & O liner *Multan* for Port Said by way of Malta.

Before they left Marseilles, Billy decided to make sure that his son was fully aware of the facts of life by taking him to a *cinéma bleu*. On their first night on board ship he also suggested that Geoffrey might like to experience his first dry martini, particularly as they would be attending many receptions and cocktail parties in the months ahead. While Geoffrey was still at Harrow, Billy had promised him £500 if he did not smoke until he was 21 and another £500 if he did not drink spirits until he came of age, which was quite a lot of money at the time. When Geoffrey reminded him of this, Billy quickly replied, 'Oh, I'll give you dispensation for the next six months. I don't want to spoil your fun.'

Despite the offer of dispensation, Geoffrey stuck to the no-smoking challenge and threw a party for all his friends with the £500 he received from his father when he became 21. Billy's ploy must have worked because Geoffrey remained a non-smoker throughout his life.

After a brief stop at Malta, the exciting part of the tour began in Cairo at the famous Shepheard's Hotel. Visits to Heliopolis races and the Gezira Club were arranged, along with trips to the Cairo museum and the exhibition of Tutankhamun's treasures. There was no shortage of cocktail parties or visits to other night spots during their stay. Sir John Cadman, the chairman of the Iraq Petroleum Company, who later became Lord Cadman, offered them the use of his aircraft and pilot when they reached Haifa and they decided to visit Jerusalem on the way, booking in at the King David Hotel. This enabled Geoffrey to see something of Nazareth, Bethlehem and the Sea of Galilee, although Billy couldn't resist the temptation to arrange some business meetings in Tel-Aviv. The memorial service for King George V took place while they were in Jerusalem and involved Greek Orthodox and Copts as well as Anglican clergy, making the occasion far more colourful, as well as ensuring a packed congregation.

They planned to use Sir John's plane to fly along the route of the Iraq Petroleum Company's pipeline, finishing up at Baghdad, where they were to stay with the British ambassador, Sir Archibald Clarke-Kerr, who later became Lord Inverchapel. The aircraft was a rather old, but usually reliable, DH Dragon Rapide biplane and took them as far as Amman, where they were to spend the night as guests of the Transjordan Frontier Force, dining in Mess before having an audience with the Emir the following day. The weather, however, gave considerable cause for alarm and their plane was forced down in a sandstorm at Rutbah Wells. Fortunately, it was not damaged and they eventually reached Al Hadithah. Heavy rain storms during the next two days kept them grounded again and they decided to drive on to Baghdad in an open Ford, an adventurous journey as the car didn't have four-wheel drive and they had to cross numerous wadis and watercourses.

Most of the army and RAF units in Baghdad were equipped with the Rootes Group's Commer trucks and Humber staff cars and each unit seemed anxious to provide the best hospitality during Billy and Geoffrey's visit. Those first few weeks of the tour proved an exciting introduction to foreign travel and the sort of business and social life Geoffrey could expect with his father. It helped to convince him that it was an exciting enough life for him to want to join the family motor business when he left Oxford.

The Dragon Rapide took them from Baghdad to Basra, where they planned to pick up the old Imperial Airways flight to Karachi, but one of the company's flying-boats had crashed in Alexandria harbour with considerable loss of life. They eventually joined the Imperial Airways flight to Karachi by way of Kuwait, Bahrein, Sharjah and Baluchistan. These were still the early days of large passenger planes and it was not unusual for passengers to be asked to jettison some of their luggage if the plane couldn't gain enough height. This happened on the flight to Karachi and the pilot announced that the plane was overloaded and it would be necessary to jettison some of the cargo and luggage while they were flying over the Persian Gulf. Geoffrey looked out of the window in time to see one of their large wardrobe trunks spinning round and round in the air before landing with a splash in the sea below.

His father turned to Morris and said, 'I've had a word with the pilot and he told me that if the luggage they have jettisoned doesn't do the trick we might have to sacrifice some passengers. We have drawn lots and I'm afraid that you have drawn the short straw.' Morris went as white as a sheet and needed several long swigs on his hip flask before the colour came back to his cheeks and he realized that Billy Rootes was pulling his leg.

As they travelled across India from Karachi to Jamnager to stay with the Maharajah Jam Sahaib of Nawanagar, a nephew of the great Ranjitsinhji, one of the greatest cricketers of the 1900s, and his brother Duleepsinhja, who also played for England, Geoffrey had his first experience of the absolute power of the rulers of the princely states and their immense wealth, compared with the squalor and poverty in the cities, where large numbers of people were forced to sleep in the streets. During their stay at the palace, he and his father dined each evening with the Jam Sahib and his large family, and enjoyed the fine oysters from their host's private oyster beds. During the day they went on shooting parties for duck, black-buck, chinkara and sand grouse and Jam Sahib organized a special expedition for them to shoot a panther.

Billy went on to Bombay with Charles Morris for meetings with the Governor, Lord Brabourne, and Geoffrey rejoined them in Calcutta for the journey to New Delhi. They had been invited to stay at Viceregal Lodge with the Viceroy, the Marquis of Willingdon. Designed by Lutyens, Viceregal Lodge and its surrounding buildings were impressive and the whole atmosphere was very formal and ceremonial. In the evening, all wore white tie and tails and before dinner were marshalled by the Viceroy's ADCs to be told whom they were to take in to dinner.

The Viceroy's staff at the time included a number of distinguished men, like General 'Pug' Ismay, Sir Eric Miéville and Captain Jack Brittain-Jones, who later became the Rootes Group's purchasing director in Coventry. He also managed the Indian cricket team when it toured England in the 1930s. Lord Willingdon flew Billy and Geoffrey to Agra in his private plane so that they could see the Taj Mahal by daylight and by moonlight, before leaving for Madras to stay with Lord Erskine, who was the Governor there.

It wasn't all play, however, and when they arrived in each Indian city Billy insisted they went to see the Rootes distributors and dealers. He allowed Geoffrey to sit in on the meetings, so that he would get first-hand knowledge of the problems and conditions.

Apart from the brief visit to the *cinéma bleu* in Marseilles, the tour so far had been of the highest moral tone, but that changed quite abruptly when they left Madras to go to Ceylon. Billy told Geoffrey that they would be meeting two ladies who would be joining them for the duration of their visit. He made no secret of the fact that Lady Castlerosse was his mistress and that he was very much in love with her. In order for them to be able to spend more time together, she had brought along a friend to entertain Geoffrey on the occasions when they wanted to be alone.

Geoffrey was very fond of his mother and it came as a shock to find that he was suddenly travelling in the company of his father's mistress, but in spite of the rather equivocal situation he became quite fond of her and was very distressed later to learn that she had committed suicide during the war. Doris Castlerosse was a very charming and elegant woman of considerable beauty. In 1936 she was still married to Valentine, Viscount Castlerosse, who had the distinction of starting the first society gossip column in the *Sunday Express*.

Her companion was an attractive woman in her 30s who was entertaining and exciting to be with, but did have some rather unusual sexual tastes. Geoffrey quickly found that he had been left in the company of an insatiable nymphomaniac and his resistance was low. His first experience of sexual intercourse occurred during a rickshaw journey between the Galle Face Hotel and the Columbo Club. His attractive companion had very fixed ideas about the uses to which rickshaws could be put and, as Geoffrey found her advances very much to his liking, he went along with her suggestions. It was a rickshaw journey he was never likely to forget.

Although both Geoffrey and his father would have liked to stay longer in Columbo, they had to catch up with their schedule and took one of the old Blue Funnel boats to Penang. Playing Mah Jong on the way helped to pass the time and take Geoffrey's mind off attractive nymphomaniacs and the hidden joys of rickshaw rides in Ceylon. Although they only had a brief stop in Penang, at the famous Runnymede Hotel, the beauty of the surrounding countryside was very evident as they drove to Ipoh and Kuala Lumpur to stay with the High Commissioner, Sir Shenton Thomas.

They paid a brief visit to the Sulton of Jodhpur and their next port of call was Singapore and the Raffles Hotel. Billy suggested that they should spend several weeks there relaxing before going on to Java. Much of Geoffrey's relaxing was done in the company of a particularly beautiful Chinese girl with the rather delightful name of Mabel Wong. Her father, S. Q. Wong, was one of the most prominent businessmen in Singapore and a director of Wearnes, the main Rootes distributors. The Air Officer Commanding Singapore, Air Commodore Sidney Smith, also had a very attractive daughter, known to her friends as 'Squeak', and she also helped to make Geoffrey's visit to Singapore memorable. Her mother Claire had been a close friend of T. E. Lawrence, of Lawrence of Arabia fame, in the days when he was Aircraftsman Shaw.

Billy certainly did his best to ensure that Geoffrey had a good time, and it must have been one of the most entertaining world tours a father ever arranged for a teenage son. There was certainly no shortage of female company. The beautiful Balinese girl dancers, bare-breasted above their sarongs, were enough to increase the pulse rate of any red-blooded young ex-Harrovian, but it was a little blonde girl from Chicago, who was staying with them in the solitary hotel, which made Geoffrey's stay in Bali more enjoyable.

On their return to Singapore, before embarking for Hong Kong, his father received a cable which was a timely reminder of the war clouds gathering on the horizon, and the first indication of the essential part Billy and the Rootes Group were to play in rearming the British army and air force. Without the initiative taken by the Government in 1936, and the immediate support given by Rootes and other leading motor manufacturers, it is unlikely that the country's sadly depleted aircraft industry could have been built up quickly enough to counter the massive German air power, and enable Britain to win the war.

The cable invited Billy to become chairman of a committee the Government was forming, with the task of setting up a shadow industry to manufacture aircraft at new and existing factories in Britain. He immediately cabled back his acceptance, and from then on the Rootes Group was in the forefront of the Government's scheme to organize the volume manufacture of airframes and aero-engines. As chairman of the co-ordinating committee, he served throughout the war with the Ministry of Aircraft Production and the Ministry of Supply, working closely with Lord Beaverbrook and playing a major part in persuading the Americans to provide additional badly needed aircraft, ships and materials.

All thought of war disappeared, however, when they reached Hong Kong and were again joined by Billy's mistress, Lady Castlerosse, and her travelling companion with the nymphomaniacal tendencies who had enriched Geoffrey's carnal knowledge when they were in Ceylon. They all stayed at the Repulse Bay Hotel and enjoyed the usual round of cocktail parties and dinners organized by the wealthy heads of large companies like Jardine Matheson and Butterfield & Swire. They lived in considerable style and luxury, even by normal Far Eastern standards, and there was never any shortage of naval and army officers to help make the parties go with a swing.

At Repulse Bay there was a raft anchored several hundred yards off-shore and Geoffrey and his companion decided to swim out and enjoy the privacy it provided. On the way back his friend got cramp, panicked and quickly became exhausted. Geoffrey managed to turn her onto her back (a position she was never usually slow to adopt) and was able to tow her to the shore and administer artificial respiration until she had recovered sufficiently for them to return to the hotel. It was a dangerous situation which could have had a tragic ending. Shortly afterwards she returned home, much to Geoffrey's disappointment.

This didn't last long, however, for soon after arriving in Shanghai he found a charming and very pretty White Russian girl, who was a hostess at one of the night clubs. There were a lot of White Russians in Shanghai who had escaped there after the Russian Revolution. Sir Victor Sassoon, who owned the Cathay Hotel on the Bund, where Geoffrey and his father were staying, was an old friend of the Rootes family. The Sassoons had just moved their vast fortune and centre of operations from India to Shanghai, and when they later moved to Nassau the Rootes family had considerable dealings with the E. D. Sassoon Banking Corporation, which they also owned.

Sir Victor's large house, a few miles outside Shanghai, was the scene of many enjoyable parties and he introduced Geoffrey to Alexandras, an exotic cocktail he always insisted on making for his guests. Victor Sassoon had also been at Harrow and took a liking to Billy Rootes's eldest son, making sure that he was able to enjoy all the benefits of life in Shanghai to the full. They went to the races together, where the large retinue of retainers, business associates and relations which accompanied Sir Victor included a rather extraordinary old uncle he referred to as 'Nunky', who seemed to be particularly knowledgeable about the form of all the horses. The racing was very good and all great fun.

Billy had business to attend to when they reached Tokyo, but that didn't prevent them from savouring the delights of a Geisha party before setting sail for Honolulu and San Francisco on one of the ships of the Dollar Line. It was a large, luxuriously equipped vessel with excellent accommodation, and the famous passengers who had chosen to travel at the same time made it a voyage which lacked nothing in entertainment and glamour. Their old friend Victor Sassoon was on board, accompanied by a very attractive Englishwoman, and Charlie Chaplin and Paulette Goddard, who were living together and married some time later. Geoffrey remembered Charlie Chaplin as being pleasant, but rather uninteresting, but Paulette Goddard, as might well be expected, made a very deep impression on him, particularly her remarkable gift of being able to communicate so well with young people. Apart from being very beautiful with her perfect skin, she had a vivacious personality and was entertaining where Chaplin was dull. Billy and Geoffrey stayed with them later in Hollywood, and Geoffrey met her again after the war in the Palace Bar at St Moritz, when she was still very beautiful and was accompanied by Erich Maria Remarque, the author of *All Quiet on the Western Front*. Another of the passengers was the tremendously talented Jean Cocteau, who made no secret of the fact that he was a homosexual and had with him a rather beautiful young man called Marcel. Along with several American film directors and distinguished figures from the world of business and commerce, they formed a very amusing and interesting collection of people.

From Los Angeles, Geoffrey and his father took the special Santa Fe train en route to Chicago, which provided luxury travel at its best. The journey from Chicago took five days, with stops at the Grand Canyon and at Albuquerque, New Mexico. They had their own drawing room, where they could sit and have meals served, and a separate compartment for sleeping, which had its own washing and toilet facilities. The train also had an excellent observation car at the back and a barber's shop, restaurant car and bar. When the train reached the Grand Canyon, a car was available to take them to the rim of the canyon, so that they could look down on the Colorado River and see the magnificent view of the Painted Desert on the other side. At Albuquerque, transport had also been arranged to take them to an Indian Reserve so that they could see something of the everyday lives of the Navajo Indians.

The glory of the Santa Fe train, now sadly only a memory, provided a fitting way of arriving in Chicago, where there were fresh surprises in store for Geoffrey and his father. They were staying at the Drake Hotel, near the centre of the city, when they received an invitation from Mr Cord, the chairman of the Cord Car Company, to lunch with him on his private yacht moored on Lake Michigan. There were a number of guests, most of whom were involved with the automotive business, and after lunch Mr Cord announced that he had arranged a little entertainment for his guests. They were invited to take part in a clay pigeon shooting competition, but instead of shotguns, they were to use the Thompson sub-machine-gun which Al Capone had used during the infamous St Valentine's Day Massacre, when he arranged for a number of rival gangsters to be lined up against a garage wall and shot.

The whole idea sounded rather macabre, but the competition was a complete failure, because the sub-machine-gun jumped about so much every time it was fired that none of the guests managed to hit a clay pigeon. Geoffrey was able to tell his friends later that he had used Al Capone's famous sub-machine-gun, but they found it difficult to believe that it had been used for a clay pigeon shoot, even in America.

Billy was in his element when they reached Detroit, visiting all the automobile plants and introducing Geoffrey to senior executives at General Motors and Chrysler. At Dearborn they spent some time with Henry Ford and his son Edsel, who was the father of Henry Ford II and whom Geoffrey got to know particularly well after the war.

While they were in the Middle West they went to South Bend, Indiana to stay with Vincent Bendix, the wealthy chairman of the Bendix Corporation, one of the major suppliers to the motor and aircraft industries. The slits for machine-guns in the two pillboxes at the entrance to the drive leading up to his home, for use in case the house was attacked during a strike, was a sharp reminder of the extremes of feeling that existed between management and labour in America during the mid-1930s.

Money bought power in America in those days, and this was very evident a few weeks later when Vincent Bendix arranged a large dinner party for them at one of New York's Park Avenue hotels. After dinner, a fleet of cars, with a siren-wailing police escort, took all the guests across New York to see Joe Louis fight Max Schmeling. It was an historic fight which Schmeling won in the 14th round. Although Louis was American and Schmeling was German, the sympathies of a large section of the crowd were with the German, because he was white and Louis was black. After the winner was announced, a tremendous fight broke out alongside the ring between a group of New York Irish and another group of blacks. It was a night to remember in more ways than one.

Geoffrey and his father were nearing the end of their world tour, but before they boarded the *Aquitania* and sailed for home, they were able to watch the *Queen Mary* dock after her maiden voyage across the Atlantic, and while they were dining on the roof of the St Regis Hotel on their last evening in New York, they saw the German *Graf Zeppelin* airship, all lit up, weaving its way between the skyscrapers to its mooring, looking for all the world like a giant floating cigar. It was a remarkable sight and a fitting end to a remarkable six months.

Geoffrey went up to Oxford in the Michaelmas term, having passed the College Entrance for Christ Church during his last term at Harrow. He hoped to read history, but his father wanted him to read modern languages because he felt that they would be of more use to him in business. After four terms studying French and German, Geoffrey persuaded his father to let him come down from Oxford and gain some experience of business life before the start of the war with Germany, which by then seemed inevitable.

While he was at Oxford he had tried to join the University Air Squadron, but he was under 21 and was unable to get his father's written consent, which he needed. It was a time of considerable uncertainty and young men of military age found difficulty in settling down. Geoffrey admitted later that he did not take proper advantage of his time at Oxford and drank and gambled too much. During the long vacations he worked in the Rootes plant at Coventry, gaining experience in the machine shops and foundry.

When he joined the family business officially in 1938, he was sent to London to work at Devonshire House and at the Sunbeam Talbot factories at Barlby Road and Acton. His brother Brian had also finished his schooling in Switzerland and the two of them shared a flat together at St James's Court. Their evenings were spent in clubs like the Bag O'Nails, enjoying the high life of London's West End to the full, but during the day they were expected to work hard like every other young apprentice. Billy had given strict instructions that they were not to expect, or receive, any favours and they had to work their way through the various departments in the same way that he had done on joining the Singer Company before the First World War.

Brian was working in the service department at Barlby Road when his father paid a surprise visit. He had gone there straight from a night club with his overalls covering his dinner jacket. The foreman took pity on him and suggested that he had better keep out of the way by sliding under the front of one of the cars on the trolley the mechanics used when they were changing the engine oil. Within a few minutes he was fast asleep, but when his father insisted on seeing where he was working, the foreman pointed to the legs protruding from the car. 'He's changing the oil, sir,' he explained. 'Is he now!' Billy replied, bending down and shouting at the prostrate figure. 'I hope you're making a good job of that!'

The shock of suddenly hearing his father's voice woke Brian up and he shot upright, striking his head on the bottom of the sump and covering his face with oil. The blood started to trickle down his forehead as he slid out from beneath the car. 'Good gracious!' Billy exclaimed when he saw the blood and, turning to the foreman, said, 'Perhaps you had better find him something less dangerous to do before he does himself more damage.' He went away chuckling to himself, fully aware of the tricks apprentices got up to, as well as the reports of his sons' riotous living.

He felt, however, that the time had come for his sons to be separated and sent Geoffrey to work at the company's Shadow Factory at Speke, near Liverpool, where they were building Blenheim bombers. While Geoffrey was there he shared digs with Barrie Heath, whose brother George worked for Rootes. The two of them had been friends since they were both small boys and they remained so until Barrie Heath's death in 1987.

While he was at Speke, Geoffrey also joined a local flying club and learned to fly in a Tiger Moth, doing eight hours' solo before it was time for him to go into the army. He joined the Territorial Army and was commissioned in the Supplementary Reserve of Officers of the Royal Army Service Corps, later to become the Royal Corps of Transport, after taking a course at Buller Barracks, Aldershot. Brian was also commissioned at about the same time in the Supplementary Reserve of the Twelfth Royal Lancers and did an attachment with them at Tidworth. Barrie Heath joined the Royal Air Force and went on to win a DFC as a bomber pilot. After the war he was knighted and became chairman of Triplex and later Guest Keen & Nettlefold.

Chapter 16

From Aldershot to Berlin

WHEN WAR BROKE out in September 1939, Second Lieutenant Geoffrey Rootes was stationed at Aldershot, where the RASC had a strange hotch-potch of impressed vehicles which even included some milk-floats. He was in the main armoury, drawing rifles and small arms ammunition, when he heard over the radio Chamberlain's expected announcement that, as Britain had not heard from Hitler, the country must consider itself to be at war.

A week later he was in France with the advance party of the RASC's First Corps, locating billets for troops to be stationed in the area round Laval. He was among the first of the British Expeditionary Force to be sent to France and was to serve the greater part of the war abroad. When Hitler invaded Belgium and France at the beginning of 1940, the First Corps were rushed up to the approaches to the Albert Canal and came under heavy aerial attack until the order came for them to retreat.

They managed to shoot down a German Heinkel bomber by concerted small arms fire but, as the aircraft crashed near the road, they had difficulty in preventing the Belgian and French refugees, who were also being strafed, from slaughtering the German aircrew. One member of Geoffrey's troop was killed and another severely wounded during their retreat through Ypres to the outskirts of Dunkirk, where they were told to smash the cylinder blocks of their trucks with sledgehammers and tip their vehicles down a steep bank into a canal in order to prevent them falling into enemy hands.

During the three days they spent at Brai Dunes they were constantly machine-gunned and bombed by enemy aircraft, but fortunately the soft ground prevented many of the bombs from doing too much damage. Geoffrey found an abandoned infantry truck containing several Bren guns, which they set up at strategic points and used to blaze away at the enemy aircraft with as they came in for their low-level attacks. The Bren guns were no match for the fast-flying fighter aircraft, but being able to fight back kept up the morale of the troops.

They were fortunate not to lose any more men, although one was posted missing under rather mysterious circumstances. He was a rather lazy little Irishman called Crosby, who was frequently drunk but was a bad soldier, drunk or sober. He somehow managed to get hold of some booze and, while still drunk, came across a .38 service revolver which he pointed at Geoffrey, threatening to shoot him, until Sgt James, the platoon sergeant, took it away from him and put the drunken Crosby under close arrest. In the general confusion, however, he managed to escape and disappeared.

Geoffrey didn't see him again until some three years later, during a pause in the battle of Mareth. He was standing by his truck when a small figure approached and said with a pronounced Irish brogue, 'Good morning, sir. I'm sorry I tried to shoot you at Dunkirk.' It was Crosby, who had turned up like a bad penny, but what had happened to him in the meanwhile remained a mystery.

Geoffrey and his troops were eventually evacuated from Dunkirk, embarking from the *Mole* onto a destroyer. They were shelled and attacked by German E-boats but eventually reached Dover safely before going by train to Tidworth, to the camp where Geoffrey had spent some time when he was in the Officers Training Corps at Harrow.

Geoffrey's younger brother Brian had also volunteered to serve in France but, much to his anger, the War Office considered that his health was not good enough for active overseas service and he was forced to spend the greater part of the war serving in England.

Immediately after Dunkirk, Geoffrey volunteered for further service overseas. He was posted to East Africa, but before embarking received some leave, which he spent with his father in London. The blitz was at its height and, along with many other well-known buildings, the Treasury received a direct hit. Billy and Geoffrey went along the next morning to find Winston Churchill poking about among the ruins with his umbrella. He was very distressed because several of his friends had been killed.

On Christmas Eve 1940 Geoffrey set sail in the *Orbita*, which was attacked by a German armed merchant cruiser soon after leaving port. Their escort succeeded in sinking her and the *Orbita* eventually arrived safely at Durban. The British troops were entertained magnificently by the South Africans and Geoffrey and his three fellow officers were the guests of the Platt family, who had a lovely house at the Izipingo Sugar Plantation. One of the Platt sisters later married Denis Compton, the English test cricketer, and another became the wife of Max Niven, David Niven's brother.

Geoffrey eventually arrived in Nairobi to be commissioned in the East African Army Service Corps and stationed at M'B'Gathi Camp, now the site of Nairobi airport. Soon after he arrived there was a major scandal when Joss Errol was murdered and Jock Broughton was accused of his murder. Several of Geoffrey's fellow officers had to give evidence at the trial, as they had been present at the party at the Muthaiga Club just before the murder. Jock Broughton was eventually acquitted, but threw himself out of a window at the Adelphi Hotel in Liverpool when he returned to England.

Geoffrey was posted to Arusha in Tanganyika to train African troops to drive trucks, quite a task as most of them had only just arrived from their tribal reservations and had never seen a steering wheel before, let alone a motor vehicle. They managed to knock the recruits into shape and Geoffrey was appointed Platoon Commander in a General Transport Company of what was really the First East African Division, but was referred to as the Eleventh to confuse the enemy. His platoon was made up mainly of Wakamba, although there were a number of other tribes represented including Luo, Kipsigi and Nandi. It was quite a mixed bag to command, but fortunately he had studied Swahili and was fairly good at languages. He was still only 22 when he had to take Orderly Room and Sick Parade in Swahili and deal with severe problems of scurvy. Owing to the very long lines of communications, they could not get regular supplies of fresh rations and consequently suffered from a lack of fresh meat and vegetables.

With several hundred troops to feed, a supply of fresh meat became vital. Geoffrey had managed to buy a BSA 8 mm rifle which took captured Italian ammunition, while he was in Nairobi, and he also had his father's faithful old Joseph Lang 12-bore shotgun. The experience he had gained shooting at Stype before the war with his father stood him in good stead, and he shot enough antelopes to provide meat for all the troops.

The campaign eventually ran its course and, with the fall of Addis Adaba, the Italian Commander-in-Chief, the Duke d'Aosta, surrendered. Geoffrey was sent back to Nairobi and posted to the Director of Military Intelligence, Middle East Command, who was Brigadier John Shearer, a friend of his father's. After retiring from the army following a distinguished career in the Indian cavalry, he became managing director of Fortnum & Mason in London.

Unfortunately, when Geoffrey reached Cairo he was informed that Brigadier Shearer had been relieved of his post, due to some miscalculations he and his staff had made about the strength of Rommel's forces. As his protégé, Geoffrey was no longer welcome in Intelligence at Middle East Command and he was posted as Transport Officer to a Field Ambulance in the Western Desert. The Eighth Army was heavily involved in battles with the Afrika Corps in the area of Gazala, Tobruk and Knightsbridge, and as Geoffrey's Field Ambulance was sandwiched between the two forces, he had to treat casualties from both sides, but he managed to come through unscathed.

He served with the 384 General Transport Company for the rest of the North African campaign and at the start of the campaigns in Sicily and Italy. At El Alamein his unit was involved in rigging up imitation vehicles with the aid of camouflage nets, in an effort to deceive the enemy and divert enemy aircraft attacks from the main British force further south. They did this with remarkable success and the enemy wasted a considerable amount of ammunition and bombs by attacking the sham vehicles and tanks.

It was a very tough battle which started with a tremendous artillery barrage, and during the long pursuit of Rommel through Cyrenaica and Tripolitania, Geoffrey narrowly escaped death when his 15 cwt truck was blown up by a mine. The presence of mind which had caused him to have the inside of the vehicle packed with sandbags no doubt saved him and his driver–batman from serious injury, even though their vehicle was damaged beyond repair.

After the capture of Benghazi and Tripoli they had to face the Mareth line on the Tunisian border, which had been heavily fortified by the Germans. Field Marshal Montgomery decided to attack across the Wadi Zigzaou with a force which became known as Wace Force and consisted of lorried infantry made up of the Sixth and Seventh Green Howards, the Fifth Durham Light Infantry, a battalion of the Argyll and Sutherland Highlanders and elements of the Twenty-third Armoured Brigade. Geoffrey was in command of the transport for the lorried infantry, which came in for a rather tough time when the tanks of the Twenty-third Armoured Brigade were unable to cross the Wadi Zigzaou as planned, due to heavy rain. Some did get across, but others were bogged down on the British side of the Wadi.

Geoffrey and his men had to leaguer their vehicles overnight while the infantry attacked. They were caught between two minefields and under heavy shellfire. The following morning they managed to re-embus the infantry, who had suffered heavy casualties, and return as ordered to an area near Medenine.

Monty decided on a change of tactics, sending the Fourth Indian Division through the Matmata hills and the New Zealand Division south by way of Foum Tatouine and through the Wilders Gap pass, named after a New Zealander of that name. This move succeeded in trapping large numbers of the enemy and Geoffrey had to take back a convoy of vehicles crammed with German prisoners of war. It was near the end of the North African campaign. Tunis fell in due course and the enemy forces in North Africa surrendered.

Geoffrey had met Monty at the start of the campaign and was delighted to see that he was using an open Humber staff car made at Coventry. Monty and the Humber became a frequent sight as he drove around, giving morale-boosting pep talks to the troops and handing out cigarettes. He was something of a showman, issuing orders of the day couched in a mixture of biblical and fox-hunting language, but his individual approach and fearless disregard for his own safety were two of the reasons for his success, although he had not been universally popular with all the officers when he took command of the Eighth Army.

After being regrouped and re-equipped at Tahag, in the Suez Canal

Zone, Geoffrey took part in the invasion of Sicily and was responsible for the transport of supplies, mainly ammunition, for the Thirteen Corps. At Foggia he hid his trucks overnight in a huge cemetery full of large and elaborate Italian tombs, some of which were several hundreds of years old. During the night there was a heavy bombing raid and many of the tombs were split open and destroyed, scattering bodies over a wide area. They made a rather gruesome sight the next morning, but Geoffrey and his convoy had to push on to the Sangro, where the next major battle was to take place. He was promoted to Captain on arrival and given command of a unit known as an Independent Artillery Platoon, RASC, whose job was to service the County of Lancaster Yeomanry, who were equipped with 5.5 howitzers.

The formation to which Geoffrey's unit belonged was the Sixth Army Group Royal Artillery, which also had an Air Observation Post Squadron equipped with Cessna aircraft. Their function was to fly over enemy lines, spotting gun positions and radioing back the information to Allied gun batteries. It was a very risky job with every chance of being shot down by Allied gunfire, within the trajectory of howitzer shells, as well as by the enemy. One of the pilots was Colin Huttenbach, a close friend of Geoffrey's from Harrow days, who had the distinction of being awarded a DFC and bar at a time when the RAF wasn't in the habit of giving DFCs to gunnery officers. Geoffrey flew with him in his Auster on several occasions, helping to spot enemy gun positions. Because the Auster was relatively slow, it was very manoeuvrable and they were able to fly in such tight circles that the enemy ME 109s had difficulty attacking them in such hilly country with its narrow valleys.

After the battle of Sangro, Geoffrey's formation was switched from the Eighth Army to the Fifth Army under the command of General Mark Clarke, and this meant moving from the east to the west coast of Italy. They fought their way up through Italy and became involved in some particularly heavy fighting as they approached Monte Cassino. Allied gunfire and bombing made so many craters that the movement of transport and tanks became nearly impossible, but the Cassino eventually fell and the advance continued. They arrived in Rome, where the capture of the city coincided with the 'D'-day landings at Anzio. Geoffrey and his men were also the first troops into Montepulciano and he celebrated the fact by buying large quantities of Vino Nobile di Montepulciano from the Barone. The wine became a great favourite of his after the war.

Their arrival at Florence provided a welcome opportunity for some relaxation. The Allied guns were in the hills to the south with the German artillery in the hills to the north, but it was decided to declare Florence an open city and life there was fairly normal. While Geoffrey and some of his fellow officers were enjoying themselves in the Piazze del Duomo, sipping iced drinks, shells from both sides were whistling overhead. It must have been a unique experience.

Seventy remarkable years

Above *The young Billy Rootes (left) and his brother Reggie with their mother.*

Below left *William Rootes, who was a pioneer motorist.*

Below right *The Rootes family band in 1872.*

Above *This 1902 de Dion-Bouton was one of the first cars William Rootes sold. It was bought by an Indian prince who had a surrey made to shield him from the Indian sun. On its return to England it was bought by Reg Hawkins of Ilchester who drove it in the RAC London–Brighton Veteran Car Run in 1966. Tommy Wisdom can be seen on the left with cap and cigarette.*

Below left *J.B. Dunlop, with the first Humber bicycle to be fitted with pneumatic tyres, talking to R.J. Mecrady. In the background is 'Conger' Walsh, who won the Bath Road 100 mile (161 km) record on a high bicycle in 1896.*

Below right *Number 13, Cope Street, Coventry, one of the houses where Billy Rootes had digs while he was a penny-an-hour apprentice with Singer.*

Above left *Sub-Lt. William Rootes RNVR in 1915.*

Above right *Billy Rootes in his office at Devonshire House in London.*

Below *Billy Rootes (fifth from right) taking part in the Car Mart Golf Tournament on 7 May 1930.*

Top *Racing driver Tommy Wisdom (left) with Dudley Noble, Rootes's first publicity manager, attending a new model launch in the early 1930s.*

Above *The Viceroy of India, Lord Willingdon, with Lady Willingdon and the new Hillman Wizard tourer which they had just purchased for use in India.*

Below *One of several Humber cars shipped out to Argentina in the spring of 1931 for use by the Prince of Wales (left) and Prince George (right). They are staying at the chalet of His Excellency the British Ambassador at Mar del Plata.*

Top *His Royal Highness Prince George (left) talking to Reggie Rootes during a visit to the Humber factory in 1931. On the right is H.L. Davey, the Humber sales manager.*

Above *The prototype of the first Hillman Minx in a village on the French–Swiss border while it was being tested by Billy Rootes (second right) and his chauffeur George Vallet (right). The car on the left is the new Hillman Wizard which carried the cameraman who photographed the testing.*

Below *Sir Herbert Austin (left) visiting the Rootes showrooms in Canterbury. Alongside him is Billy Rootes.*

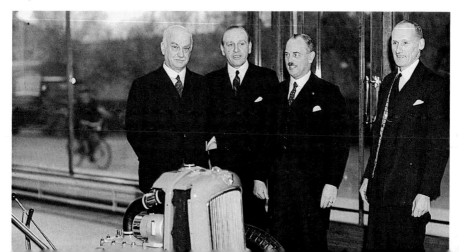

Above *Billy Rootes with his Humber Snipe sports saloon and his younger son Brian with his Humber Blue Streak bicycle in March 1933.*

Left *His Royal Highness the Prince of Wales trying out the Humber tricycle owned by his grand-father, King Edward VII, when he visited the Humber factory at Coventry in July 1934. With him are Colonel J.A. Cole (left), Joe Chaldecott, the Rootes sales director (centre), and Billy Rootes.*

Below *His Royal Highness the Duke of Gloucester's Hillman seven-seater saloon being landed in Egypt ready for the start of his tour of the Middle East and Australia in 1934.*

Above *The launch of the Aero Minx at the Devonshire House showrooms. Reggie Rootes is second from the left and Billy is fourth from the left. The well-known racing driver Freddie Richmond, who later became the Duke of Richmond and Gordon, is on the far right, alongside Colonel J.A. Cole.*

Below *The Prince of Wales arriving at the Olympia Motor Show in October 1935 in his new Humber Snipe.*

Bottom *Geoffrey Rootes (carrying cameras) and his father (right) in India during their world tour.*

Above left *The inimitable Charlie Morris, who was Billy Rootes's travelling secretary and valet for 30 years, accompanied him on many overseas visits, including the world tour in 1936.*

Above right *Former motoring editor Captain Edgar de Normanville, whose famous overdrive units were used in many Rootes cars.*

Below *A youthful Hughie Green, of 'Opportunity Knocks' fame, takes delivery of his new Hillman Minx saloon surrounded by some of his fans in 1932.*

Top *Gracie Fields with her Humber limousine on the way to the studios for another day's filming.*

Above *The famous entertainers of the 1930s and '40s, the Weston Brothers, Kenneth and George, taking delivery of their new 3-litre Talbot saloon.*

Below *The well known Crazy Gang comedians Flanagan and Allen, who were frequently top of the bill at the London Palladium, chose this Hillman Minx drop-head coupé in 1935.*

Left *Among the first Hillman Wizard owners were the record-breaking British flyers, Jim and Amy Mollinson.*

Below *Music hall star Nellie Wallace was another keen Hillman owner. She is seen here with her new Minx drop-head coupé.*

Bottom *The celebrated actress Gertrude Lawrence, after taking delivery of a new Humber Pullman Cabriolet de Ville.*

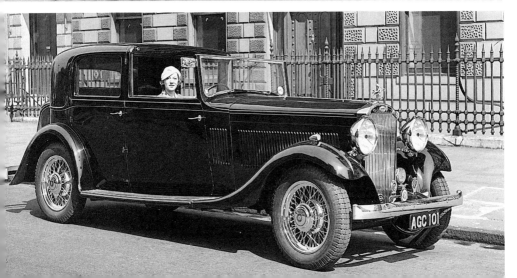

Above *Captain E. Molyneux was a famous dress designer who had this Humber named after him.*

Below *Geraldo, whose dance bands became famous on radio before the war and who went on to have his own television shows, was the owner of a Humber de Ville which he had painted ivory.*

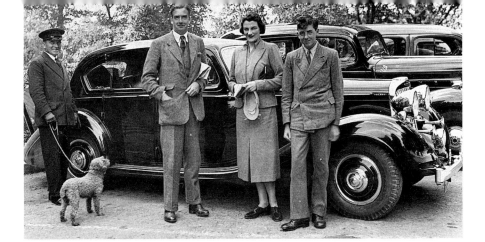

Top *Rootes cars were popular with politicians: Anthony Eden had his Talbot 3-litre saloon shipped to Ireland when he spent a holiday in Killarney with his wife and young son.*

Above *Billy Rootes made an early sale at the Earls Court Motor Show in 1938 when he persuaded Penelope Dudley Ward to buy the new 4-litre Sunbeam Talbot saloon. She was the actress daughter of Freda Dudley Ward, who was a close friend of the Prince of Wales and founded the Feathers Clubs.*

Left *The well-known racing driver the Hon. Brian Lewis talking to Billy Rootes (right) at the launch of the new Humber Super Snipe at Crystal Palace race track.*

Above *Billy Rootes gets down to watch the hill climbing performance of the new Humber Super Snipe at the Crystal Palace race track during the launch demonstration before a crowd of motoring personalities and journalists.*

Below *The British Prime Minister Neville Chamberlain driving away in his Hillman at Croydon Airport on his way to make his famous 'Peace in our time' speech at the House of Commons on 31 March 1938 after his meeting with Hitler.*

Bottom *Herr Hitler showed considerable interest in the latest Sunbeam Talbot when he visited the Rootes Group stand at the 1939 Berlin Motor Show with the other German leaders. Billy Rootes is second from the left.*

Top *The specially designed overhead conveyor which enabled aeroplane fuselages to be taken from one part of the shadow factory to another without disturbing the work going on below at Speke.*

Above *Blenheim bombers lined up on the airfield alongside the Rootes shadow factory at Speke in readiness for their first test flight.*

Below *By July 1939 work was in progress at Rootes's new shadow factory at Ryton-on-Dunsmore, near Coventry, which was going to be used for aero-engine production. After the war the factory became Rootes's main car production plant, and now produces Peugeots. Billy Rootes (third from the left) is seen discussing plans with the builders.*

Above *King George VI visiting the new Rootes aero-engine plant in Coventry with Queen Elizabeth and being met by Reggie Rootes.*

Below *When a German bomb hit Devonshire House, extensive damage was done to offices on the top floor and the boardroom, seen here being inspected by the two Rootes brothers.*

Bottom *Billy Rootes with his sons Brian (centre) and Geoffrey at Stype in 1942 when they were on leave from the army.*

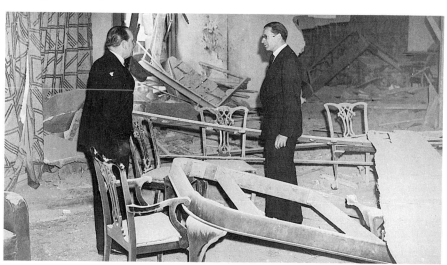

Above General Sir Bernard Montgomery's famous Humber staff car 'Old Faithful' was well to the fore when as Commander-in-Chief of the Twenty-first Army Group he had his first meeting on French soil with Lt. Gen. O.N. Bradley of the American forces.

Below Sydney Camm, the designer of the Hurricane fighter (left) with H.G. Wells and Billy Rootes.

Bottom Pilot Officer Duncan Smith (left) receiving a cheque for £15,000 from Billy Rootes for the purchase of two Spitfires to join the Motor Industry Fighter Squadron. In the centre is H.S. Stanley, the organizer of the Fighter Fund. On the right is Joe Chaldecott.

Above *Field Marshal Viscount Montgomery of Alamein touring Rootes's Stoke factory at Coventry in his wartime Humber staff car 'Old Faithful' during a visit to the Group's factories. Billy Rootes is seated on his right and Geoffrey Rootes is in the front passenger seat. The chauffeur is Sgt Mitchell who took charge of the Coventry demonstration fleet.*

Below left *Billy Rootes leaving for his investiture at Buckingham Palace in 1942. He was knighted for his war work.*

Below right *Reggie Rootes (centre) outside the new premises of Rootes Motors Inc. in New York.*

Top *Joe Chaldecott (left) visits the company's sales organization in Manila for the launch of the Hillman Minx there.*

Above *During a 40,000-mile (64,360 km) world tour of the Group's overseas sales and manufacturing organizations during the early part of 1953, Reggie Rootes visited the assembly plant of Rootes Australia Limited in Melbourne. He is seen here inspecting an early Humber model from the company's museum. With him are George Laird, director and general manager Rootes Australia; L.B. Flight, advertising manager; S. Bramley, foreman in charge of the company's garage; and Bill Betts, the regional manager of the Rootes Export Division at Devonshire House.*

Left *Reggie Rootes talking to Jim McDiarmid, the driver of 'Old 21', the seven-ton Commer truck which had covered 300,000 trouble-free miles (482,700 km) over indifferent Australian roads in four years.*

Above *Reggie Rootes being interviewed by BBC television before the opening of the thirty-third International Motor Show at Earls Court in November 1948. A model of Rootes's new Sunbeam Talbot 80 is alongside him on the turntable.*

Below *The Sunbeam Talbot 80 sports saloon was Rootes's first completely new post-war car and its design owed much to the company's aircraft experience. Billy and Reggie Rootes are seen here with the car in the Devonshire House showrooms.*

Top *John Bullock and Charles Fothergill of the* News Chronicle *competing in the RAC Rally with one of the works Sunbeam Talbot sports saloons. They are seen here during a timed ascent of Bwlch-y-Groes in the Welsh mountains.*

Above *The 1954 Hillman Californian, which was derived from the Hillman Minx for the American market.*

Below *The Hillman Minx in sleeker post-war form.*

Top *The Hillman Super Imp, which had many competition successes.*

Above *The tough little Hillman Husky, which was the star of* Husky be my Guide, *written by best-selling Australian travel author Fred Thwaites.*

Below *The four-cylinder Humber Hawk, which was roomy and reliable.*

Above *The Sunbeam Rapier was a worthy successor to the Mark III Sunbeam and won races and rallies.*

Below *The sporty Sunbeam Alpine was also available with a hard top and was later fitted with a more powerful Ford V8 engine to become the Sunbeam Tiger.*

Bottom *The luxurious 3-litre Humber Super Snipe saloon.*

Above *The Super Snipe seen here and the Humber Hawk were both available as estate cars.*

Below *The Humber Sceptre was the first of the smaller post-war Humbers to be mass-produced in larger numbers.*

Bottom *The Singer Vogue took the place of the old-fashioned Singer Hunter, with its horse-head mascot, wooden facia and drawer complete with tool kit.*

Top King George VI visiting the Rootes Group stand to look at the new Hillman Minx convertible at the first British Motor Show held in New York in April 1950.

Above Billy Rootes giving a press conference after landing in New York in 1951 when he was chairman of the Dollar Export Council. On the left, mopping his brow, is Joe Chaldecott.

Left Mayor D.H. Mackay presenting Billy Rootes with a white stetson which symbolized the hospitality and friendliness shown to him by the city of Calgary, Alberta. Billy also received many awards and accolades in America, including being made adviser to the state of Texas.

Top *Princess Margaret visiting the Rootes stand at the Earls Court Motor Show in 1950. Third from the left is Dickie Webb, the Rootes reception manager in Coventry, who looked after all the important visitors to the factories for nearly 30 years.*

Above *Norman Garrad with Stirling Moss (right) and his co-driver Desmond Scannell studying the route for the 1952 Monte Carlo Rally. They were competing in works Sunbeam Talbots.*

Right *Admiral of the Fleet Earl Mountbatten talking to John Panks (left) and Billy Rootes when he visited the Rootes stand at the British Exhibition in New York in June 1960. It was the biggest exhibition ever staged abroad by Britain and was organized by Billy Rootes.*

Top *Lord Rootes with Prince Philip and Vice-President Nixon looking at the model of the Statue of Liberty during their tour of the New York World Fair.*

Above *J.E. Scott, the general sales manager of Rolls-Royce, Billy Rootes, and Dr Llewellyn Smith, managing director of Rolls-Royce, share a joke before the annual luncheon of the British Automobile Manufacturers Association held during the New York Motor Show in April 1960.*

Below *Billy and Reggie Rootes receiving the news that they had been successful in their bid for the Singer Motor Company.*

Above left *Billy Rootes and his wife Ann leaving their London home for Buckingham Palace and the investiture on 12 July 1955. Billy was awarded the GBE for his work as chairman of the Dollar Exports Council. He later took the hereditary title of Baron Rootes of Ramsbury.*

Above right *Although Rootes didn't win the Monte Carlo Rally outright until 1955, they won the RAC's Dewar Trophy in 1952 for the company's remarkable successes with Sunbeam Talbots in the Alpine Rally, which was considered to be the most outstanding engineering achievement of the year. Wilfred Andrews, the RAC chairman, is seen here presenting the magnificent trophy to Billy Rootes.*

Below *Billy Rootes, an apprentice with the Singer Motor Company in Coventry as a young man, watches an apprentice at his own company's Ryton plant, 21-year-old Wreford Fenn, as he checks the wheels of a Sunbeam Alpine which has just left the assembly line.*

Top Geoffrey and Marion Rootes attending the annual dinner and dance of the Institute of Automobile Manufacturers at Grosvenor House, London.

Above Reggie Rootes welcoming Harlow H. Curtis, the president of General Motors, when Rootes organized a get-together for American automobile chiefs visiting England in September 1954. The chairman of Vauxhall Motors, G.N. Vansittart, is on the left, with (second from the right) Walter E. Hill, the Vauxhall Motors managing director.

Left Billy Rootes shares a joke with American president Harry S. Truman.

Top *Belgian motoring journalist Paul Frère, who won the 1960 Le Mans 24 Hour Race, being presented with the Rootes Gold Cup by Billy Rootes at the Guild of Motoring Writers Annual Dinner in London. On the left is Laurie Cade, the Guild's senior vice-president.*

Above *Billy Rootes with his favourite dogs in the grounds of Ramsbury Manor, his Wiltshire home.*

Right *The Prime Minister, the Rt. Hon. Harold Macmillan, out shooting with Billy Rootes on the Rootes estate at Glenalmond in Scotland.*

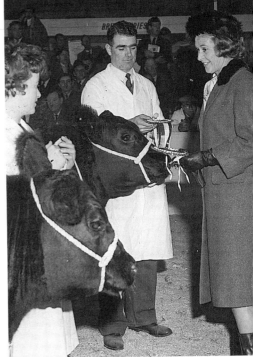

Above left *A keen farmer and Hampshire Down sheep-breeder, Billy Rootes is seen here with his prize-winning lambs at the Royal Windsor Show in 1954.*

Above right *Billy Rootes's Aberdeen Angus cattle were famous throughout the world and he was president of the Aberdeen Angus Society. Brian Rootes's wife Bet is seen here presenting rosettes at the Royal Smithfield Show in London.*

Below *Ron Clayton, who was responsible for taking Rootes Group photographs for more than 30 years, is presented with a silver tankard by John Bullock, Liam Hunter and Bill Elsey during a Devonshire House party.*

Above *Billy Rootes shows a customer some of the hundreds of trophies won by Rootes cars in races and rallies throughout the world which were on view in the Devonshire House showrooms.*

Below *Billy Rootes surveys the day's output of cars for export from the Rootes Ryton-on-Dunsmore plant. With him is George Bryan, the dispatch foreman.*

Top *Billy and Reggie Rootes discussing future developments with Rupert Hammond (right), the Group's financial director.*

Above *The last photograph taken of the Rootes brothers together was at the Singer Chamois launch in Devonshire House in October 1964. Left to right are Geoffrey Rootes, Reggie Rootes, Billy Rootes, Timothy Rootes and Brian Rootes. Billy Rootes died on 12 December that year.*

Left *Geoff Rossiter was chosen to make the presentation to Reggie when he retired as chairman on 5 April 1967. A farewell party at the Ritz Hotel in London was attended by many who had been with the Group before the war. Lady Rootes is in the centre.*

After going northwards towards Bologna, he spent the winter of 1944–5 in the mountains in the neighbourhood of Castel del Rio. The Germans were in control of most of the lateral roads and had mobile guns which they could move along the roads and shell the Allied positions. The bad weather and heavy snows made getting ammunition up to the gun positions very difficult, even by pack mules. Ron Varney, who was commanding 376 Artillery Company, was taken ill and invalided home and Geoffrey was given his command with the acting rank of Major.

Eventually spring came, along with VE Day and the enemy surrender in Italy. Geoffrey was posted home and then sent to the Rhine Army Headquarters, BAOR, where he served in an administrative capacity until it was time for him to be demobilized. While he was with the British Army of the Rhine, however, he was instructed to accompany his father, who had been sent there with an Allied Mission to examine the possibility of dividing Berlin into various Allied sectors, with particular reference to the engineering industry. They stayed with General Lucius Clay, who was in command of the American troops in Berlin, and both were shocked to see the results of the Allied bombing of a city they had known so well before the war. The Adlon Hotel, where they used to stay, was only a shell. A floor waiter was wandering among the ruins completely dazed and shell-shocked and groups of middle-aged women were trying to move rubble with their bare hands. It was a sight which brought home the tragic reality of war.

Geoffrey was eventually demobilized in March 1946 after six-and-a-half years' service in the army. He had been in the thick of the fighting for much of the time but, at the age of 29, he was still in good physical shape and was ready to resume civilian life.

Chapter 17

Cars and trucks
and aircraft

BILLY AND REGGIE Rootes had been preparing for the war they felt
was inevitable for nearly three years and, by the time Chamberlain
made his historic announcement on 3 September 1939, arrangements
were already in hand for staff at Devonshire House to be moved to
Stype as soon as London came under heavy attack from the air. Plans to
put the Rootes factories on a war footing the moment hostilities began
had been finalized a few months after Billy and Geoffrey's return from
their world tour. The new shadow factory at Speke was also in full production.

With his brother, Billy had visited Speke, near Liverpool, in May
1937 to inspect the site where they were planning to build Britain's first
shadow factory for the production of bombers for the Royal Air Force. It
was to be an entirely self-contained production unit with its own power
plant and ancillary services. At the time of their visit, the site was just a
very large cabbage field, but they gave the go-ahead on their return to
London and work progressed so rapidly that the first complete aircraft
came off the production line at the new factory in September 1938.

Building and equipping the factory had been a gigantic task and
a remarkable feat of organization, particularly at a time when many
people in Britain had been lulled into a sense of false security and the
urgency of the situation was lost on them. Apart from all the construction work, a vast collection of intricate plant and machinery had to be
obtained, set up and brought into full working order in a matter of
months. Supplies of raw materials needed to be maintained. The factory
had to be staffed and a housing estate with more than 1,500 new houses
built to accommodate many of them. Apart from the new factory and
outbuildings, it was also necessary to construct many miles of new con-
crete roads and runways.

The layout of the factory enabled raw materials to be brought in at
one end and finished aircraft to come out at the other, ready to be
flight-tested from the adjoining aerodrome and then flown on to their

new squadrons. In planning the factory, the Rootes brothers had been able to draw on the wide experience they had gained from their frequent visits to America. A special feature was the electrically operated overhead railway, located high up in the roof of the main assembly shop and erecting hall, which allowed large aeroplane sections and even entire airframes to be transported from one section of the building to another without causing any interference to the work being done in other areas below.

Targets were achieved from the start and output increased steadily, until within 18 months the factory was turning out bombers at a rate that was 40 per cent higher than originally planned. The Bristol Blenheim bombers being made there were mid-wing cantilever monoplanes with retractable undercarriages and carrying a crew of three. They were powered by two Bristol Mercury VIII engines, each developing 840 hp with a take-off power of 920 hp, giving the bombers a maximum speed of 295 mph (475 km/h) and a range of 1,900 miles (3,057 km).

When Sir Kingsley Wood, the Secretary of State for Air, visited the factory in April 1939, he described it as 'the best-equipped and probably the largest of its kind in the world, forming one of the most important units in the Government Factory Scheme for the rapid expansion of the Royal Air Force'. His tour of the plant involved walking several miles through the various departments, watching the bombers being manufactured stage by stage until they were ready for testing.

Billy Rootes recognized the publicity value of the visit and the effect it would have on the morale of the workforce. With the support of the Air Ministry, he planned the press facilities down to the last detail, ensuring that reporters had good news stories and that the photographers were able to get their pictures back to London in time for the following morning's national newspapers. Arrangements were made for the photographers to go ahead of the official party, accompanied by guides who were briefed to take them speedily from one photographic point to the next without causing any inconvenience to the Minister and his party, and extra staff were also available to help newsreel men with their cumbersome equipment. Each area where the photographers were allowed to take pictures had been carefully planned and reconnoitred to ensure that they showed the latest long-nosed Blenheims in full mass production and the finished machines being wheeled out of the factory before taking off on their test flights.

Cars were available so that the photographers could send their pictures on the 4.05 pm train from Liverpool, which got in to Euston at 7.30 that evening, in good time for the early editions. Later pictures were put on the 5.25 pm train, which arrived in London at 8.40 pm. Extra telephones were available so that reporters could telephone through their stories immediately following the Minister's press conference. Sir Kingsley's impressions of the factory and the glowing terms he used to describe the efficiency of the Rootes Group appeared in all the

early editions the following morning, along with graphic photographs of
the aircraft leaving the factory. All this attention to detail paid dividends and resulted in glowing reports in newspapers and magazines and
on the newsreels. It was a typical example of Billy Rootes's ability to get
maximum publicity from an important event.

During the first months of the war, the factory at Speke produced one
in every five bombers built in Britain. When the other manufacturers'
factories got into full production, the ratio was reduced to one in every
seven, but between 1 September 1939 and 30 April 1945, when the war
in Europe ended, Rootes built a total of 4,447 bombers. This represented
3.66 per cent of all the aircraft built, including fighters, bombers, reconnaissance aircraft, transport planes and trainers. It was a remarkable
performance, considering that the five companies of the Hawker
Siddeley Group built 30,641 and the five Vickers factories produced
30,152 of the 121,400 aircraft manufactured during the period. De
Havilland was responsible for 6,957, Bristol 6,310, Miles Aircraft 5,335,
Airspeed 4,673, Fairey 4,391, Blackburn 3,260 and Westland 3,031.
Among the other motor manufacturers involved, Morris Motors built
2,785, Austin 1,605 and Standard 1,514.

A great deal of the credit for the record-breaking performances
achieved at Speke was due to Rupert Hammond, who was sent there on
a two-week assignment at the start of the war and stayed there for the
next four years, running the factory and keeping production going,
despite shortages of raw materials and repeated attempts by Hitler to put
the factory out of action.

To reduce the risk of enemy bombers being able to put more than one
factory out of action at a time, a second Rootes shadow factory was built
on a 60-acre site at Ryton-on-Dunsmore, on the outskirts of Coventry,
which came into full production in 1939. Known at the time as the
Number 2 Aero Engine Shadow Factory, it turned out complete sets of
components for Hercules engines at a rate of 800 a month, as well as
250 complete power plants. By 31 December 1943 three extensions had
been built, and the covered factory space had increased to 925,214 sq ft.
There were 748 staff, of whom 315 were female, and 5,362 hourly-paid
employees, of whom 1,793 were female, an indication of the important
part women were playing in Britain's factories, particularly in the
Coventry area.

The Number 1 Aero Engine Shadow Factory had also been built in
Coventry, at Stoke Aldermoor, not far from the car plant. Production
had started there in 1937 and by the early 1940s an additional five
extensions had been built and 675 sets of components for Hercules
engines were being produced there each month, as well as 170 sets for
Mercury engines and a further 100 for Pegasus power units. The Stoke
Aldermoor plant covered 246,000 sq ft, and of the 444 staff, 209 were
female. There were 2,292 hourly-paid employees and 654 of those were
women.

The director in charge of both engine plants was Harold Heath, the brother of the Barrie Heath who had been in digs with Geoffrey Rootes in Liverpool before the war and who was then serving as a bomber pilot in the Royal Air Force. The two Rootes factories produced more than 50,000 aero-engines between 1939 and 1945 and repaired a further 20,000 made by other manufacturers. The total Rootes contribution to the war effort during that period was quite staggering, considering that their other factories built 60 per cent of all the army's armoured cars and 35 per cent of all scout cars, along with 3,500 other armoured reconnaissance vehicles. More than 20,000 vehicles imported from America in knocked-down form were assembled and 12,000 others were repaired. Quite apart from the many thousands of Hillman and Humber staff cars, Rootes also made 300,000 bombs, 5,000,000 fuses and 3,000,000 ammunition boxes. Altogether, 11 per cent of the total wartime output of wheeled vehicles came from Rootes factories. The Talbot factory at Barlby Road in London had also been turned into a repair plant for Rolls Royce Merlin engines.

Billy and Reggie Rootes worked unceasingly for the war effort, and Billy also took on the responsibility for a number of Government committees involved in increasing production in Britain. In May 1940 he was appointed chairman of the Shadow Aero-Engine Committee, a move which had a rapid impact on aero-engine production generally. The War Office had also asked him to visit France in January 1940 to advise them on the servicing and maintenance of vehicles for the British Expeditionary Force, and the Under Secretary of State at the Air Ministry wanted him to investigate the motor transport situation of Royal Air Force units in France. Many of the vehicles concerned were Humbers, Hillmans and Commers and Billy was keen to organize a major unit overhaul and exchange scheme, to speed up the heavy repair operations and introduce important economies.

He was accompanied to France by Bernard Winter, the Group's engineering director, and after being there for nearly two months they gave detailed reports to the War Office and the Air Ministry which uncovered a number of major failings in the way in which the transport systems were being handled, particularly by the army. They reported that, with the exception of the Royal Army Service Corps, there was a lack of knowledge of motor transport requirements and this was vital in what was by then a completely mechanized army. The Royal Army Ordnance Corps, which was responsible to the various units for the maintenance of their vehicles and operating their workshops, had placed too much importance on obtaining officers with engineering degrees. The result was that those who had been chosen mainly because of their electrical, civil and mechanical engineering qualifications did not have the necessary experience to organize and operate a Motor Transport function efficiently.

Billy suggested that, in order to solve the problem quickly, a number of carefully selected, experienced men from the motor industry should be given special intensive training in army methods and discipline, and sent to France as soon as possible. In order to keep the general staff well informed of all the problems, a special advisor should also be appointed who would be able to influence inspection procedures and instructional facilities.

Too many skilled mechanics were having to do fatigues and guard duties, instead of being allowed to get on with the repair and maintenance of vehicles. This was an important waste of time and talent when other men were available to do these tasks who did not have the skills so urgently needed. The report gave examples of red tape damaging the efficiency of the army's mechanical transport system and made suggestions as to how this could be overcome. It also emphasized the need for closer co-operation between all the motor manufacturers supplying vehicles to the forces.

The army didn't take too kindly to all the criticism, but urgent measures had to be taken to solve the problems and the majority of the recommendations were put into effect. The visit also gave Billy Rootes and Bernard Winter an excellent opportunity of getting first-hand knowledge of the way in which Rootes vehicles were performing in action, and the modifications which would be needed in order to make future models more efficient.

Soon after their return to England, Devonshire House received a direct hit from a German bomb, badly damaging the boardroom and several offices. Billy moved his personal staff across to Claridge's Hotel in Brook Street, and worked from there until the offices and boardroom had been rebuilt.

In 1940, on the night of 14/15 November, under a bright full moon, waves of German bombers tore the heart out of Coventry, dropping more than 50 land mines, 1,200 high explosives and 35,000 incendiary bombs. The following morning Billy Rootes was summoned by Winston Churchill and given the task of getting Coventry back into action again as quickly as possible.

He agreed and immediately drove to Coventry to see the damage and form a Reconstruction Committee, under his chairmanship, which could draw up plans for bringing life back into the badly shocked city. His first points of call, however, were the Rootes factories which had been damaged. An eye-witness account of the situation published afterwards in the *Dictionary of National Biography* stated:

'On the morning after the blitz, Rootes was to be found on an upturned box outside his plants addressing his workforce, encouraging them to clear up the mess and promising that there should be work for all. The former apprentice was demonstrating, as he was to demonstrate time and again, his thorough relationship with the motor industry and his abiding loyalty to the Coventry community. His drive and assertiveness and his qualities of leadership in rehabilitating industry had consequences both locally and nationally. Many recommendations were usefully applied in other bombed cities and William Rootes's impact through his Coventry Industrial Reconstruction and Co-ordinating Committee contributed greatly to Coventry's economic recovery'.

During the weeks following the blitz, most of the homeless were housed; a new transport system was organized; many miles of temporary water mains and sewage pipes were laid; essential raw materials were brought into the city and supplies were maintained so that within a short time the assembly lines in all the factories were again working to full capacity.

Billy thought it would give encouragement to the workforce if they were able to fight back. He paid for three Spitfires and became President of an appeal to raise the £100,000 needed for the motor industry to have its own squadron of fighter aircraft. He persuaded Viscount Nuffield, Lord Austin, Lord Perry and Lord Kenilworth to be patrons, and the secretary of the fund, as well as being one of the leading instigators, was H. G. Starley of Champion Sparking Plugs. Colonel Arthur Waite agreed to act as chairman of the Organizing Committee.

A sum of £105,000 was quickly raised, thanks to the support provided by all sections of the automobile trades, and it had been the President of the Motor Factors' Association, Mr C. H. G. Hobday, who made the first contribution. A sectional drawing of a Spitfire was used to raise money through factory and dealer organizations, so everyone was able to contribute, including many schoolchildren who learned about the fund through BBC broadcasts. A rivet cost sixpence, a sparking plug eight shillings, a petrol tank £40 and an engine £2,000. Lord Beaverbrook, who was at that time still Minister of Aircraft Production, agreed that anyone donating £5,000 could have the privilege of naming one of the fighter planes.

Billy Rootes gave a luncheon in London on 29 August 1941. Attended by many distinguished leaders of the motor industry, and with Lieutenant-Colonel Moore Brabazon, Minister of Aircraft Production, as the principal guest, it was to celebrate the purchase of 21 Spitfires and the completion of the Motor Industry Squadron.

All the aircraft were given names. There was 'Lord Austin', 'Champion', 'Nuffield', 'William E. Rootes', 'Rootes Shadow' and 'Rootes Snipe'. Brown Brothers had named their Spitfire 'The Dominant Factor'; Dunlop Rubber called theirs 'Pericles'; Ford employees named their plane 'Go To It' and Joseph Lucas workers decided on 'King of the Air'; ERF had 'Sun Works'; the Motor Agents' Association's plane was called, not surprisingly, 'M.A.A.'; the Motor Factors' Association had 'The Gay Gordon' and the Scottish Motor Trade Association, not to be outdone, chose the name 'Caledonian'; Jack Olding decided on 'The Cat'; S. Smith & Sons had 'Smithfire'; Vauxhall and Bedford dealers chose 'Wyvern I', with the company having 'Wyvern II'; members of the Society of Motor Manufacturers and Traders decided on 'S.M.M.T.'; and another group of people in the motor industry wanted their Spitfire called 'H. G. Starley'.

Until the squadron was finally disbanded in April 1945, it was in the thick of the fighting in Britain and also did two years' service overseas. Although the original Spitfires were later replaced by the latest Mustangs, powered by Rolls-Royce Merlin engines and made in the Packard plant, the squadron retained its coat of arms with the bar sinister, which resulted in its pilots being nicknamed the 'Bastards of the Air'.

In July 1941 Lord Beaverbrook had invited Billy Rootes to join him as his deputy at the Ministry of Supply and become Deputy Chairman of the Supply Council, answering directly to him, and with full authority to act as an administrator. Billy turned down an invitation also to be Director General of Production at the Ministry because, as he explained to Lord Beaverbrook, he had relied for some years on production experts, and felt that the Minister should look for someone with first-class production experience.

It was agreed that he would be able to retain all his directorships, that the appointment to the Supply Council would only be for as long as it took him to improve the supply situation and that as soon as his work was completed he would be allowed to retire in favour of someone else. Within four months, however, Billy was appointed Chairman of the Supply Council, with additional responsibilities which kept him fully occupied for the next three years.

He and Lord Beaverbrook were close friends and had worked together at the Ministry of Aircraft Production. When he had resigned the Chairmanship of the Shadow Aero-Engine Committee, Lord Beaverbrook wrote: 'What you have done you have done brilliantly. You cannot be praised too much, or spoken of with too much enthusiasm. All through my association with you at the aircraft ministry I derived nothing but inspirations from my contact with you. To the gratitude I feel there is necessarily added on immense admiration for your energy and leadership.'

They proved to be a formidable pair, full of determination and with insatiable appetites for hard work. Their achievements together during the next two years ensured that the Royal Air Force received aircraft in the numbers it badly needed and that the army was equipped with the latest tanks, transport and equipment. Billy Rootes made several trips to America and Canada to persuade the governments of both countries to increase their aid to Britain. His astute business acumen and wide experience of North American business methods, as well as his contacts within government and industry, proved invaluable in opening up new lines of communication and negotiating the delivery of urgently needed materials and equipment.

In November 1942, at the request of the British Government, as Chairman of the Supply Council, he led a delegation of senior officials from the Ministry of Supply and the War Office to America and Canada. Their objective was to cut through much of the red tape which was holding up urgent supplies, and to co-ordinate the work of the British Supply Mission, the British Army Staff, the British Raw Materials Mission and the Inspection Board of the United Kingdom. The failure of these organizations to agree, or to keep each other informed, had led to confusion, duplication and misleading directives as to Britain's top priority requirements.

It was a mission which had an important bearing on the help Britain received from America and Canada for the remainder of the war, and the speed with which urgent decisions were made on both sides of the Atlantic. The importance of this aid can be judged by the fact that during 1943 the supply of munitions, explosives, equipment and materials from America to the Ministry of Supply exceeded $5,000 million, or £1¼ million. This was during a year when the Ministry's total expenditure over the whole field of production in Britain was less than £1 million. The Canadian Government also supplied a further £300 million worth of aid.

The British delegation had to contend with proposals to increase the size of the American armed forces, which would have reduced the amount of aid available to Britain. Reports from Washington suggested that the American army was going to be increased in size to 13 million, a figure so clearly beyond the possibilities of overseas movement as to become unreasonable, but by the time the delegation left, the size of the increase had been reduced to 7.5 million, including 2.2 million air force personnel. This was a much more reasonable figure and one which would have much less effect on the future availability of American aid.

It was the first occasion that a co-ordinated approach had been made to the highest American authorities, enabling an overall programme of aid to be discussed. Arrangements were made to co-ordinate the work of the British Supply Mission and the British Army Staff, which it was hoped would lead to more accurate forecasting and smoother working procedures. What was previously a disjointed group of individual organizations, all trying to get priority supplies for themselves, was replaced by an efficient organization of a calibre able to negotiate and handle such a vast amount of business.

Billy Rootes was also critical of the organization of the Ministry of Supply in London, which he felt showed a lack of sufficient breadth of understanding, commercial drive and vision in solving problems. He recommended that changes should be made which would introduce a greater sense of urgency and lead to better co-ordination and more forceful action. Not every member of the delegation was in agreement with his suggestions, but they did solve many of the problems and achieved greater efficiency and progress.

When the other members of the delegation returned to England, Billy Rootes decided to stay on until the end of December for further meetings with Government officials and to visit seven of the plants in America and another eight in Canada which were producing tanks, tank engines, guns, small arms, ammunition, wireless, electrical and optical apparatus, marine engines, locomotives, airframes and aircraft engines. He wanted to investigate the latest North American production techniques and schedules which he felt could also be used in Britain to save time and enable the country's war programme to move ahead faster.

He was particularly interested in the Ford system of treating armour plate and in a giant press the company had which could treat 80 tons of plate in an eight-hour shift. Henry Ford agreed to provide similar equipment to help the British war effort. He told Billy that American manufacturers were also relying less on high-alloy steels and had replaced bolting and riveting techniques with casting and welding procedures which were simpler, reduced man hours and speeded up production. Agreement was reached for a greater interchange of ideas and information on new production methods between manufacturers in Britain and North America, which continued throughout the war.

Before he left America, Billy Rootes also dealt with the low morale which existed among the 3,198 staff employed there by the British Supply Mission, the British Army Staff and the Joint Inspection Board, many of whom were American. In common with American Government departments, there was a high turnover in staff which, at the time of his visit, was running at the rate of 70 per cent each year. 'Long periods of duty in Washington tend to produce a certain despondency of mind which does not fortify one in negotiations,' he told Lord Beaverbrook on his return. Bringing the three organizations closer together, reducing numbers and providing incentives for the more hardworking and loyal members of staff, along with the appointment of a director general in overall control, led to a much happier and more efficient organization in Washington.

Billy Rootes was knighted in 1942 for his achievements and the outstanding contribution made to the war effort by the Rootes Group in producing record numbers of aircraft, vehicles and supplies for the British forces. The part played by his brother Reggie during the war was also not overlooked and he received a knighthood in 1945.

Chapter 18

The fight for German know-how

APART FROM THE problems of getting their own factories back into peacetime production, Billy and Reggie Rootes, along with other British motor manufacturers, wanted to ensure that German industry would not be used again as an instrument of war, or become a major competitor in overseas markets. They were still angry at the way in which Opel and other companies had been able to dominate so many markets before the war, because of the unfair subsidies they had received from the German Government. At the same time they were concerned that the Russians had already taken advantage of the situation in Germany and had stripped many of the factories belonging to leading industrial companies, including BMW, of their most modern equipment and machine tools for use in Russia. They had also persuaded a number of Germany's top engineers and designers to go and work for them.

The British Government was caught flat-footed and the Russians brought off a major *coup* when they got Ingenieur Augustin, Germany's number one backroom boy in the engineering field and a permanent civil servant, to go and work for them, and head a special design and development branch of their Kommissariat for Heavy Industries. They gave him an apartment in Griefswalder Strasse, in the Russian sector in Berlin, but by then he had already persuaded some 40 leading engineers to go and work with him.

Billy Rootes asked his friend Sir Percy Mills, the head of the Economic Division of the Control Commission for Germany, if he could find out what had happened to five of the German engineers who had particular knowledge of the motor industry which he felt would be of benefit to the Rootes Group. If they could be found, he hoped that the Board of Trade would help him to bring them to England to work. This he felt would speed up the process of getting information about the latest German advances in research, design, and production developments and techniques. The engineers he was particularly interested in were Walter Schilo of BMW, Dr Richard Bruhm and Karl Frydag of

Henschel, Eduard Winckler of Auto Union and Dr Ferdinand Porsche of Mercedes.

Sir Percy Mills agreed, but Billy Rootes's hopes of benefiting from their knowledge and experience were rather dashed when he received a reply from A. W. G. Bechter of the Control Commission's Economic Intelligence Section. In a confidential report he gave details of their whereabouts, but warned that those engineers who were already working for the Russians, although not under contract, were being so highly paid and so well looked after that it would be very difficult to persuade them to work for British companies. The average salary being paid to German engineers by the Russians was between RM 10,000 and RM 12,000 (reichmarks) a month, but in addition they were supplied with treble the normal food rations, plenty of cigarettes, and all the fuel they needed for a number of cars which had been placed at their disposal.

It also appeared from the report that none of the engineers he wanted would be available. Walter Schilo was very distressed at the death of his wife and had been left with four very young children. He didn't want to leave Germany, however tempting any offer might be. Dr Richard Bruhm had been connected with the Opel works at Russelsheim, but during the war had been chief production manager of Auto Union. He was reported to have strong Nazi leanings and had been taken into custody by the British Military Government authority at Fleckeby in Schleswig-Holstein and was still there under detention.

Karl Frydag had been a director of Henschel Flugzeugwerke AG at Berlin–Schonefeld, but for most of the war he had been head of the department for the design, development and production of aircraft fuselages for the whole of the German aircraft industry. His department was part of the Reich's Air Ministry. He had fled from Berlin in April 1945 and taken refuge in Austria, but had returned to Germany the following month and was now living in a small village in Upper Bavaria. His close connections with the Nazi Party were only because, as a Government official, membership of the party was obligatory. The works at Schonefeld had in any case been stripped of all plant and equipment by the Russians and there was little of value left. Eduard Winckler, who had been with Auto Union before moving to Opel, had joined the Wehrmacht, but had failed to return from the Eastern Front.

Contrary to general belief at the time, Dr Ferdinand Porsche had not been responsible for the design and development of Germany's Tiger and Panther tanks, but he was entitled to full credit for the development of the successful Auto Union racing cars and the Volkswagen. Before that he was for some years chief engineer with the Daimler–Benz Company at Stuttgart and had been credited with the design of the rear engine type of Mercedes car which was the forerunner of the Volkswagen. There was no doubt that he had been a close confidant of Hitler, with whom he had had direct personal contact during the war, and between 1943 and 1944 had been working on a number of important projects involving the development of those of Germany's secret weapons which demanded some form of jet propulsion, although his efforts to increase the range of the VI missiles during this time had not been very successful. At the end of the war he had been placed under close arrest by the American Military Authorities at Stuttgart, and as his connections with the Nazi Party were well known, it was very unlikely that he would be released to come to England.

Billy Rootes's attempts to get machinery from Germany were also unsuccessful, due mainly to the inability of the Board of Trade to cut through red tape. Sir Percy Mills tried to help Rootes get two Keller die-sinking machines from the Volkswagen plant, but in the end Billy wrote to him in January 1946 explaining that he couldn't afford to wait any longer and because of the interminable delays had approached some friends in America. Although they were his competitors, they had now supplied him with a new Keller for the Rootes die shop in Coventry.

The British Government was anxious to rebuild some of Germany's badly damaged factories as soon as possible to meet her essential needs, and this included getting her motor industry going again. Help was requested from various trade associations in Britain, including the Society of Motor Manufacturers and Traders. The Control Commission in Germany was also very short of technical personnel, particularly people with automotive experience, and this time Sir Percy Mills approached Billy for help in recruiting suitable staff.

Billy Rootes arranged for an SMMT advisory panel to be set up under the chairmanship of Sir Peter Bennett, with himself as deputy chairman. The other members were Sir Miles Thomas, Sir Patrick Hennessy and C. B. Nixon of Leyland. Their task was to visit Germany to review the industrial situation there, particularly as it affected the motor industry. At the instigation of the Ministry of Supply they spent nearly a month in Germany, visiting factories before reporting their findings back to the Government. The SMMT panel had also been asked to investigate the commercial methods the Germans had used both before and during the war and advise on means of controlling the German industry's future trade, both at home and overseas. The Government wanted advice on what steps it should take to prevent Germany from transferring her physical assets or technical experience to other countries, such as India or Spain, in an attempt to break away from Allied control and re-establish the German automobile industry elsewhere. It was during this visit that Billy Rootes made such scathing references to the Volkswagen 'Beetle' and its potential in export markets. As I have already said, he lived to regret his remarks later when the car made such large inroads into both British and overseas markets, including America, and more than 20 million of them were sold before the design was finally scrapped.

The Society of Motor Manufacturers and Traders also set up another committee in December 1945 which was of particular importance to

Britain's motor manufacturers. With Reggie Rootes as chairman, its brief was to look into reparation claims against Germany and to ensure that the claims made by individual companies received the industry's full support.

Although Billy Rootes was no longer officially involved with the Air Ministry, the Ministry of Supply, or the Board of Trade, there was one additional task he undertook for the Government when war ended. He was asked by the Treasury for his views on the changes he felt should be made to the Civil Service to improve its business efficiency.

Despite the regard he had in general for the Civil Service, based on more than 20 years' experience serving on various committees and over-seas missions, he was shocked at the amount of inefficiency he found there. There was 'a lack of spit and polish', and a generally unkempt atmosphere in public offices. Reception arrangements were very bad and the reception staff badly dressed and inattentive. He felt that the impression they created was bound to be unfavourable, which was par-ticularly unfortunate in the case of overseas customers. He pointed out that slovenly offices affected the outlook of the staff and emphasized the attention paid to these matters in his own organization, where the dif-ference in the attitude of the staff was obvious. He felt that good work-ing conditions created a sense of pride of achievement, kept staff brighter and more enthusiastic, and were important factors in attracting recruits.

He was also critical of the Civil Service tea breaks: 'In my company, office staff are either allowed a definite tea break so that they can visit the canteen, or tea is brought round by a waitress dressed in a neat uni-form, but cups and saucers are not left lying about offices after the tea breaks are over'.

There was also criticism of the 'excessive caution' which he felt could be traced to Parliamentary control and ministerial responsibility. The Civil Service would eventually be forced to react to public pressure and demands from business organizations for quicker action in solving prob-lems. The slow tempo of work, due in part to a reluctance to take risks, was reflected in the large number of staff employed at the lower levels, compared with the small number at the top. Too many people were serving on committees who were not in a position to make decisions and senior officers spent too much time reading documents and not enough time on constructive thinking and the management of their branches.

The lack of good shorthand typists and the tendency to look down on shorthand typing work was also counter-productive. Billy revealed that his own secretary was paid £800 a year, a considerable salary in 1946, making her one of the highest-paid secretaries in London. Little wonder that she never left and was able to buy shares in the company when it went public! Billy Rootes was also critical of the Civil Service tele-phone service and its standards of speed, efficiency and courtesy compared with the standards set by business organizations, even though the equipment provided was usually as good as any to be found in commercial concerns.

The slow rate of promotion was, he felt, killing the important qualities of energy, initiative and enthusiasm among the younger members of the staff, and he suggested that unsuitable staff should be retired early to make way for more able men. Senior officers who carried real responsibility and worked efficiently could then be better paid and given more free time, so that they could develop their contacts with the commercial and industrial world, which was necessary if the present sense of isolation in the Civil Service was to be broken down. The practice of taking papers home in the evening was, he said, 'deplorable'.

Lunch breaks were too long and he suggested that small luncheon rooms where visitors could be entertained would save executives a great deal of time, because they wouldn't have to go out in the middle of the day. There was a need to increase output, but not necessarily to increase working hours, which in many instances were already too long. What was required was better leadership from the supervisory staff, who should be setting higher standards.

The report was bound to annoy many of the die-hards in the Civil Service, but having been asked for his recommendations Billy was not prepared to waste time on delivering a series of platitudes in order to please senior officials. He was also keen that the country's Civil Service should be in a better position to serve industry during the difficult times ahead, and this was particularly necessary in overseas markets.

As soon as the war ended, Rootes had begun planning a fresh attack on overseas markets, and the process of stripping their Coventry factories of all their wartime paraphernalia so that they could be retooled and got ready for peacetime production. Skilled workers returning from the forces had to be absorbed back into the workforce and given the training necessary to bring them up to date with the latest production methods. The war had brought many advances in techniques and the development of new equipment.

The Rootes brothers were also quick to appreciate that there were a number of very capable regular army officers whose organizing experience and large number of important contacts would be of value to the group. One of those was Major-General Sir Leslie Williams, one of Britain's key men responsible for the supply of materials and equipment for D-Day. He joined the board of Rootes Limited and was given the task of centralizing the company's London sales and service organization, and making their Barlby Road depot at North Kensington, where Sunbeam Talbot cars had previously been produced, the largest motor trading and servicing establishment in London, offering a 24-hour service to all Rootes customers. The value of Sir Leslie's rank and extensive army contacts was also not lost on Billy and Reggie, who wanted to ensure that Rootes continued to get a large share of the cars and trucks still being bought by the army. For the past 30 years Major-General Sir Leslie Williams had been involved with the purchase of vehicles and all types of ordnance equipment for Britain's armies in every part of the world.

Two of those returning from the war were Billy's sons Geoffrey and Brian, who were now ready to play their part in the development of the group of companies their father and uncle had built into a remarkable motoring empire during the 1920s and '30s. Reggie Rootes' son Timothy, who had been apprenticed with Humber Limited at Coventry for two years from 1942 to 1944 after leaving Harrow, was also due to return to the Group as soon as he was demobilized. He had been to Sandhurst and seen military service with the army in the Middle East between 1944 and 1947.

Brian Rootes, who was demobilized from the Twelfth Royal Lancers with the rank of Major, had married Elizabeth Margaret Philips in February 1944. Bet Philips was a widow whose husband had been killed very early in the war. She was the attractive daughter of Humphrey Barclay, the domestic chaplain to King George VI, and already had one son, Simon. Bet and Brian later had another son, Bill. Geoffrey also married a widow, Marian Slater, whose first husband, Wing Commander Garth Slater, had been killed towards the end of the war. Marian had two children by her first marriage, Christa and Colin, who were six and four respectively at the time she married Geoffrey at St George's Church, Hanover Square, on 15 August 1946.

Billy Rootes had been the matchmaker here. He had met Marian at a VE Day party given by Sir Peter and Lady Farquhar and had invited her to a welcome home party for Geoffrey which he and his wife were planning at Stype. A number of Geoffrey's old friends had been invited, including Vernon and Nicky Coats. After being at Oxford with Geoffrey, Vernon Coats had joined the Oxon and Bucks Light Infantry, winning a Military Cross at Anzio but also being severely wounded. His wife Nicky had been injured when a German bomb hit the famous Café de Paris in London, killing Snake Hips Johnson, the West Indian band leader, and all but six members of his band. One of the survivors was the pianist Yorke de Souza, who later played at the 500 Club in Albermarle Street when it was owned by the actors John Mills and Dickie Attenborough. It became a favourite haunt of many Rootes executives, including Brian and Geoffrey, during the 1950s and '60s.

When Geoffrey met Marian Slater that weekend at Stype, he fell deeply in love with the vivacious young war widow and proposed to her soon afterwards. Their marriage lasted for 44 years until his death in 1992. Colin Slater and Brian's step-son Simon Philips became close friends and shared a flat together when they were living in London.

Marion and Geoffrey spent their honeymoon in Denmark, touring in his old pre-war Talbot 10. The conditions there were a welcome change from the austerity which still existed in England and they stayed for a while with Axel de Kaufmann, the head of British Motors, the Rootes distributors in Copenhagen. He had a very pretty wife called Inge and one of their three attractive daughters married John Chaldecott, Geoffrey's second cousin, who also worked for Rootes.

When Geoffrey and Marian returned from honeymoon they rented a cottage at North End, near Newbury, which was conveniently close to Stype and not far from London for when Geoffrey started working at Devonshire House. Later that year there was quite an upheaval at Rootes when Harold Heath, an old friend of the family who was managing director of Humber Limited and responsible for running the Coventry factories, decided to leave, taking with him another senior executive, Alan Botwood. As a result, Reggie Rootes moved to Coventry and Geoffrey went with him, moving with Marian and the children into the company house at 54 Kenilworth Road, Coventry. Geoffrey spent much of his career with Rootes at Coventry, eventually running the Manufacturing Division after his uncle returned to London. The works director there at the time was Bill Hancock and Bernard Winter was the director of engineering. He was a brilliant engineer and designer who had served in the First World War as a dispatch rider and had taken part in the retreat from Mons.

Although the end of the war provided Rootes and other companies in the motor industry with the opportunity to reorganize, this was made more difficult by a serious shortage of supplies of almost every description. The Government was being placed under considerable pressure from other industries and the motor industry had to take its turn in the priority queue for raw materials. The only way in which motor companies could qualify for sufficient allocations of steel was to hit their export targets. It was hard going and those companies who were not allocated enough steel to enable them to continue building cars and trucks, among them Singer Motors, had to turn to making other products. To make matters worse, motor manufacturers were having to rely on the models which would have been launched in 1940 had the war not intervened. It was at least two years before new designs were ready and in the meanwhile the pre-war models had a series of 'face-lifts' to try and give them some sort of fresh appeal, particularly overseas.

Rootes was no exception but, despite the lack of new models, they still managed to export up to 80 per cent of their car and truck production, a figure well in excess of the 50 per cent target set by the Government. Billy Rootes's enthusiasm for selling into overseas markets during the 1920s and 1930s instead of relying on the more lucrative home market certainly paid dividends during those difficult years immediately after the war. Most of the network of overseas companies and other sales outlets which he had built up before 1940 had survived in some form or other. Their task now was to get their export division fully operational as quickly as possible.

Chapter 19

The North American challenge

WITHIN A FEW weeks of the end of the war, Billy Rootes had set off on what was to be an extensive tour of America, to investigate the market potential there and take a closer look at the way in which American companies were tackling their post-war problems. It was a vitalizing experience and on his return he urged others in industry to do the same, particularly those who he suggested 'were feeling complacent and satisfied that now the hostilities had ended everything in Britain's industrial garden would be lovely'.

The report he prepared for his brother Reggie, who had been elected the first post-war president of the Society of Motor Manufacturers and Traders, contained a timely warning of the problems Britain's car and truck makers had to solve and the need for an urgent change of outlook. It was a far-sighted look into the future and gave a clear picture of the situation facing British motor manufacturers. He told Reggie he was convinced that Britain was already falling well behind America and didn't appear to have that country's energy or vision to appreciate how fast the world was moving. Britain also lacked the bold leadership necessary for what he referred to as 'these adventurous times'. He emphasized:

> 'America today is alive to the surge of its tremendous economic power. I have a feeling that they will leave nothing undone to become the most efficient instrument in world trade. We must now, without delay, realize the implications of this new attitude. Before 1939, American industrial plans centred around their internal markets, but war demands completely re-energized American industry and their potential is now at least 50 per cent greater than in 1939. They will have to find a vent for that increased productive output and can only do it by planning to export as they have never done before. I am convinced that, unless there is an industrial renaissance in this country, our economic future will be in jeopardy. Equally grave is the fact that any sag in our economy, and particularly in the export

field, will have a disastrous effect on the countries of the British Commonwealth. Further, America, sooner or later, will become rather tired of helping us over stiles we no longer have the spirit or zest to climb.

It is no good our indulging in an orgy of self-pity. It is true that we have been completely submerged in warfare, while America has never been 100 per cent at war, and that we have been bogged for years in a slough of control and governmental direction. We have lost many lives and among them the men who could have reinforced our leadership today. But we cannot build on regrets or reshape our future by day-dreaming of what might have been. The blunt fact is that in industry we need production and yet more production. We appreciated that this was necessary in the war years but many people now seem to imagine that production no longer matters! Yet this is vital if we are to reduce costs and be an effective competitor in world markets.

The cost of any volume product in Britain today is so ridiculously high that we cannot hope to compete with America and it is only in specialized products that we are on an equal footing.

The war has now been over for more than six months, yet we still have nearly all the controls which were enforced on us during the war years. What a contrast to the States! It is time that many of our politicians realized that a business cannot be built on red tape. It demands leadership and inspiration and it would be far more apposite if some of our political mentors could show a little of this refreshing spirit, instead of merely wailing of austerity, or worrying whether we are firmly clamped in our industrial or social yoke.

Iron and steel costs are perilously high. Coal, iron and steel are the very sinews of our economic existence and the price level must be such that we can start producing at competitive prices. In America during the past 20 years iron and steel prices have only increased by £1 a ton, apart from the 5 per cent rise recently granted by the American Government. Yet in Britain iron and steel prices have gone up approximately 50 per cent since 1939.

The motor industry is a good example of the resulting difficulties. From information I gathered in America the increase in the cost of building a car there is only 10 to 20 per cent more than in 1939. Our increase in costs are out of all proportion and the cost of making a car in Britain now is not 10 per cent or even 20 per cent more than in 1939, but 60 to 80 per cent higher. The rise in costs of materials is mainly responsible for the uncompetitiveness of our products and amounts to approximately 70 per cent of our costs.

When the initial world shortage of motor products has been appeased, it is difficult to see how Britain will be able to compete, because even before the war we were not competitive in the world markets so far as prices were concerned. There is an idea here that if iron and steel costs have increased by only 50 per cent, people should not necessarily have to pay more for their cars. The truth is, of course, that manufacturers are being forced to pass on the increase in cost. Any who did not would inevitably end in the bankruptcy court!

There is all the difference in the world between the present outlook of the average American and that of the average Briton. The whole of America, from the worker at the bench to the top executives, think progressively and have the ambition to do things quickly. All American producers are contemplating increased production and working towards that target. They are all planning enormous capital expenditures with a view to better mechanization and a radical improvement in the quality and quantity of their products.

The American worker appreciates that his personal prosperity is bound up with that of the organization for which he works. He is eager to accept more modern methods and modern machinery which he knows will create more effective production and marketing which, in turn, will bring him a greater reward.

The British worker, on the other hand, is still suspicious of change and in the main has failed to realize the simple economics that if the price of goods can be lowered by more effective production methods, more can be sold and there will be a greater share of the profits available for him. I know that responsible labour leaders are fully aware of this fact, and I rejoiced the other day to see that one said quite bluntly that if the workers were to have a bigger share of the cake, the cake must be made bigger.

It is true that this unfortunate outlook on the part of many of Britain's workers is due to the unhappy industrial policy of the past, but this is 1946 and they must realize that their country's welfare is, in the end, their welfare, and in this hour of need it is part of the nation's welfare too. They must appreciate that this betterment in the long run will turn, not on 'going slow' but on 'going fast'.

One advantage we do have in Britain is the excellent machinery so painstakingly built for negotiation between worker and employer. To an Englishman, some of the incidents which occur during strikes on the other side of the Atlantic are fantastic. At one of the Ford plants I saw an instance where 250 police were called in to quell a strike disturbance. When they arrived they found the workers in such an aggressive mood that, to save further trouble, the police permitted themselves to be put under lock and key in the local barracks! To our orderly minds, such a situation is all but unbelievable, but I cannot help wondering why, having such an excellent negotiation machine, we do not use it to the full!

Unofficial action outside that splendid machine in the long run will only lead to chaos in negotiation and a complete breakdown in our established methods of settling disputes. We have still a long way to go before we reach that degree of enduring understanding between America and ourselves which alone can guarantee world peace and prosperity. I took in a typical cross-section of the American people during my visit. There is definitely a lack of understanding as to either the reason for or the gravity of our economic plight.

Prejudice against us has been hardened in many quarters by the belief that our present form of government is of an extremist character and will work against all those principles the average American holds dear. We must be clear on one unalterable fact. It is useless our bleating that Britain has to export in order to live. The American standpoint is that commerce goes to the successful and, if we wish to command their attention, it will have to be on the basis of our achievements rather than on a recital of our woes.

After years of our cramped, confined, fettered and overtaxed motor industry, a glimpse of the American automobile industry is a revelation. I am quite certain that our industry could achieve comparatively just as much if our government had the right outlook. It is a fact that no British Government yet has realized the value of our industry. The British motorist is looked upon as little more than an easy source of government revenue. Yet I found that, in America, following agitation there, even the nominal five dollars a year war tax on automobiles has been abolished.

The American outlook is that the automobile industry is not only the creator of employment but also a constant asset in improving living conditions by providing adequate transport for its people. A car for every worker is already an American reality. With us it is merely a pious hope and will remain so until a government comes along which, by reducing taxation and the cost of raw materials, will enable British manufacturers to turn out cars at prices within the reach of the average working man's pocket. Sooner or later, if we are to truly raise our standard of living, this ambition must be realized. Why not sooner?

It is, however, useless to talk about cars for workers until we have sufficient roads to carry those cars. America's conception of road building is an eye-opener. The Triborough Bridge development in New York, for instance, has resulted in a bridge with four vehicle tracks in each direction, with enormous viaducts and flyovers so that traffic is not impeded. It virtually lifts transport into the air above the many obstacles below. Yet we have been content for years to leave our traffic jammed and bogged in road strips we have the temerity to term arterial highways.'

It was the first of many visits which Billy Rootes paid to America after the war, and he was able to draw on his experiences during those visits to develop his own business philosophy and ensure that the changeover of the Rootes factories from wartime to peacetime production took place with the minimum of fuss and made use of all the latest production methods. The factory at Speke, which had broken production records for the output of bombers during the war, was taken over by the Dunlop Rubber Company and Rootes concentrated on turning the Ryton-on-Dunsmore factory into one of the most modern car production plants in Europe.

In 1947 they decided to enter the North American market and appoint distributors in America, Canada and the Caribbean. With typical thoroughness, Billy spent some months there, researching the requirements of the market and setting up the distribution network he felt would create the best impact in such a large and demanding area. His was a different approach to the attitude shown by some of the other British manufacturers and on 7 December he wrote to his brother from New York: 'I don't endorse the Austin policy of blowing a great blast, and inviting somewhat critical comment, but there is sound business to be created in the United States, Canada and the Caribbean.'

He realized that keeping even a limited number of distributors supplied with enough cars and spare parts would place a big strain on the factory until the development work there had been completed. As a result, he decided that their first entry into the market would be restricted to setting up distribution in Chicago, Kansas City, Los Angeles and San Diego, San Francisco, Philadelphia, Washington, Dallas, St Louis, Portland and Seattle. When business in those areas became established on a sound basis, additional distribution areas would be sought.

New York was included in his plans, but finding the right distributor there was proving difficult. He looked at Messrs Fergusons but didn't feel that their organization was up to Rootes's standard, and decided to concentrate on Messrs Inskip. They were the Rolls-Royce and Bentley distributors for the whole of America and had been selling British cars for some years. His problem was that they sold MGs in the eastern counties and Billy didn't like Rootes being involved with MG. This was probably due to his unfortunate relationship with Lord Nuffield. In the end it was agreed that Inskip would sell Rootes cars in the territory represented by Manhattan, Long Island and the section north of the city up through Westchester County, but not the west side of the Hudson River, namely New Jersey.

Rootes's plan was to sell 2,000 cars during their first year in the North American market, by starting off in a more modest way than Austin, and then to build on their success. It was a policy which proved to be correct and reflected the wealth of experience and knowledge of the American automotive market which Billy had built up during his many visits there. It was what many other British manufacturers lacked and they paid the price.

He used his friendship with 'Boy' and 'Buzzy' Scheftel, and their considerable influence, to obtain office space in New York at a time when it was almost unobtainable. With the Scheftels' invaluable help he rented 2,000 sq. ft of offices overlooking the square in front of the Plaza, towards Central Park. The all-in cost was $6 per sq ft, well within his budget, and that figure included air-conditioning and all the services to the building, with the exception of office cleaning, electric light and telephones. He even persuaded the landlord to pay half the cost of erecting the partitions! Billy Rootes planned to use the offices in New York for the sales and service representatives covering Canada and the Caribbean as well, until the time was right to open up additional offices in Toronto or Montreal. He gave instructions to Price Waterhouse to start an Incorporated Company for Rootes in America and appointed legal advisors and a tax expert. While he was in Washington he also set in motion an investigation into the patent situation for the word 'synchromatic', which he wanted to use.

He considered the possibility of Tim Bailey, who had accompanied him to America, staying on to run the American company. He was a very capable young executive who went on to play an important role in the company's export organization, but Billy felt that it would be unfair to put him in charge of such an important new venture when he lacked sufficient business experience. He valued Tim Bailey's potential as a future senior executive, however, and suggested that when he returned to England in April for his wedding he should remain there and be given an opportunity to gain more management experience. He could then be used to advantage in other overseas appointments, which at the same time would also open up new opportunities for him. It was another example of Billy's willingness to recognize ability in young executives and enable them to gain the necessary experience to succeed.

The man he chose to be the company's manager in New York was Norman Garrad, who had plenty of sales experience, having joined Clement Talbot in 1931. He was with that company when it was bought by Rootes in 1935. He was an ideal choice not only because he had sufficient business experience, but also because he was a Sunbeam Talbot enthusiast and the company's early sales successes would rest mainly on that marque. Billy planned to let Norman Garrad stay in America for nine months until his younger son Brian had gained enough experience to take over.

Billy had a high regard for the outspoken young Scot which stemmed from their first meeting in London some 20 years previously and the time they had subsequently spent together in Scotland. Norman Garrad was one of several Talbot executives whom Billy had sent for in 1935, soon after buying the Talbot company. He wanted to find out which of them had the necessary aptitude for promotion, and saw each one privately at the Talbot plant in Barlby Road, taking a careful note of how they behaved during the interview.

When it was Norman Garrad's turn, he walked into the large boardroom to find Billy Rootes seated at the end of a long table. There was no handshake, just a welcoming smile and 'Please be seated', and 25 years later Norman Garrad told me that he still remembered their conversation at that first meeting as though it had only just happened.

Having motioned him to a seat, Billy Rootes said, 'So you are Garrad. You've been with the company for four years and are earning £550 a year.' Then, looking straight at him very hard, he added, 'Well now, I have something to say to you. If I don't like the way you work and the business you create in the next three months you will not be here after that time—is that clear?'

The remark infuriated the young Scot, who was brimful of confidence and objected to being told that he was now being put on trial. 'Quite clear, Mr Rootes,' he replied. 'I know you now own this company, but I have some news for you. If I don't like the way you run it I most certainly will not be here in three months!' Billy Rootes looked at him for what seemed a very long time, then suddenly said, 'That's all, Garrad, close the door as you go out.'

Norman Garrad didn't like the sound of the word 'out' and told Jack Scot, who was waiting outside for his turn to be interviewed, that he thought he had just talked himself into a quick dismissal by his rather hasty and pugnacious response. The drive back to Scotland provided him with little comfort and for the next few weeks everything seemed very quiet. There was no response to his interview, but six weeks later he was instructed to return to London to attend a sales conference where Billy was to talk about the company's future prospects.

Some 300 tense and rather nervous members of staff assembled at London's Mayfair Hotel. When Billy arrived with his brother they made their entrance down the long flight of stairs to the ballroom where the meeting was to be held. As they approached the stage, he suddenly saw Garrad and made a bee-line for him. 'Hello, Garrad,' he said, shaking hands. 'How am I doing? Are you satisfied?'

'Oh yes, sir!' Garrad replied, completely taken aback. Billy Rootes patted him on the shoulder and said, 'That's good, and by the way, you are not doing too badly either,' then walked away smiling. Describing the incident again some years later, Norman Garrad said, 'What a man. From that moment on I was his slave for life—and have lived to prove it!'

It was in the mid-1940s that Norman Garrad saw so much of Billy Rootes during his frequent visits to Scotland, and gained such an interesting insight into his character. During those visits Billy usually stayed at the Royal George Hotel in Perth, which was owned by Norman's friend Willie Steele, so he was able to make sure that his chairman was well looked after despite the rationing. The visits inevitably meant working long hours because they started early and worked late and Norman was living about 22 miles from Perth at the time.

Arriving home in time for dinner one evening after a tiring day visiting dealers, he found a message asking him to return to Perth as quickly as possible. When he got to the Royal George Hotel he was instructed to go straight up to the bedroom. As he entered the room, Billy disappeared into the bathroom, clad only in his underpants, and appeared soon afterwards carrying two glasses and a very large hip flask, one side of which contained whisky and the other side brandy.

'Sit down on the bed and let's have a drink, Garrad.' It was more an instruction than an invitation. Billy poured out two large drinks, sat down on the bed and said, 'I'm glad you answered my call so quickly without moaning about having to drive back to Perth again this evening, but I want you to be the new sales manager of Sunbeam Talbot Limited and move to Coventry. Will you accept the job!'

Norman Garrad accepted without hesitation and the two of them had dinner together but, as Garrad was leaving to drive home at about midnight, Billy said, 'Good, I'm glad that's settled. See you here for breakfast at 8.15 am'. During breakfast the next morning Billy suddenly put down his paper and asked, 'Do you know anybody who deals in antiques?' He was told that there was a Miss Maime McLeish who only lived about half a mile away, and insisted that they set off straight away to pay her a visit, even though he was warned that Miss McLeish didn't like being disturbed until 10 am and was very strict about opening hours.

Instead of the usual antique shop, she kept all the fine antiques displayed at her large house, and visitors were able to walk round at their leisure and see each item in its true setting. Vallet brought the car round and followed Norman's directions until they arrived at the house just before nine o'clock. The car had hardly stopped before Billy jumped out and rang the bell. The big oak-panelled front door was opened by an old-fashioned Scottish housemaid, who told him, 'I'm sorry, sir, but Miss McLeish doesn't see anyone before ten in the morning.'

'But I'm a prospective customer,' Billy replied. 'Aye sir, I ken fine, just come back at ten,' and with that she closed the door.

When he rang the bell next time it was dead on ten o'clock and the same old housemaid answered. 'Good day, sir, do you want to see the pieces?' she enquired, letting them into the hall. 'You can go from room to room and when you want to see Miss McLeish just pull that bell cord and she will join you.'

They spent the next hour looking at antiques, noting down the various items which Billy wanted to buy. When Miss McLeish arrived, Billy gave her the list and said, 'Miss McLeish, I am a businessman and will give you a cheque now for £800 for a quick deal.' Without batting an eyelid Miss McLeish replied, 'Sir William, all my pieces are clearly marked and if you had decided to spend £9,000 there would still be no reduction. Good morning, Sir William. Please close the door as you leave. Goodbye, Mr Garrad. I look forward to seeing you again some time.'

Billy Rootes stood his ground and, using all his undoubted charm, replied, 'But of course I was only joking, Miss McLeish. Here is my cheque for £980. It is a pleasure doing business with you.' As they got back into the car he turned to Norman Garrad and said, 'Smart woman,

that. Knows her business and people!' He later became a very good customer of hers after buying Glenalmond House, his estate in Scotland.

Billy Rootes paid another visit to America in 1947, but on that occasion he was accompanied by his younger son Brian, who was being
groomed to become head of sales and marketing for the group while
Geoffrey concentrated on the manufacturing side of the business.

The first 500 cars to arrive in America in 1948 were all Sunbeam
Talbots, specially produced for the North American market with all the
necessary modifications to lights, indicators, bumpers and overriders,
heaters and trim. The majority of them were convertibles, but plans
were well advanced for what Billy referred to as 'a really snappy sports
tourer', which he hoped would give Rootes an additional 3,000 or so
sales, particularly on the west coast. But in a press interview on arrival
at Southampton on 22 June 1948, after another visit to America and
Canada to see how sales were progressing, Billy Rootes complained bit-
terly about the lack of Government support.

'The thing that disturbs me most overseas is the utterances of
Government officials. Every time a man like Hugh Dalton is put back
into the Cabinet and says we are going to seek ways and means of
nationalizing industry, we are antagonizing the very people we are
relying on. Through the European Recovery Plan every American
taxpayer has a stake in the United Kingdom, but the reason why this
recovery plan is now being questioned there is partially due to statements made by members of the British Government. Unless Britain,
by greater production, can start to pay her way, this country is in for
the most terrific disturbance it has ever had.

Of paramount importance is Britain's dollar deficit and it is vital
that we increase our exports to dollar countries. High on the list of
goods that Americans and Canadians are prepared to buy from us is
automobiles, but the cars we export from Britain must cost less than
those built in the States. Americans expect to buy a full-sized motor
car equipped with radio, heater and a new range of accessories for not
more than $1,500 [£375 at the 1948 rate of exchange]. Britain has,
consequently, got to lower production costs by between 22 and 25 per
cent.

To do this, British factories will have to produce to the maximum
and a greater supply of materials must be made available, steel in
particular. I suggest that the method of the allocation of steel should
be overhauled, so that those industries which can bring in dollars can
be given definite priority in steel supplies. If we could increase production and lower costs then America could become a permanent
market'.

Chapter 20

New models and the aircraft influence

THE RACE BETWEEN British car manufacturers to launch their new model range had become more apparent towards the end of 1947, when there was a real urgency to replace the face-lifted, pre-war designs with sleeker and more exciting cars, which they hoped would see them into the 1950s. It had been a desperate two years for the design teams, not only because so much depended on the success of those first post-war models in re-establishing reputations and increasing market shares, but also because they were being asked to achieve in two years what would normally take three or four.

There was also no real logical progression for them to work on, because there had been a gap of nearly six years when motor manufacturers had had to concentrate all their efforts on producing aircraft or war vehicles, and designers had had their minds set on more urgent targets. Billy Rootes felt, however, that this wartime experience could still be put to good use and instructed his designers to consider what aerodynamic benefits might be gained by using the shapes of modern aircraft fuselages.

Ted White, who had been responsible for the styling of pre-war Sunbeam Talbot models, was one of those given the task of carrying out Billy's instructions. Having been concerned with aircraft forms during the war, and realizing that the motoring public had also been influenced by aircraft designs for the past five years, he also felt that a car incorporating similar shapes should quickly achieve public acceptance. Along with Ted Green, who had been a colleague of his at Talbot for more than 20 years, he set about styling a Sunbeam Talbot with sufficient aircraft influence to give it maximum sales appeal, particularly in America, and succeeded beyond his wildest dreams.

They decided to retain the characteristic Sunbeam Talbot radiator grille, which had been very popular before the war, but in a softer and more rakish style, and this time the bonnet forms were curved down to meet it. The new car was also notable in that for the first time all the lamps would be mounted flush into the metalwork. The wings, or fend-ers, would also no longer be separate components, but would be merged into the body form and the body would be full width, without the usual running boards. For Sunbeam Talbot this was a radical departure from all previous customs and practices, but Ted White admitted later that he was influenced to some extent by a Packard model which had been pro-duced just before America's entry into the war.

Having styled the radiator and frontal appearance to their satisfac-tion, they concentrated on the front wings and came to the conclusion that an aircraft-type 'drop tank' form might merge in well with the nose housing the headlamps. The idea worked successfully and when they came to tackle the side treatment they decided that a flowing reveal, or roll, should be taken from the bonnet for the full length of the car. This was then carried round the back, where it appeared on the break between the boot lid and the spare wheel access door—a very practical location. The rear wheel opening seemed to disrupt the fuselage lower form, so detachable covers were styled to continue the line of the sill through to the rear.

It was becoming obvious to Ted White and Ted Green that, apart from the radiator grille, the car bore no family likeness to previous Sunbeam Talbots on its lower half so, in order to preserve some 'house style' and continuity, they decided that the top of the car should inherit some of the flavour of the previous model. As a result, the roof and win-dow area, with the reverse slope on the quarter-light, appeared as a very much more flowing form of the previous model, sitting on top of the 'fuselage'. Inside, the instrument panel was also novel and showed air-craft influence, along with good ergonomics.

Although the final exterior style was a mixture of rather odd ingredi-ents, it was very well received by the media and the public when it was launched in 1948, and has since been accepted as being rather a classic. Soon after the design of the Sunbeam Talbot 80 and 90 had been com-pleted, the styling of all Rootes cars was transferred to the Group's head-quarters at Coventry. The name of the Acton activity was changed to British Light Steel Pressings, who then became suppliers of body shells and components to the assembly plants at Coventry.

The new Hillman Minx Magnificent was introduced in September 1948 and was designed to strike a logical balance between the require-ments of the home and export markets. It was easily exported in CKD form, which meant that it could be 'completely knocked down' and transported in pieces for assembly at Rootes plants overseas.

Although the full-width body was of the unitary construction well known on the Minx and first introduced in 1936, the designers had gone much further than before. The inside valances of the front wings, the facia board and other features were all welded together in one piece with the body and the chassis frame, giving greater strength but also making the car lighter, despite its additional width. A lighter body also gave the new Minx considerably increased performance and roadability. Billy Rootes claimed it was 'the first medium-sized car that I have ever driven and been satisfied with. That doesn't mean that I can't find any faults because we are always striving for perfection, but it is a really fine motor car'. He emphasized that the Minx was not intended as a cheap car, but a quality model offering the best value for money in the medium-car range.

The styling of the new car was partly the work of Raymond Loewy, a distinguished American industrial designer whom Billy Rootes had met before the war and had employed in 1939 to develop new shapes for Rootes models. Loewy had signed an agreement with Studebaker in 1937 and although there was not time during 1939 for him to produce anything new for Rootes, there is no doubt that the first post-war Hillmans were influenced by the Studebaker models which he was working on at the time. Many people in the motor industry gained the impression that Loewy, who had opened an office in London, influenced the design of all the post-war Rootes cars, but this was not so, although the marked similarity to Studebakers shown by a number of Hillman based models, particularly in the 1950s, was certainly due to Raymond Loewy Associates.

The Minx Magnificent, known also as the Phase III Minx, was economical to run and had a good top gear performance. It had independent front suspension for the first time, but still used the well-tried, 1,185 cc side-valve engine which had been designed in 1930 for the first Hillman Minx. Although this engine remained in production until the mid-50s, the Minx Phase IV, which went into production in the autumn of 1949, had an enlarged, more powerful unit of 1,265 cc. A Phase V version of the car was launched in October 1951, but little more was changed until 1953. The saloon and drop-head coupé models both proved very popular and although they were not particularly exciting mechanically, they achieved considerable success in a number of export markets.

In 1947 production of all the Humber models had been transferred from the old Humber Road factory at Stoke to the far more modern Ryton-on-Dunsmore plant a few miles away. Until then, the Humber Hawk and Humber Snipe models, although they had been announced as new in 1945, were really the 1939 and 1940 models and were rather similar to the large Hillmans of the pre-war period. The Hawk had Evenkeel independent front suspension and was powered by the side-valve, 1.944 cc four-cylinder unit fitted with an aluminium cylinder head and using the same gearbox as the Hillman Minx. The 1945 Snipe had the 2,731 cc, six-cylinder engine previously used for the Humber 18 hp produced between 1935 and 1937. It was not particularly successful, probably because it came between the Hawk and the Super Snipe models which were more popular and had a much better performance, being powered by the larger, six-cylinder, 4,086 cc engine rated at 100 bhp.

The other outstanding model in the Humber range was the Pullman, which had been built for military purposes during the war. After being given a face-lift in 1945, it was launched as the new Humber Pullman. It had considerable appeal as a large, luxury saloon, particularly with company chairmen and civic dignitaries. It was also popular with wedding companies and undertakers and sold well until 1948, when it was replaced by a longer wheelbase version with a semi-razor edge, seven-seater body. This version, however, was quickly replaced by an entirely new and more rounded Thrupp & Maberly limousine body which was both large and impressive. It was a favourite model for use by embassies and government departments and the Humber Pullman Mark II and III remained in production until 1953.

There was also a Humber Imperial version, which was mechanically identical to the Pullman and shared the same Thrupp & Maberly body style but had different seating arrangements. With the row of forward-facing occasional seats folded down, the Imperial had a very spacious rear compartment giving almost 3 ft (0.9 m) of leg room.

When production of the Pullman and Imperial series finished in 1954, because the assembly line at Ryton-on-Dunsmore being used for their production was wanted for another model, there was an uproar from government departments, embassies, hire car people and many large companies, because there was nothing to take their place at anything like the price. It was one of the few marketing mistakes which Billy Rootes made when it came to gauging public demand, and the demise of the Pullman and Imperial models had a much bigger effect on sales than was originally thought possible. Without a large, luxury Rootes car at the top end of the market, many companies changed over to other makes because they wanted to standardize with one make of car throughout the model range.

One of the most outspoken critics of the decision to drop the Humber Pullman was the Prime Minister, Winston Churchill. He and Billy Rootes had a lot in common, as well as a high regard for each other which went back to the war years. Their friendship continued when war ended, and Winston Churchill always bought Humber cars. He was furious when Rootes decided to stop producing the Pullman, which he preferred to any other car because there was plenty of room for him to stretch out in the back. The only option was a new Rolls-Royce, but within a short time he was on the telephone complaining to Billy that not having a Pullman was making his motoring a misery because the new Rolls didn't have enough room. He emphasized that their friendship was being placed under severe strain and he wanted something done quickly to solve the problem.

Billy tried to explain that the Pullman assembly line had been taken up to make room for another model, but Churchill would have none of it. 'Rubbish, Billy,' he roared down the phone. 'I always looked upon you as a man who knew how to solve problems. Don't tell me you're going to let me down in my hour of need! I'm one of your best customers and I want a Pullman.'

With all the jigs and tools destroyed, there was no way of building a new one and the only answer Billy could suggest was for them to find one which had a very low mileage and persuade the owner to sell it back to the company, so that it could be stripped down to the last nut and bolt and rebuilt until it was the equivalent of a new car. The task took several weeks, with almost daily messages of complaint from Churchill, asking what was happening and when was his Pullman going to be delivered. It turned out to be the most expensive Humber ever built, but Churchill was delighted and still had it when he died.

It wasn't the only occasion when Churchill got the better of Billy over cars. They were both keen farmers and Billy wanted some of Churchill's pigs. He planned to test for himself the prototype of the New Humber Super Snipe estate car, which was due to be launched later in the year, and had it delivered to his home at Stype, near Hungerford, on the same weekend that he was due to drive over to Chartwell to see the pigs. The drive from Hungerford to Kent seemed to provide an excellent opportunity for him to try out the new model and when he arrived he parked it out of the way by the side of the house. The door was opened by Randolph, who made the delightful remark that his father was in the study 'writing one of his impromptu speeches'.

Billy was taken to see the pigs, the price was agreed but, to Billy's dismay, after lunch Churchill insisted on seeing him out to his car. 'That's just what I want, Billy,' Churchill exclaimed on seeing the new estate car. 'It's what I need for my painting holiday. Can I have it delivered to me on Monday? I'm leaving for Italy on Tuesday. How lucky you came over when you did!' Despite all his protests, Billy knew there was nothing he could do. He should never have let Churchill see the prototype, but the only response he got from his friend was, 'No car, no pigs, and the deal is off!'

Although the new Humber Super Snipe estate car wasn't due to be announced for some months, the prototype was checked over and delivered to Churchill in time for his painting holiday, but for the next month Billy had to put up with telephone calls from Rootes dealers on the Continent asking for details of the new Humber which the British Prime Minister had been seen driving across Europe. It was not a subject which any of his colleagues felt it wise to mention, particularly when the new Humber was being discussed and the question of new model security was on the agenda.

Despite all the shortages and Government restrictions, work on the Rootes factories had been completed by 1950, and they had a good new model range. The Rootes brothers felt that the time had come for them to show the world that they were really back in the business of making quality cars and trucks, and made plans for the Humber Jubilee Convention. The first Humber bicycles had been made in 1868 and, although between 1895 and 1900 the company made motor cycles, motor tricycles, motor quads and some other types of motor vehicles, it was 50 years since the company had started producing Humber cars in what was then looked upon as volume production and they were seen on the roads of Britain for the first time. Some had even found their way abroad, like the ill-fated model shipped to India in 1900.

The Jubilee took nearly 12 months to plan, but by September everything was ready. Rootes entertained more than 7,500 guests at their Ryton-on-Dunsmore plant in Coventry, as well as 5,000 employees and their families. The Convention Hall had the appearance of a motor show, with every Humber, Hillman and Sunbeam Talbot model on view as well as Commer and Karrier commercial vehicles. Exhibits round the hall illustrated the other activities of the company including public relations, advertising and marketing, design and engineering, with particular emphasis placed on the worldwide activities of the Group.

The guest list was very impressive and included ambassadors and diplomats, representatives of the Dominion and Colonies, Government officials, service chiefs, distinguished industrialists and representatives from the 120 different countries which were importing Rootes cars and trucks. They included importers from the north to the south of the Western Hemisphere; from Northern Europe to the South African Cape; from the Near East to the Far East and from Australia to New Zealand.

Needless to say, all sections of the British and overseas media were well represented, but there were also a number of guests whom Billy Rootes had invited personally, who had been involved with his own business career during the previous 30 years or so. Colonel Cole, who had retired as chairman of Humber in 1943, but had remained on the board, was there and so was Bill Hicks from Truro, who took delivery of one of the first Humber cars to be made in 1900, and Len Davey, who led the sales campaign, and Sam Wright, one of the first testers. Frank Rollason, who was Billy's foreman when he was a Singer apprentice in 1910, was also there and so were Harry Marston and George Tysoe from his early days at Singer. It was George Tysoe who had persuaded him that the new Singer 10 was going to be a world-beater.

On the Saturday, when the Distributors and Dealers Convention took place, there were also 50 people who had been selling Humber cars from the early days and who had helped to build up the business. It was evident that the Rootes brothers had gone to great lengths to make sure that nobody was forgotten who had helped them in the past and whose help they would need in the future.

Special trains from London arrived each day and guests were given an opportunity of seeing the work being done in all three Coventry factories, with conducted tours taking place throughout the day. They also saw, for the first time, the products of Tilling Stevens, the Maidstone company which Rootes had purchased only that month, along with its associate company, Vulcan Motors Limited.

Tilling Stevens were pioneers of the petrol electric motor vehicles and had been since 1897, when Mr W. A. Stevens went into partnership with a Mr Baker. After he retired, a limited liability company was set up in 1906 with the title W. A. Stevens, but in 1912 the company was reformed as Tilling Stevens Limited, as a result of its association with Thomas Tilling Limited, the London bus operators. A public company was registered with the title of Tilling Stevens Motors Limited in 1919, but the title reverted to Tilling Stevens Limited in 1937. It was quite a progressive company, producing a variety of automobile parts and products in an imposing five-storey building with some 227,000 sq ft of floor space. There was even a fully equipped surgery in the charge of a trained nursing sister, with weekly visits from a local doctor and surgeon to look after the health of the workers, who also had the benefit of an excellent sports ground nearby.

In another part of Maidstone the rebuilt Romney Works was ready for the installation of new equipment and plant. It was to be an entirely self-contained offshoot of the main factory, covering some 30,000 sq ft and mainly devoted to experimental and prototype work in connection with the revolutionary new TS3 diesel engine. It was this engine which particularly interested Billy Rootes, because it could be run on almost any type of fuel, quite apart from petrol and diesel, and had obvious potential for use in military vehicles and in countries where regular fuels were in short supply. It later proved to be quite a successful marine engine. The TS3 was fitted to Commer trucks for some years, but being a three-cylinder, two-stroke engine with horizontally opposed pistons, it was inclined to be rather noisy. It could have achieved greater popularity if there had been more people wanting trucks with engines of somewhat unconventional design, capable of running on creosote or paraffin as well as ordinary fuels.

The engine did, however, lend itself to a range of publicity gimmicks, although not all of them successful, as I found out a year or two later during the Scottish Motor Show at Kelvin Hall in Glasgow. Rootes had new trucks on show there which were powered by the TS3 engine and as we were in Scotland I thought it would be a good stunt if we ran the engine on Scotch whisky. The president of the show was a man called Melvin, who was also the head of our main dealership in Glasgow. His son John was a friend of mine and another keen rally driver.

It seemed to me that many of our dealers in Scotland were also involved in the Scotch whisky business and had their own distilleries, so I asked John if he could find one who could supply us with some really high proof spirit, of the type usually only sent for export. A large box containing a dozen or so bottles of the best Scotch whisky was delivered to my hotel the next day and John and I set off for the Melvin Service Station, where I had arranged for one of the new TS3-engined Commer trucks to be available with an empty fuel tank, so that we could carry out our experiment.

I wanted to make sure that the engine really would run on whisky before attempting to demonstrate the fact to the press, particularly as the Tilling Stevens engineers I had spoken to thought that whisky would work, but were none too sure. The main problem, they felt, would be the amount of water still left in the whisky, but they considered it would be worth a try and so, to the amazement and horror of the Scottish mechanics at Melvin's, we poured the contents of half-a-dozen bottles into the truck's fuel tank and pressed the starter. After several attempts, with nothing more than a few coughs and splutters to show for our trouble, we gave up the idea.

By then it was lunch-time, and I put the remainder of the whisky in the boot of John's car before we departed to the Midland Hotel to drown our sorrows and satisfy the inner man in true Scottish fashion. It was mid-afternoon when we returned to the show and made our way to the Melvin stand, but before we reached it John's father, who was well over 6 ft (1.8 m) tall and usually the kindest of men, saw us coming from some way off and made a bee-line for us, waving his arms in the air.

'Where the hell have you been?' he asked his rather surprised son.

'I've been having lunch with John Bullock.'

'And what were you doing before that?'

'We were trying to run the TS3 engine on Scotch whisky at our service station.'

'And what did you do with the whisky?'

A look of understanding suddenly came over John's face. 'Oh, I've got the rest of the bottles in my car. John gave them to me, but you're welcome to have some if you like.'

His father looked even more angry and I thought he was going to break a blood vessel. 'I'm not interested in the whisky in your car. What did you do with the whisky in the fuel tank of the truck?'

'We left it there for the driver to drain out when he came to collect the truck and fill it up with diesel. What did you expect us to do with it?'

'You damn fool! The mechanics drained it themselves after you'd left and they are all as drunk as owls. I've just had to go round and close the place down for the remainder of the afternoon. I hope you two haven't got any more bloody silly ideas!'

John and I thought that discretion was the better part of valour and took refuge back at the hotel. It seemed best to leave his father to cool off without our company until the next morning. We found out later that the mechanics had shared some of the whisky with the petrol pump attendant, who became so full of bonhomie and the joys of the occasion that he started giving away petrol 'with the compliments of Mr Melvin as it's motor show time'! When a regular customer came on the Melvin stand after lunch to thank John's father for such a magnanimous gesture, the response was hardly what he had expected. John Melvin senior left the stand and headed for the exit at considerable speed, ashen-faced and tight-lipped, hoping to get to his service station before the word got round that the Melvins had gone mad and were giving away petrol.

Having borne the brunt of his wrath, John and I decided to at least get some worthwhile publicity for Rootes, Melvin's and the TS3 engine, and gave the story to the morning papers. In the end we got almost as much publicity as we would have had if our experiment had worked, and it paid for the whisky.

Because of its design, which did away with the need for a cylinder head, the TS3's low overall height made it ideally suited to the under-floor method of installation which had become particularly popular in coaches. The engine was also light, economical and very reliable, mak-ing it the obvious choice for the Beadle coaches Rootes produced from 1954 onwards, when the well-known Dartford coachbuilding firm of John C. Beadle Limited also became a member of the Rootes Group.

With so much publicity being given to the cars it was, perhaps, natural that the considerable success of the Rootes Commercial vehicle business was frequently overlooked. Commer trucks became well known through the world for their quality and reliability, and the large assembly plant at Dunstable which went into production in 1954 was one of the most modern in Europe. Commer trucks were first exported to America before the First World War and in 1948, when the new range of 8 cwt to 7 ton vehicles became available, exports to America, Canada and the Pan-American countries started again. There were regular shipments to South Africa, India and Australia, as well as to the Continent of Europe. The Karrier municipal vehicles were the leaders in their field and had the market virtually to themselves in many countries.

Chapter 21

Solving the dollar crisis

THE BRITISH MOTOR industry's serious shortage of sheet steel and other raw materials continued until well into the 1950s, but even more serious was the lack of sufficient electrical power to allow manufacturers to mechanize their factories to the level where they could meet the output performances per man being achieved in America. Because home market sales were also still being restricted, production costs were much higher than they would have been if manufacturers had been able to deal with the home market demand, increase production and spread the overheads more evenly. There were still three and four year waiting lists in Britain for some models.

This had the effect of restricting exports and Billy Rootes was particularly critical of a Government policy which urged motor manufacturers to earn more foreign currency, and dollars in particular, but didn't give them the freedom and materials they needed to do so more effectively. In 1945 he had predicted that Britain would be capable of producing three-quarters of a million vehicles a year before 1950. Few believed him, certainly not the government of the day, but his forecast was correct and by the late 1940s he was predicting that if restrictions were lifted British manufacturers could produce a million cars a year, with a large percentage of them going for export.

His experience of the North American market had an important bearing on Rootes's export policy during the years following the war. He saw the traffic congestion in American cities as a golden opportunity for the smaller European cars to carve a substantial niche for themselves in America and also to make inroads into the Canadian and Latin American markets. The visits he and his brother made to those areas immediately following the war only confirmed this view, and despite all the restrictions and problems being created by the Government, they went ahead with their plans to increase exports and to make the dollar markets their top priority.

It was certainly a bold move, in the light of some of the major setbacks which other manufacturers had experienced in America and Canada, mainly because of insufficient knowledge of the market and a failure to do enough research. Rootes had started selling cars in Canada in 1937 as a result of a close friendship between Billy and Robert Fennell, a leading businessman in Victoria, who had encouraged them to set up an office there with his help. After the war, Robert Fennell visited England to discuss the North American market opportunities with the Rootes brothers and this led to the formation of Rootes Canada, with offices in Montreal and with Robert Fennell as president. In 1951 they opened a new million-dollar plant in Scarborough, a suburb of Toronto, and stocked it with more than a million dollars' worth of service parts. It became the focal point of Rootes's operations in Canada, with further parts depots being set up in Vancouver and Montreal to provide the essential back-up facilities required to service more than 200 Rootes dealers throughout the country.

From quite modest beginnings, by the early 1950s Rootes had a nationwide service organization serving Canadian business and industry. An indication of their success, quite apart from the sale of cars to the public, was the fact that within a short time more than 30 Canadian municipal authorities were also operating Rootes vehicles.

· The American market was also tackled with similar determination, and much of the Rootes post war success there was due to the skill and determination shown by Billy's younger son Brian, who had moved to New York from London in 1948 when it was found that the climate there was better for his asthma. It was soon evident that he had inherited his father's flair for salesmanship. He had been sent to the Argentine, Uruguay and Brazil before the war, to get first-hand knowledge of conditions in some of the overseas markets and to develop his talent for selling.

On arrival in New York with his family in 1948 he took a small apartment, which also served as an office, and began the task of building up a sales and service network that would cover the whole continent. This meant endless visits to dealers and during the next five years he flew more than half a million miles until by 1953 he had created an organization of 800 Rootes dealers, with parts depots throughout the country. The company took elegant new offices in New York and by the early 1950s, 25 per cent of all the Rootes Group's export sales were going to the United States, no mean achievement as the Group was selling 75 per cent of its output abroad and Coventry production records were being broken each year.

Brian had also been closely involved with the organization of the British motor industry's successful automobile exhibition in New York in 1950, which his father had helped to instigate. Billy Rootes was the chairman of the British Motor Manufacturers Association and in less than two months, with Gottfried Neuburger as the show's executive director, he managed to stage a star-spangled event at the Armory, at 25th Street and Lexington Avenue in New York, which lasted from 5 to

10 February. The New Yorkers loved it and the list of specially invited guests read like a *Who's Who?* of American society, from the Charles Amorys to the Randolph Hearsts. There were bankers, lawyers, industrialists, heads of film studios, international publishers, radio, television and film personalities, embassy officials, heads of travel agencies. Every aspect of New York society and business life was represented, even down to the chief receptionist of American Airlines, who was undoubtedly going to be useful to Billy and his business friends during their visits to America. Ed Cueno, the Counsel for the Auto Workers Union, was another of the guests whose presence was a shrewd move, in view of the concern being expressed in some quarters about the effect that imports of foreign cars might have on America's own automobile industry.

In his message of welcome, Billy Rootes emphasized the fact that extended trade between America and Britain was an essential factor towards the recovery of world trade and an assurance of peace. Cars on show included Allard, Austin, Daimler, Bentley, British Ford, HRG, Healey, Lea Francis, MG, Morgan, Riley, Rolls-Royce, Rover, Standard Vanguard, Triumph and Wolseley. Rootes showed their new Hillman Minx Magnificent as well as Sunbeam Talbot and Humber Pullman models and the latest Commer Express delivery vehicles. There were Triumph and Ariel motor cycles and a range of products from Smith Motor Accessories and Lucas Electrical Services also on view. The show was an outstanding success and paved the way for the first International Motor Show with American and foreign cars being displayed together.

The American market, however, was not Brian's only responsibility. He also directed sales in the Central American market from Mexico down to Panama, Venezuela, Cuba, Haiti and Puerto Rica. They were years that provided many opportunities for him to display his ingenuity and enterprise. At one time the Mexican Government placed a complete embargo on imports of British cars. Rootes was anxious to assemble cars there with local labour, but the Government refused to allow even one complete car into the country so that arrangements for assembly could be discussed. Brian left New York in a Hillman Minx and drove the 3,000 miles to Mexico in five days, crossing the border in the car as an ordinary tourist. The authorities were sufficiently impressed and surprised at his arrival to consider his scheme—a move that led to the establishment of the Group's assembly plant in Mexico.

On another occasion, after discovering that a pippin red shade of lipstick was fast becoming all the rage with American women, Brian borrowed a spare lipstick from his secretary and sent it home to his father with the suggestion that the design team and the company's colour consultants should experiment with the same shade for the latest Rootes models. As a result, pippin-red-coloured cars not only became bestsellers in dollar markets, they also topped the list in many other countries.

In 1952, Hillman Minx sales were running at a record level and plane loads of dealers and their wives were flown to Britain to see the country and the Rootes factories. One dealer alone sold more than 1,000 cars and still wanted more.

The post-war successes of the Rootes Group overseas, and in the dollar markets in particular, had not passed unnoticed, and in 1951 the Government invited Billy Rootes to head the country's export drive in the essential dollar markets. It was a challenge which he accepted with enthusiasm. Apart from being demonstrably patriotic, for more than 30 years he had been urging other British companies to follow Rootes's example and sell more goods abroad. The country's urgent need for dollars made this even more crucial and even his sternest critics agreed that there was no better man to be the chairman of Britain's influential new Dollar Exports Council. No-one had more drive or enthusiasm, or a better knowledge of the dollar markets, and his capacity for hard work was beyond question.

His marriage, however, had suffered because of this seemingly insatiable appetite for work. He was frequently away, and when he was at home there were usually business guests to be entertained and more proposals to be discussed. Even holidays abroad were turned into opportunities for meetings with Rootes personnel and business colleagues. He seemed unable to relax away from the office and never missed any opportunity to deal with business matters. Although he thrived on the pressure of work which seemed to come so naturally to him, anyone who didn't share his enthusiasm, or couldn't stand the pace, soon found life very difficult.

His marriage to Nora was dissolved in 1951, after they had been married for 35 years. They remained on good terms and she continued to live at Stype for several years, before moving to a smaller house in London where she died in 1964, two months before Billy's death the same year.

The divorce caused considerable distress to Geoffrey and Brian, who were particularly upset when their father married again a few months later. Lady Ann Peek was attractive and extremely wealthy, but there were some very difficult sides to her character which did not endear her to Billy's sons, or their wives, and they had very little to do with her socially. Ann had been married to Sir Francis Peek and before him to Sir Charles Mappin. She seemed to make Billy happy and was certainly an elegant hostess at his country estates in Hungerford and Scotland and at their London town house in Shepherds Close.

It quickly became obvious that Ann enjoyed leading her own life and had her own wide circle of friends. This did have some advantages, because she didn't complain when Billy's work kept him away from home and his Dollar Exports Council activities meant frequent trips to America and the other dollar areas. She had little to do with any of the social activities of the Rootes Group on the occasions when the wives of other directors were present, and was rarely seen at company or dollar export functions.

Peter Young was a most capable chief executive of the Dollar Exports Council for some years and coped very well with the demands of Billy's heavy workload. He put up with the long hours involved with a remarkable amount of good humour and fortitude. We became good friends as a result of the time we spent together on dollar export matters. This often meant working with Billy late into the night, planning conferences, lunches or dinners, or making arrangements for overseas trade delegations. It was rewarding and interesting work, but called for considerable stamina as well as an ability to think quickly at the end of a long, hard day in order to keep up with Billy's sharp business brain. No matter how late the hour, he never seemed to become tired or miss any important point.

I was saddened when Peter Young finally felt that he had to choose between his marriage and the job. I lost a good friend and Billy lost a very good executive through his refusal to come to terms with the fact that there were occasions when family life must come first, even before earning dollars! The final crunch came one evening when Peter had arranged to take his wife out to dinner and the theatre on their wedding anniversary, but because there was a dollar exports meeting planned for that afternoon, had arranged for her to come to Devonshire House at six. Despite Peter's protests and frequent reminders from me that his wife was waiting for him and that it was their wedding anniversary, Billy insisted on continuing the meeting until after eight o'clock.

It was one occasion when his charm did not work. Naturally enough, Peter's wife was furious about the whole episode and he resigned the next day. I don't think it occurred to Billy that a wedding anniversary demanded any special celebration. He put Britain first and felt that everyone else should do the same—even if it was their wedding anniversary. He was such a brilliant and fascinating man who could show remarkable kindness and generosity, that it was pity he had such a blind spot when it came to the demands of married life. I realized this early on in our association and did all I could to make sure that my marriage didn't suffer. My wife and I agreed that when Billy was in England he would have my undivided attention, but that when he was away we could get back to leading a normal family life. It was a policy which worked very well for more than 20 years, and most of his other close colleagues planned their lives the same way.

Another of Billy's failings caused problems on occasions, and that was his lack of any real sense of humour. Writing speeches for him could be difficult because of this, particularly if they called for some light relief. Jokes had to be explained to him and even then he often got them wrong. I also found out that he seemed to have a poor knowledge of the Bible. Many of the speeches I wrote for him when he was chairman of the Dollar Exports Council were aimed at persuading people running small businesses to tackle the rather daunting American market. On one occasion I suggested that they should remember what happened to David and Goliath. David was successful because he made sure that he had the right ammunition and hit the giant Goliath in the right place at the right time. This was proof that even underdogs could win against seemingly impossible odds if they planned their strategy properly.

Billy read the speech and looked puzzled. It was soon obvious that he didn't know who David and Goliath were and for all he cared they could have been two General Motors dealers. I persevered, trying to explain the reason for drawing the parallel, and in the end he grudgingly agreed to leave it in the text. Unfortunately, when he came to give the speech he got David and Goliath mixed up, although the rest went over very well. I was trying to keep out of sight behind a pillar at Devonshire House, but when he saw me he rushed across the room and said. 'There you are, John, I knew it was a damn silly story. We should keep off religion in future. It doesn't go down well with business people, you know.' I never made any reference to the Bible again.

My predecessor at Rootes had been Toby O'Brien, one of the most outstanding public relations men of the day, who had previously been head of public relations at Conservative Central Office. He had a brother, also called Toby, who was head of public relations for the Post Office. Toby was an exceptionally good speech-writer and had a knack of producing phrases for Billy Rootes which made headlines. His was a hard act to follow when he left to form his own consultancy. It was Toby O'Brien who thought up the slogan that British businessmen should 'Add two noughts to their thinking and take the starch out of their boiled shirts when selling in the American market', and Billy used it to good effect on a number of occasions long after I had joined the company.

At the time that the Rootes brothers invited me to join them I was working as a public relations consultant with Sidney Barton, whose chairman Mike Williams-Thompson had been Chief Information Officer at the Ministry of Supply after the war. He had quite remarkable contacts in the Government and industry and had built up a reputation in Fleet Street as a brilliant publicist and organizer. He certainly brought a new conception of public relations to Fleet Street and was liked and admired by all sections of the media. I learned a great deal from him, but the offer made to me by Billy Rootes when Toby O'Brien left seemed too good to miss. The job would have been much more difficult, however, had it not been for the valuable experience I had gained from working with Mike Williams-Thompson. It was some months before Billy Rootes accepted the fact that Toby O'Brien was no longer working for him, and whenever there was a particularly important speech to be written he usually rang Toby for advice. One day when he did so Toby was abroad and I was left to write the speeches from then on.

John Wilcox was a newspaperman before accepting my invitation to join the Rootes public relations team and soon proved an excellent deputy. He later became head of public relations for the International Wool Secretariat and was also managing director of a successful West End consultancy.

He was one of a number of journalists I brought into the Rootes public relations department whose daily newspaper experience proved very valuable. When I took over, Jackie Masters and Rowland Rouse were the two press officers, but neither of them had any journalistic or writing experience. Jackie Masters looked after the press fleet and was a delightful old man in his late 70s who had been brought into the company by Dudley Noble in January 1944 to work as his assistant. He was a veteran car and motor cycle enthusiast and had been secretary of the Motor Cycling Club which ran the historic trials from London to Exeter at Christmas, to Land's End at Easter and to Edinburgh at Whitsun, which Billy Rootes used to take part in. He had been working for the Hotels and Restaurant Association and his delightful wife Bee had taken a wartime job running the bar at the George & Dragon at Wargrave, in Berkshire, where Dudley Noble and his wife were living. Bee was always the life and soul of any party and lived to be nearly a hundred, still enjoying her regular tipple of gin and sherry mixed in quantities which would have ensured most people of an early death, long after Jackie had died.

It was very unfortunate that Jackie Masters and Rowland Rouse didn't get on together, because this led to petty jealousies and created a bad atmosphere. The arrival of fresh blood and a number of very able young executives like John Wilcox, Liam Hunter, John Rowe and, later, Mike Trestrail, who looked after publicity for our Commercial Vehicle Division, soon changed the situation, and during the 1950s and '60s Rootes was acknowledged to have one of the most successful public relations teams in the motor industry.

Rowland Rouse spent most of his time looking after Kalanag the magician and his wife Gloria, who travelled the country with their act, the highlight of which was making a Hillman Minx disappear on the stage. They had been doing this for some time and had reached the stage where most of their performances took place at second-rate theatres. The illusions was done by mirrors and some of their equipment seemed to have been around for some time as well. I decided that the cost of supplying Kalanag and his wife with transport, along with the free meals and flowers which appeared each week on Rowland Rouse's expenses, as well as his own disappearing act for three or four days each week to look after the publicity, was too high a price to pay. When I put an end to the whole deal, Rowland Rouse quite understandably took considerable umbrage. He was then in his late 60s, but his knowledge of Rootes and the motor industry did prove very useful, and he remained with the company for some time.

Our chief librarian was Jeannette Wilkinson, whose team of girls did an excellent job of supplying us with facts and figures and keeping our extensive photographic library up to date. Tom Mulcaster looked after the company magazines, including *Modern Motoring* and *Travel*, which he produced each month for the benefit of Rootes owners.

We were also very fortunate to have Billy Elsey as advertising manager. He had joined Rootes before the war at the age of 15 as a page-boy, complete with pillbox hat, working in the Devonshire House showrooms. During the war he was a bomber pilot, with many raids over Germany to his credit. When he returned to the company he rejoined the advertising department and his flair and organizing ability soon led to him being put in charge of all the group's advertising and marketing. It was a wise decision and he remained with the company until his untimely death while still in his 50s. He proved to be an excellent colleague and was well liked throughout the motor industry.

After Billy Rootes became chairman of the Dollar Exports Council, the speech-writing load increased considerably as hardly a week went by when he was not called upon to speak at lunches, dinners or some other function to do with the export drive, in addition to his commitments for the company. With so many speeches to write each week I began to run out of fresh ideas and felt that John Wilcox, who was extremely amusing as well as being a very able writer, should take over some of the speech-writing. I knew that Billy wouldn't normally allow anyone else to write his speeches for him, but if I was away from the office when the next speech was needed, he would have to let John Wilcox have a go. I disappeared to the Press Club and the ploy worked. From then on he produced a number of excellent speeches and I was able to spend more time on company activities.

The only time I ever heard John complain was after he had spent some time writing a rather lengthy speech for a Dollar Exports Conference where the theme was again the problem of selling in such a large and complex market as America. To liven the speech up, he suggested that the swings and roundabouts of selling in the American market could be likened to a metronome, with the pendulum swinging from one side to another, and then added, 'and in case you don't know what a metronome is, it's a dwarf on the Paris underground'.

Billy read the speech through carefully and stopped when he came to the mention of the metronome. 'What's all this, Wilcox?' he asked, shaking his head.

'It's just a little joke, sir, which I put in to lighten the speech up a bit,' was the rather exasperated reply.

'Hmm!' said Billy, picking up the telephone and pressing the button for his brother. 'Reggie, could you come in for a minute? There's something I need your advice on.'

When Reggie appeared a few moments later, Billy asked him if he knew what a metronome was.

'Yes, Billy' came the reply. 'It's an instrument you put on a piano for beating out the time in music.'

Billy gave a grunt. 'That's what I thought it was, but this fool Wilcox thinks it's a dwarf on the Paris underground.'

Despite his lack of humour, Billy Rootes was quite brilliant when it came to making speeches, or when he had to appear on radio or television. The problem was that he would try to involve himself with too many facts, particularly when he was talking about the situation in other industries. I always tried to give him as few facts to remember as possible, because his strength of personality and enthusiasm drove home points more forcefully than any amount of figures could do.

The half-hour BBC radio programme 'In Town Tonight', which went on the air every Saturday at 7.30 pm, interviewed important and interesting people who had just arrived in London, and the producer usually wanted Billy to appear when he got back from one of his overseas tours. On one occasion he had just landed at London Airport after leading a delegation of bankers and businessmen to Latin America and had rushed to the studio with his travelling secretary, Charlie Morris, who was armed with a mass of trade figures. They were seated in the waiting room before the start of the programme, with Morris having to look up the latest figures for the export of items like whisky, textiles and clothing, and Billy busily scribbling them all down on a piece of paper, when Danny Kaye walked into the room. He was due to take part in the programme and he and Billy had met on a number of occasions in Hollywood.

'Hello, Billy,' he said, taking a seat alongside Morris. 'You look as though you are an old hand at this sort of thing. Tell me, do you ever get nervous?'

Billy shook his head. 'Not really, Danny. I'm having to appear on radio a lot now, on both sides of the Atlantic.'

Danny Kaye smiled. 'You're a lucky man, Billy,' he replied. 'I'm also making a lot of broadcasts, but I still feel nervous.' Then, taking the mass of papers that Morris was still searching through, he threw them into the air and grinned, 'There now, Billy,' he said, patting the horrified Billy on the back, 'that makes us even. Now we're both nervous.'

Before Billy could reply, the door opened and they were ushered into the studio to take part in the programme, with Morris frantically trying to get the papers back into some sort of order. Needless to say, the programme went very well and Billy Rootes gave an excellent interview without the need for any notes.

The incident did nothing to spoil the relationship between Billy and Danny Kaye, and he did get his own back by selling the American a car. Billy realised that a mass of scribbled figures are of little real value during a radio or television interview and would have been more of a handicap than a help so he appreciated that helpful action from a true professional.

In November 1954 Rootes earned an additional $2 million in Britain from a contract placed with the Group by the American army to recondition 4,500 American military vehicles. Under 'Operation Swappo', as the contract was known, the United States Army Ordnance Authorities in Britain and on the Continent arranged for thousands of American vehicles to be repaired and then handed back to the American military authorities for further use in Europe. A spare parts convoy of 26 American cargo transporters, each 42 ft (12.8 m) in length and with a carrying capacity of 16 tons, made its way across 500 miles (804 km) of European roads from Mannheim in Germany to London. On arrival at the Rootes Group Service Station at Ladbroke Hall in North Kensington, six of the cargo transporters went north to Manchester, where the Group Service Station there also carried out some of the vehicle reconditioning under the same contract. A separate section at both repair depots, along with the necessary personnel, had been set aside for the operation.

The convoy was believed to have covered more miles to its final destination than any other American Army convoy in peacetime. Manned by one driver per transporter, it left Mannheim at six o'clock one morning and drove across Europe to Dunkirk where the transporters crossed the Channel on a British ferry for Dover. On Continental roads the transporters were not permitted to travel at night, but in Britain they were not allowed to travel by day.

When they arrived in London the police escort brought them into Ladbroke Hall, where the unloading of each of the trailers by Rootes Group personnel went on throughout the day and at night by floodlight. They also had to unload 500 tons of spare parts for the trucks to enable the contract to be completed on time.

During the nine years that Billy was chairman of the Dollar Exports Council, Britain's dollar earnings increased every year and so did the number of companies opening up fresh markets for their products in America, Canada and Latin America. Billy was made a GBE in 1955 and a baron in 1959 for his dollar export activities and continued to play an important part in increasing dollar earnings when the title was changed in 1960 to the Western Hemisphere Exports Council.

Chapter 22

The Orly affair and Piccadilly capers

AS A JOURNALIST and a former news editor, keeping good stories out of the media has always been rather an anathema to me, but there are bound to be occasions when the publication of a photograph, or a particular story, could be disastrous to a company or an individual. Something happened in November 1956 which could have spoilt Billy Rootes's chance of being made a baron and have severely damaged his international reputation.

He had been persuaded by his wife to go on a shopping expedition to Paris but the visit turned into a nightmare which was totally unexpected and rapidly got out of hand. Raymond Dane was the Rootes public relations man in Paris and as I knew that he was well able to deal with any day-to-day problems which might arise while Billy was there, I had decided to remain in England, catch up with some of my social life, and enjoy a peaceful few days with my family. Working for Billy was like holding a tiger by the tail. Life was hectic. Keeping pace with a workaholic with unlimited energy and enthusiasm entailed long hours, but his brilliance and charm made him an exciting man to be with and he always commanded considerable affection and loyalty from his senior staff. Those of us who were close to him, however, never missed the opportunity to recharge our batteries while he was away, with the certainty that if we didn't do so we would have difficulty in keeping to his demanding schedule when he returned.

Raymond Dane had been a Hollywood PRO who had served as a colonel in the American army during the war, married an attractive French girl and settled down in Paris. He spoke fluent French and within a short time had turned into a true Parisian. He even looked French. I had spoken to him before Sir William and Lady Rootes left for France and told him to telephone me if he had any problems.

My wife and I had arranged lunch for some of our friends and were enjoying a relaxing weekend when the telephone rang at our home in Surrey. The first of the guests had arrived and I thought it might be

Raymond Dane ringing to say that everything had gone according to plan and Sir William and his wife were on their way back to London. The telephone operator asked whether I would accept the charge for a Paris call and I presumed that this was because Raymond was 'phoning from the airport and didn't have enough change.

I accepted the charge and a rather subdued voice the other end of the line said, 'Is that you, John? I haven't got much time, but it is essential that you get on the next plane to Paris. Bannerman will book you on the flight and meet you at the airport'.

Billy Rootes's voice was unmistakeable, but I was surprised at the urgency in his call. It crossed my mind that it might be a hoax, but before I could explain that our lunch guests had just arrived and I couldn't leave until that evening, he said, 'Don't worry about francs, John, Bannerman will have money for you. I must ring off now. See you later'.

The line went dead and I put a call through to Mordant Bannerman in Paris. As it was Sunday morning, I hoped he would be at home. He ran our French company and was a good friend of mine. We had both served in the Royal Air Force during the war and he had commanded a bomber squadron with considerable distinction.

His wife answered the telephone and seemed relieved to hear me. 'Thank goodness you have 'phoned, John. Mordant's had to go to the police station with the company lawyer, but he asked me to let you know that he will meet you at the airport and has booked you on the 14.30 flight'.

'What is the company lawyer doing at the police station?'

'Mordant will be able to tell you all about it when you arrive, but Sir William and his wife have been taken into custody and Mordant and the lawyer are trying to get them released on bail'.

I began to understand why Billy had been so insistent that I should catch the early afternoon plane, but I still felt rather stunned at the news. For the French police to take into custody one of Britain's most distinguished industrialists and his wife, the situation must have been serious.

I decided to take a chance and put a call through to Joan Harrison, who was the head of the *Daily Express* Bureau in Paris. The only woman foreign correspondent for a national newspaper at the time, she was a first-rate journalist and there wasn't much of importance went on in Paris that she didn't know about. I knew her well and could easily think of an excuse for telephoning her if she hadn't heard about Sir William's visit to the police station, without making her too suspicious.

As I had suspected, however, Joan was already well informed. She gave a laugh when she recognized my voice. 'Hello, John. I guess we will be seeing you over here somewhat rapidement. No doubt you have heard that your nice Billy Rootes and his wife are in the nick charged with assault.'

'Assault!' The whole thing was becoming more absurd and difficult to believe, but I knew that Joan would tell me the truth.

'Yes, assault. It seems that Lady Rootes slugged a customs official with her handbag at Orly Airport and Sir William also got arrested when he went to help. Let me know where you will be staying and I will let everyone know.'

There wasn't any time to waste, as the Monday morning papers would obviously carry full reports of the incident. 'Joan, I will do better than that. I will treat you to a slap-up dinner at Maximes if you will pass the word around that I will be in the Long Bar of the George V Hotel at six tonight and will be pleased to buy all British foreign correspondents a drink. By then I will be able to tell you our side of the story.'

Billy Rootes always had a suite at the Ritz and I didn't want to run the risk of meeting newspapermen there in case they bumped into him. I also felt it would be wise for him to keep out of the way of the press for the time being. The Long Bar of the George V was a favourite watering-place which all the foreign correspondents knew well.

My wife Jean was used to quick changes of plan from the days when I had been a newspaperman and had left to cover stories at short notice, but even she was not ready for my announcement that I had to leave for the airport immediately, because the chairman and his wife were being held by the Paris police. Fortunately, our guests were good friends and accepted the situation without a murmur of complaint, although I think that some of them thought I was pulling their legs at first.

Jean offered to pack my bag so that I was able to have a quick drink with our guests, but as they sat down to lunch I made my excuses and drove off to the airport, with very mixed feelings. I always enjoyed Paris, but I had the feeling that this trip would be rather an exception.

Mordant Bannerman looked relieved to see me, and I soon realized why. He'd also been looking forward to a peaceful Sunday, having said goodbye to Billy and his wife at the airport, but by the time he had reached home their 'plane had left without them and they were in police custody. With the help of the company's lawyer he had secured their release on bail and they were now back in their suite at the Ritz.

The problem at the airport had apparently begun when Lady Rootes had insisted on leaving her maid to see her luggage through customs and had gone on ahead, carrying her rather large handbag. She was stopped by a woman customs officer, but refused to show her the contents of the bag. The customs officer tried to grab the bag and, in the struggle which followed, she unfortunately let go of it just as another member of the customs staff arrived on the scene. The bag hit him in the mouth, and when Billy arrived to see what was happening, the gendarmes took him into custody along with Lady Rootes.

I liked Ann Rootes, but knew how difficult she could be in situations she didn't like. Another woman grabbing her handbag was a sure recipe for trouble. She had a number of friends in Paris who made up the modern jet set there and who were suspected of being involved with drugs, which were fashionable at the time. That may have been one of the reasons why the customs officials were so interested in her handbag, but there was never any evidence that she had been involved with drugs and certainly nothing was found in her handbag, which made the whole incident even more ridiculous. It was unfortunate that the language problem added to the difficulties and within a matter of minutes everything had got out of hand.

When I arrived at the Ritz it was evident that Billy appreciated the seriousness of the situation, but Ann was far from despondent. Her suggestion that we should go to Maximes was fortunately turned down by him, who saw the wisdom of them both keeping out of the limelight until I had been able to talk to the press and see whether we could minimize the bad publicity as soon as possible.

Before leaving for the George V Hotel I got Billy's agreement to invite all the British newspapermen to lunch the following day. A private room would enable everyone to talk to him individually over drinks and I knew that Joan Harrison would be good company for Lady Rootes and prevent her from saying anything which might be used against her. Discretion was never her strongest point.

The Long Bar was packed with familiar and, I hoped, friendly faces. Joan had done her job well and every national newspaperman in Paris was there. The only person missing was the staff man from Reuters. They had quite a large staff in Paris and Joan had only been able to leave a message with the news desk and didn't know who would be coming.

There was a tap on my shoulder. Standing there was a young reporter who had worked for the *Evening Despatch* in Birmingham when I had been news editor of the paper at the end of the war.

'Hello, David, what are you doing here?' I said. I presumed he was in Paris on holiday but couldn't believe my luck when he replied, 'Waiting for you to buy me a drink. I'm working for Reuters'.

David Richards had been one of two university graduates who had joined the *Evening Despatch*, and I had saved their jobs on a number of occasions when they had been rather economical with the facts in some of their reports. They both wrote well, however, and John Egan went on to work for the *Daily Express* in New York. Reuters was important because the agency would be supplying the stories for most of the British provincial papers who did not have staff men in Paris, and some of those papers were published in areas where Rootes had factories and a large labour force.

I was able to explain what had really happened at the airport. It was fortunate that Billy Rootes, on his frequent visits to Paris, had always been on good terms with the press and was genuinely liked. Joan was also on my side and, as the owner of another large handbag, the contents of which she admitted she really would not want anyone else to see, engendered considerable sympathy for Lady Rootes's stance. The

Brits were united on one thing—the whole incident had been badly handled by bloody-minded French officials.

The invitation to lunch the following day was looked upon as being a typical gesture by Billy Rootes, and I promised that he and his wife would answer any questions, once they had been given an opportunity of recovering from their ordeal in the hands of the French police. The inference was that the French authorities had been unnecessarily heavy-handed in their behaviour towards one of Britain's best-liked industrialists, and one who had been responsible for producing many of the aircraft and fighting vehicles which had led to Germany's defeat and the liberation of France. The British correspondents went off to write their reports; I managed to get the last table at Maximes and felt every justification for celebrating a job well done. Champagne always seems to taste better when there is cause for celebration and there was no doubt that the reports of the incident in the next morning's papers would be fair and suggest that it was all a storm in a teacup. We were certainly in good company, with one of my favourite film stars, Rita Hayworth, dining at the next table with her husband, Aly Khan.

Joan insisted on a memento of the occasion and had a photograph taken of us enjoying more champagne at Rootes's expense. The photograph was delivered back to us in the form of dozens of book matches which she swept into her outsize handbag. As Joan was a heavy smoker, I didn't expect the matches to last long, but I could have bought a quality lighter for much less and it would have caused less trouble.

When the cigars were being handed round after lunch the next day, she produced one of the book matches to light her cigarette. Ann Rootes, who was sitting opposite, was quick to notice the incriminating photograph and asked if she could keep it as evidence that public relations was one big jolly. The next few days, however, were to prove her wrong.

Although the British press had played down the story as we had hoped, the French legal system was making it difficult for Billy and his wife to leave Paris until their case had been heard, and that could take some time, because the customs officer who had been struck by the handbag was now claiming substantial damages for teeth which he claimed had been loosened. He was certainly taking full advantage of the situation and seemed to be enjoying the publicity. His claim made sure that the story wasn't going to die a natural death and continued to make headlines. Our French lawyers were also having a field-day and persuaded Billy that my activities should be restricted while they worked behind the scenes to try and arrange a settlement.

My regard for Billy Rootes, which had always been high, was increased even further by his behaviour during the next few days. I knew that sooner or later he would have to appear with his wife before a magistrate at the Palais de Justice, the French law courts, and decided to see what could be done to make the visit less of an ordeal. Unlike in England, where it is an offence to take photographs in the precincts of a court, in France photographers are allowed to take photographs inside the building. Raymond Dane and I spent a morning finding our way round the building which seemed to have much in common with a rabbit warren.

There was certainly no way of anyone being able to get in or out without being photographed at will. As that was the case, it seemed sensible to make sure that the photographs were to our advantage and we agreed that instead of rushing along the corridors trying to miss photographers, which was the usual practice, we would provide a photo call, so I let it be known that Sir William and his wife would pose for photographs outside the court. The idea was that they would arrive in their chauffeur-driven Humber Pullman and let the press photographers take all the shots they wanted, before walking arm in arm into the court, as though they were going to have their passports renewed.

The French photographers were very co-operative and appreciated the arrangements, but I was rather concerned to see that Joan Harrison's Scottish photographer, who had been sent from London by the *Daily Express*, was nowhere to be seen. I couldn't believe that he would have missed such an opportunity, particularly as I had told him our plan when I had had a drink with him the previous evening.

After all the photographs had been taken, Raymond Dane and I led the way into the large ante-room where defendants and witnesses had to wait before going before the magistrate. As we entered the room I could see the *Daily Express* photographer standing on a table in the corner and waving Raymond and me out of the way. I looked round. Behind us were two gipsy women who quickly fell in alongside Sir William and Lady Rootes so that they could be photographed together.

It was obviously a posed photograph of Sir William and Lady Rootes and the two women waiting to see the magistrate. I learned later that the gipsies were a mother and daughter who were seeking permission to visit their husband and father who was being held on a murder charge. It was the sort of photograph which a good national newspaper photographer would have thought up and I should have realized that he wouldn't have been satisfied with an arm in arm shot outside the court. We had fallen right into the trap.

As Billy and Ann went in to see the magistrate, I grabbed Raymond Dane and we ran through the corridors to the front of the building. Top news photographers in those days always used Speed Graphic plate cameras and I guessed that Jock would be sending the plates back to London to be developed. It didn't take long for us to find the motor cyclist who was waiting in a side street to take the plates to the airport. I counted out 100,000 francs in front of the rather puzzled French motor cyclist and told him that if he gave the packet he was about to receive several sharp blows on the ground as soon as he was out of sight, I would know that he had done so, and that if he met me the following morning at eleven o'clock in the café opposite I would have another 100,000 francs for him. In those days 1,000 francs was worth a little less than £1 sterling, so I was taking the risk that he would do as I asked for the equivalent of about £200, still quite a lot of money for a delivery rider in France.

Out of the corner of my eye I could see the *Daily Express* photographer coming out of the Palais de Justice and Raymond and I slipped away before he saw us. It was now all up to our friend the motor cyclist and his standard of moral values, which I hoped would not be too high.

The damaging photograph did not appear in the Paris edition of the following day's *Daily Express*, but I was worried that it might have been used in some of the later editions, so I rang Keith Howard, the paper's news editor in London. He was an old friend and a brilliant news editor, having been a protégé of the famous Morley Richards. We had sailed together and his wife was one of my eldest daughter's godmothers. Despite our friendship I knew that his first loyalty would be to his paper, in the same way that I was being loyal to my company and our chairman.

'Thanks for not using a photograph of Billy Rootes today,' I said when he came on the line.

'It wasn't for want of trying', he replied, with what I took to be an admission of defeat. 'Jock rang to say that he was sending us a very good exclusive, but the plates were broken when the package arrived. It must have been some ham-fisted handler at British Airways.'

I caught a taxi to the Palais de Justice and went across to the café where I had arranged to meet the motor cyclist, but as I walked through the door I was horrified to see Jock sitting at one of the tables, going through his copy of the *Daily Express*. He looked up as I came in and I tried not to look too cheerful. 'Hello, Jock. What are you doing here? Can I get you a cognac?'

'Can you make it a double? I paid two gipsy women 50,000 francs to pose with Sir William and his wife and the paper hasn't used the picture. Can you believe it? I'm worried that they won't now repay me the 50,000 francs. All the way over here for nothing.'

I bought two large cognacs and told Jock that I would be back in a minute to help him drown his sorrows. Fortunately for me, the motor cyclist was right on time so I didn't have long to wait. I shook him by the hand and gave him an envelope containing the other 100,000 francs. As he rode off, I went back into the café to enjoy the first of many large cognacs with an understandably very disappointed photographer.

I was particularly relieved that we had managed to prevent the photograph from being published, because it would have seriously damaged Billy Rootes's image at a time when we were hoping that his outstanding achievements for the motor industry and the Dollar Exports Council would be rewarded with him being awarded a baronetcy. He was the innocent party in an incident which had been allowed to get out of hand by the French customs officials and the police.

After the customs officer who had unfortunately got in the path of the flying handbag had been suitably compensated for his pain and suffering—something which should have been handled more expediently by our French lawyers—all the charges were dropped and we were able to return to London.

In order for Billy and his wife to do so with the minium of fuss and publicity, I suggested that we should catch the midnight flight from Paris to Heathrow, which was usually only used by tourists. By the time it arrived all the photographers who were based at the airport would have gone off duty. He liked the suggestion, although Ann didn't appreciate having to fly tourist, and she was even less pleased when she was told that we should take only hand luggage with us on the flight, so that there would be no hold-ups in customs either end. Billy even insisted that I should leave behind a rather expensive new French coffee percolator which Jean had asked me to buy, so Mordant Bannerman's wife received an unexpected present. French coffee percolators were very good, but very expensive, and it was a gift that she felt was in keeping with the title I had earned in Paris of the last of big spenders! It was a title which stuck with me for some time, but as Billy pointed out, whenever it was suggested that I had spent more than had been necessary, 'Don't worry, John, we could have had a failure at half the price.'

Getting Billy and Ann from the airport to their house at Shepherds Close, just off Park Lane, was my next problem, because he refused to let me arrange for a car to meet them and urged me not to tell anyone, including his chauffeur and other members of their household staff, that they were returning to England in case word reached the press. 'You have a car at the airport. Would you mind taking us home? You are welcome to stay the night.' Billy was clearly pleased with the suggestion. On the surface it was an obvious solution, but it presented me with quite a problem.

At the time I left home for the airport, the only car I had had available was the specially hotted-up Hillman Minx which George Hartwell, the head of Hartwell Motors, the main Rootes dealers at Bournemouth, had built for me. George was a former racing driver and a very able competitor in rallies and hill climbs who had been very successful with a similar car in Britain and on the Continent. He set up a new course record for touring cars in the 1,300 cc–1,600 cc class over the twisting 13-mile (21-km) circuit of the Mont Ventoux Hill Climb in the French Alps with his own Minx Special in July 1957.

By the clever use of overdrive, the Hartwell-modified Minx had eight forward gears, twin carburettors, a specially designed aluminium cylinder head, and sounded like a small Ferrari. It also went like a scalded cat, and there weren't many cars that could stay with it at speeds from 0 to 60 mph (0–96.5 km/h) while its top speed was more than 100 mph (161 km/h). The fact that it was such a wolf in sheep's clothing made it great fun to drive, and rather different from the run-of-the-mill transport which other senior Rootes executives drove. I felt it wise to keep it under wraps as much as possible, particularly as I knew that Billy didn't approve of hotted-up versions of his brainchild, the Hillman Minx.

There was no way out, however, and I was obviously going to have to give a lift to the chairman and his wife in a car I would have preferred to have kept to myself, at least until I had been able to have some more fun with it. I thought that, as it would be dark when we arrived, he wouldn't see the twin exhausts and other more visual modifications, and if I could warm it up gently before bringing it round to the main airport entrance, and manage to keep the revs down, he might not notice the more powerful note of the engine.

My luck was out. Not only had it been snowing and freezing hard, but Billy insisted on them both coming with me to collect the car, rather than wait in the airport lounge where they might be seen and recognized. I gave the engine full choke, but every time I pressed the accelerator there was a loud roar from the engine, and I had to lift my foot off so that it conked out again. By this process the engine took some time to warm up, and we drove to London at a sedate pace in a high gear, so that the revs would be kept down to a minimum.

After dropping them off at Shepherds Close, I made my apologies and was relieved to be able to drive on home at a reasonable speed, without having to worry about the noise of the engine, or the car's acceleration. I felt rather relieved that, apart from asking why I had such a small and relatively low-priced car instead of one more in keeping with my position as an executive of the company, little had been said and I had managed to steer the conversation away from cars, and on to other, less delicate, matters.

My relief was short-lived, however. As soon as I arrived at my office the following morning, John Routly, the company secretary, came to see me. 'Sir William rang first thing to say how shocked he was to find you driving a rather grotty-sounding Hillman, and insisted it is replaced immediately with a new Humber Super Snipe. He's obviously well pleased with the way things went in Paris and the way you handled the press. Congratulations!'

John Routly was a close friend and we were used to working closely together. We'd managed to deal with difficult situations on a number of occasions by taking action which other members of the board might not always have approved of had they known. I told him about the Hillman and the fact that it was actually worth much more than the Humber Super Snipe he was suggesting as a replacement, but on this occasion there was nothing to be done but fall in with the chairman's wishes.

'More than my job's worth, John, not to replace that car for you. I've never heard the old man so insistent. He wants your new car delivered immediately, so if you will just choose the colour and any extras you want I will take the necessary action. I have to tell him what I have done about it when he arrives in the office later this morning'. I gave in. John Routly was right, and it was back to more sedate transport whether I liked it or not.

I did manage to arrange a compromise. John Routly agreed that I should pass the Hillman on to my deputy, John Wilcox, which meant that I was able to borrow it on occasions.

Soon after the dust had settled on the Orly Airport affair, John Routly and I were involved in an amusing situation which could also have led to some unfortunate publicity if the facts had become known. Halkin House, in Halkin Street, which was only a few hundred yards away from our headquarters in Piccadilly, was open 24 hours a day for petrol and was also a main service station for Rootes cars. Many of the large Humber Pullmans used by ambassadors and civic dignitaries were parked overnight there, as well as being taken there for service. The building also contained palatial offices and reception areas, expensively furnished with deep brown leather chairs and sofas.

One morning, the Devonshire House receptionist came into my office and asked whether I would see someone who wanted to talk to me about a rather confidential matter, which he didn't feel he should discuss with anyone else. Inwardly I gave a groan. The editor of one of our Rootes magazines had until recently been having an affair with his teenage secretary, which might not have mattered, except that he was already married and the father of seven children! The secretary's father had threatened dire action if I didn't do something about the situation, and rather than sacking a very good editor and putting the father of seven children out of work, I had had the secretary moved out of harm's way.

'Does the man look like an angry parent?' I asked, hoping that my solution to the problem of the over-sexed editor and his nubile young girlfriend hadn't gone amiss. The receptionist assured me that if the visitor in reception was a father, the child would still be very young. 'He's really rather dishy,' she admitted, adding, 'He doesn't look married', which probably accounted for her plea that I should see him, even though he hadn't made an appointment and I was due to leave shortly for a meeting.

The young man who walked into my office was smartly dressed and well spoken. As I ushered him to a chair he apologized for taking up my time, but explained that he had to leave London that afternoon. He felt, however, that he had some information which would be of concern to Rootes if it became public knowledge.

I had already just taken steps to prevent an irate Hillman owner, who was trying to have his car replaced, from allowing his rather elderly wife to do a strip-tease in the road outside our offices while he held up the traffic with his car, which was plastered in placards complaining about the treatment he was receiving. The man was quite mad and his poor wife would probably have caught her death of cold without any chance of getting her picture in the papers.

What, I wondered, could this fresh information be? Was he another irate Hillman owner threatening some publicity stunt in order to get his way? It was quite the reverse. He didn't own a car, although his father always bought Rootes products, and he was on leave from the army. He'd recently been commissioned and had come to London with another young second lieutenant to enjoy the bright lights before being posted. It was in the days when ladies of easy virtue could be found at every street corner in Piccadilly after dark, and they had both submitted to temptation after a lengthy session in one of the bars.

The two women they picked up took them by taxi to the Rootes Halkin Street offices and were let into the building by the petrol pump attendant, who was handed some money as they entered. The third-floor reception had a number of large couches, which were obviously in regular use by the women, while others took their clients into the back of the Humber Pullmans, which were parked in a reception bay clearly visible through the swing doors. The plush seats of the Pullmans were obviously being put to a more profitable use than just being resting places for ambassadorial bottoms on the way to civic functions.

As I tried to picture the transformation of a busy reception area by day into a house of ill-repute at night, I couldn't help chuckling at the thought that this was an example of private enterprise which Billy Rootes knew nothing about, but which had obviously turned one of his petrol pump attendants into an entrepreneur with a real eye for business. It couldn't, however, be allowed to continue. The young lieutenant refused my offer to settle his hotel bill, or to entertain him to lunch. It was, he explained, a matter of conscience as far as he was concerned. His father had a business in Manchester and he hoped that if the same sort of thing was happening there, someone would tell his father before it became public knowledge, and the company suffered any bad publicity.

When I told John Routly and suggested that as a lawyer he should take the necessary action to nip in the bud such immoral use of Rootes property, even though Billy Rootes always encouraged private enterprise, he also saw the funny aspects of the situation. We thought of all the possible headlines—'Rootes house of ill-repute forced to close', or 'Brothel most successful area of our business, says wealthy motor magnate', or perhaps 'Rootes new open-all-hours policy proves successful'.

We decided to employ a private detective to keep watch on the Halkin Street premises, and he caught the petrol pump attendant and his team of prostitutes red-handed. The man was fired and the locks were changed on the building. We didn't press charges, because the resultant publicity would have done more harm than good to the company and to the Rootes name, which had already been tarnished by the Orly affair. Halkin Street went back to being just another Rootes depot, before the temptation to turn it into something more profitable got the upper hand. The petrol pump attendants were more carefully screened in future and the Humber Pullmans returned to their proper use. John Routly and I decided to keep the knowledge to ourselves and nobody at Halkin Street was ever any the wiser.

Chapter 23

Competing in Europe and elsewhere

ALTHOUGH CONSIDERABLE EMPHASIS was being placed on the dollar markets, the sale of Rootes cars and trucks in Europe, as well as in Australia, New Zealand, South Africa and India, also increased considerably with the introduction of the new post-war models. Brian Rootes returned to London in 1953, having passed over the New York operation to John Panks, and became responsible for overseas sales, working closely with his father and Joe Chaldecott. His drive and enthusiasm had a great deal to do with the success of the company's export division during the next 10 years.

Rootes were always looking for fresh markets and for ways of overcoming import restrictions and increasing their market penetration. Barter deals were pioneered by Billy and Brian Rootes and on one occasion, after the company had negotiated a deal with the Norwegian Government to allow some hundreds of additional Hillmans to be sold there, I was given the task of helping to market 50,000 cases of canned Norwegian sild worth some three million kroner. More than 50 million sild were involved in the first deal and the fish, similar in size to small sardines, were eventually distributed by Armour & Company of London and Simpson Roberts & Company of Liverpool, two of the country's leading canned goods importers and distributors. They went on sale at about a shilling a tin.

Sild had been sold in Britain before the war in quite large quantities, but persuading British housewives to change their buying habits after the war was no easy task. In the end we got rid of all the sild and must have done our jobs quite well, because it is a fish which is still being sold in British supermarkets. Many similar deals followed, but this was the only fishy one—most of the others involved accessories, like tyres.

In 1953 a visit to the Ryton-on-Dunsmore factory by His Imperial Highness Prince Akihto, the Crown Prince of Japan, was arranged to announce plans for Rootes Group products to be assembled over there by the Isuzu Motor Company, one of the country's largest truck manufacturers. The negotiations had been conducted by Joe Chaldecott, who spent some months in the Far East doing the groundwork. The visit had to be cancelled at the last minute when the Crown Prince went down with a fever, but the deal went ahead and it was agreed that the cars and trucks would be merchandized throughout the Japanese islands by Yamato, a company owned jointly by the Isuzu Motor Company and Rootes. This tie-up did much to increase the export of all Rootes products in the Far East.

As a further increase in the Rootes Group's export drive, a new £2,400,000 public company was formed in Australia to allow substantial expansion in the manufacturing facilities at the Fisherman's Bend plant, where Hillman, Humber and Sunbeam Talbot cars and Commer and Karrier trucks were being assembled. Rootes was the first company to establish a motor car factory in Australia, when in 1946 they took over the Fisherman's Bend facilities which had been built to manufacture armoured fighting vehicles.

Despite his asthma, Brian Rootes drove himself to the limits, frequently making do with only an hour or two's sleep during visits from overseas dealers or groups of foreign journalists. A full day's work in the office would often be followed by a dinner and late night entertaining, with Brian as the effervescent and always popular host. He never forgot anyone's name and never missed an opportunity to be at the centre of every party or to promote Rootes and the company's products worldwide.

It was the same during his frequent visits abroad. He always preferred to size up market opportunities for himself rather than rely on reports from other people, and he insisted that his staff did the same. With his father having to spend much of the day on dollar export matters, Brian and I were frequently called to evening meetings at Devonshire House, which could go on until midnight. Senior executives didn't usually go home while Billy was still in the office, because he might well ring for them to join in discussions or provide urgent information at any hour during the evening.

There were occasions, however, when Brian felt that he had spent enough time in the office for one day and we devised a ploy together which usually worked. At about seven o'clock he would say to his father, 'John Bullock and I have some matters we must discuss tonight and need to get away now.' This usually resulted in our both being let off the hook and we could disappear for a quiet drink before going home, for what would be an early night when Billy Rootes was in town.

We came unstuck one Friday evening when Brian had a new chauffeur who didn't know the ropes. We had left 'the Green Belt' where Billy and Reggie Rootes had their offices on the first floor of Devonshire House (it was always known as 'the Green Belt' because of the colour of the thick Wilton carpeting) and had slipped out of the side entrance into Stratton Street where Brian's car and chauffeur were waiting. After passing his briefcase over to the chauffeur, Brian told him to wait while we went for a drink in the Cascade, a restaurant and night club in Mayfair Place, at the rear of Devonshire House, which was usually very quiet early in the evening. We were enjoying a couple of large gin and tonics when we heard Billy's voice and his unmistakeable step as he came down the stairs into the bar.

We were caught red-handed. Billy let out a grunt. 'So that's where you and John hold your meetings, is it, Brian?' he muttered, looking round the bar which was empty apart from Brian and me. 'That's right! Come and join us for a drink, father. We've finished our business and were thinking about going home, but we will stay if you would like a drink.' I was relieved that Brian was dealing with the situation so well, although I needn't have worried because in the many years that we worked closely together he never once let me down. He was in a much better position to deal with his father than I was on those occasions.

Billy started back up the stairs and called down, 'I haven't got time to sit around drinking while there is work to do. See you both on Monday.' Brian turned to me and laughed. 'There you are, John. We've been officially given the rest of the evening and the weekend off. Let's make the best of it.'

There was a sequel which put an end to the Cascade as far as we were concerned. We found out later that as Billy was leaving the office he had noticed Brian's chauffeur waiting outside in Stratton Street and had warned him that, because of our meeting, he might have to wait some time. The chauffeur replied that he thought that might be the case because he had seen the two of us going into the Cascade. After leaving us in the bar, Billy said to the doorman, 'You don't seem to be doing very well, there are only two people in the bar at the moment.'

'You're right, sir,' replied the doorman. 'If it wasn't for those people from Rootes I don't know what we would do in the evening.'

On the Monday morning Billy asked the cashier's department to let him know how many members of the Rootes staff had credit accounts with the Cascade. The answer was two—Brian and me! We never went there again, and a few weeks later the Cascade closed. Pity they didn't have a brighter doorman.

Brian Rootes was always great fun to work with and I was frequently impressed by his remarkable determination and ingenuity. His work for the Group took him to almost every country in the world, but China did prove a stumbling block for a while. The Chinese Government had purchased a number of Humber cars and Commer trucks, but when Brian applied for a visa on the grounds that he wanted to see for himself how the vehicles were performing, the official at the Chinese Embassy turned down his request with an excruciating smile and the assurance that all the cars and trucks were working to everyone's entire satisfaction and a visit would not be necessary.

Visiting China then became a challenge which Brian found difficult to resist. In the end he decided to enter the country from Hong Kong as a tourist and took one of the company's Far East representatives with him for company. When they arrived they broke away from the tourist party as soon as they could, because Brian wanted to visit a typical Chinese restaurant rather than the more up-market hotels and eating places included on their tour.

The only problem was that neither Brian nor his companion spoke a word of Chinese and the waiters in the places he wanted to visit didn't understand a word of English. They overcame the problem first by peering through the windows of restaurants. When a table became vacant they dashed inside and sat down, smiling cheerfully at the rather surprised Chinese at the other tables. Then when they were asked what they wanted to eat, Brian would either quack like a duck, snort like a pig, or sit there flapping his arms up and down and repeating 'cock-a-doodle-do' until the waiter got the message. I never found out how they ordered fried rice, but according to Brian they managed to eat quite well and didn't suffer any ill-effects from their novel method of ordering. No doubt the Chinese thought they were just two eccentric Englishmen who normally behaved in that extraordinary way when they visited a foreign country.

Overseas motor shows were always exhausting because Rootes had official lunches and dinners every day, quite apart from the usual press conferences for the British and overseas media and the various other activities to do with the shows. All the members of the Rootes family were usually present and I fielded a strong public relations team to ensure that we got the maximum publicity. We had our own Rootes companies in every major capital in Europe, which made organizing functions overseas a lot easier. I also employed a number of public relations consultants who provided us with on-the-spot publicity services for each European company, and they helped us to ensure that translations of press releases and speeches were always correct.

Brian's Swiss education proved useful on a number of occasions, including the time at the Geneva Motor Show, during one of the new model announcements, when he was called upon to hold a press conference in three languages. The Rootes press lunches in Paris were looked upon as being one of the highlights of the show, and Billy Rootes, who had been made the first honorary member of the Guild of Motoring Writers because of all his support for the guild and the motoring press, always fined members £1 if they turned up at the lunch not wearing the official guild tie. All the proceeds went to the Guild Benevolent Fund and he usually added a generous additional contribution from the Rootes family. He also presented the guild with a magnificent gold trophy which is still awarded annually for the most outstanding achievement in the field of motoring by a member of the Guild during the year.

In 1945 Billy and Reggie were the first guests of the Guild, when it was know as the Motoring Correspondents Circle, at a luncheon at the Cheshire Cheese pub in Fleet Street. The chairman of the Circle was Laurence Cade of *The Star*. Others present were Mrs Kay Petre (*Daily Sketch*), Major Oliver Stewart (*The Tatler*), Ronald Strode (*Kemsley Group*), James Stuart (*Evening Standard*), F. J. C. Pignon (*Daily Mail*), J. N. Bennett (*Daily Herald*), Jack Jellen (*The Scotsman*), Basil Cardew (*Daily Express*), Sidney Henschel (*Financial News*), John Prince (*The Times*), Alan Tomkins (*Sunday Dispatch*), the Hon. Maynard Greville (*Country Life*), Frank Hardy (*Irish Times*), Ralph Feilden (*The Recorder and Imperial Review*), W. A. Gibson Martin (*Liverpool Journal of Commerce*) and Dudley Noble (*The Queen*).

Antony Johnson (*Daily Mirror*), John Prioleau (*The Observer*), Tommy Wisdom (*Daily Herald*) and Robert Walling (*Evening Standard*) were still in the Forces, and Jack Bergel (*Evening News*) had been killed in a flying accident.

Billy told me that his honorary membership of the Guild was an honour he valued greatly in view of the close friendship he had enjoyed with members of the motoring press since he started the company.

Billy knew, however, that all the motoring writers were in Paris to work and so he always made sure that there was a good story for the following morning's papers. In 1953, for example, it was the new world-wide overseas delivery scheme, whereby Rootes customers could choose the car they wanted before leaving home and have it waiting for them at the airport at the other end of their journey, fully taxed and insured. When they returned home, the car was either shipped back for them or repurchased at a prearranged price.

The worldwide overseas delivery and repurchase scheme did present some problems in Britain because of the large number of customers who ordered left-hand-drive cars in case they wanted them shipped home. When they changed their minds and the cars had to be repurchased, the Rootes sales staff had the difficult task of selling cars with steering on the left in a country where everyone drove on the left-hand side of the road.

Peter Warrilow, who was the sales manager at Devonshire House, and like his brother Cyril had been with the company since pre-war days, told me one week that his staff had managed to sell six of the scores of left-hand-drive Sunbeams which had been repurchased from members of the American forces. I suggested that we do some simple market research to find out who had bought the cars and, armed with that knowledge, we could perhaps advertise in the right place to attract more customers. All we could find out, however, was that the cars had been bought by women with West End addresses, and they had all paid cash so we couldn't trace them through hire purchase agreements.

The answer dawned on me a few days later when I was coming out of the Ritz Hotel and saw a smart left-hand-drive Sunbeam coming slowly along Piccadilly with an attractive girl at the wheel. The girl smiled and invited me to join her but, perhaps understandably, took exception when I said that I was more interested in her car than her offer. I had found out why women had been buying the repurchased Sunbeams. The left-hand-drive obviously made kerb-crawling and picking up customers much easier, but I still hadn't solved the problem of where to advertise for more customers, unless a notice in a shop window in Shepherds Market might have been the answer. I decided that on this occasion Peter Warrilow—who was always helpful in finding journalists good second-hand cars—and his salesmen would have to do without the help of the public relations and marketing department.

It may have been because Billy Rootes, although he did have some engineering training, was always a salesman at heart and Reggie Rootes was mainly an organizer, that the Rootes Group always seemed to have too many models and model variations during the 1950s, and this did sometimes cause problems. Sales demands always seemed to have priority over engineering and production, no doubt because Billy was determined to give the motoring public just what they wanted, both in Britain and abroad. Rootes salesmen couldn't use the excuse that there wasn't a suitable model for every occasion and every customer.

He also knew the value of publicity and the boost to sales which competition successes brought to the company. Norman Garrad was an outstanding competitions manager and did wonders with his small but talented competitions department in Coventry, and they produced a regular list of awards in every major international rally, along with class wins at Le Mans and in the gruelling Mille Miglia Italian road race.

In 1952 the outstanding successes of the Sunbeam Talbots in the gruelling Alpine Rally was acknowledged to be the most outstanding engineering achievement of the year and won for Rootes the Royal Automobile Club's Dewar Trophy. It was presented to Billy during a luncheon at the RAC by Wilfred Andrews, the club's chairman, before a distinguished gathering of motoring and motor industry personalities. Rootes continued to win Coupe des Alpes and team awards in Alpine rallies for the next 10 years.

The following year, the Sunbeam Talbot team in the Monte Carlo Rally won the Charles Faroux Challenge Trophy, which was awarded to the nominated team of three cars achieving the best aggregate performance, irrespective of size or price. It was the first time for 21 years that the award had gone to a British manufacturer. They won the team trophy again in 1954 and then won it outright in 1956, a remarkable performance in what was acknowledged to be the toughest rally in the world.

The company's greatest success however, came in 1955 when a privately entered Sunbeam Talbot saloon driven by two Norwegian drivers, Captain Per Malling and Gunnar Fadum, won the Monte Carlo Rally outright. Per Malling was the 40-year-old technical director of the Technical Department of the Oslo police, who was driving in his fourth

Monte Carlo Rally. His co-driver, 36-year-old Gunnar Fadum, was the manager of a bread factory and vice-chairman of the Sports Committee of the Royal Norwegian Automobile Club and the Norwegian Rally Drivers Club.

Their victory did much to increase Rootes sales in Scandinavia and enabled Philip Lorraine, who was our public relations man in Sweden, to set up a publicity tour of Scandinavia which also established good relations with the press in Denmark, Norway, Sweden and Finland that lasted for more than 20 years. Philip Lorraine was an English journalist who had previously worked for *The Times* in London but had moved to Stockholm when he married his wife Gun, a successful Swedish journalist. He spoke fluent Swedish, along with several other Scandinavian languages, and was chairman of the Anglo-Swedish Society. Although the win in the Monte Carlo had been with Norwegian drivers, it was good for Scandinavian motor sport generally and enabled us to gain a much wider benefit from their success.

Before leaving for Stockholm I spent a week in London organizing special appearances by Per Malling and Gunnar Fadum and arranging publicity for their car. When the victorious Sunbeam Talbot arrived in England from Monte Carlo to be displayed in the Devonshire House showrooms, it was covered in the usual thick layer of mud and dust from the rally and had been taken overnight to the Rootes Service Station at Ladbroke Hall, in North Kensington, for safety. The manager there, on learning that the car was going to be put on display, unfortunately had it washed and polished, so the following morning I had to have it taken to Surrey and driven for several hours across a neighbour's farm and down muddy lanes until it again looked the part. It didn't seem to matter that when it did go on view later that day it was covered in good old Surrey mud, not the mud and muck collected during the drive across Europe to Monte Carlo.

After the winning Sunbeam had been on display for a few days, we allowed it to be driven by a few carefully chosen motoring writers whom we knew would not damage it, before it was shipped to Norway for the celebrations there. One of them was John Bolster, who was a colleague of Gregor Grant's on *Autosport* magazine and was also a successful racing driver. He later became a well-known television personality with his deerstalker hat and long handlebar moustache, and his easily recognizable voice was a feature of many pit commentaries and interviews during Grand Prix motor races. He nearly lost the car, however, when he left it in Hyde Park while he went to quench his quite substantial thirst in the nearby Steering Wheel Club in Brick Street. When he returned he found two rather determined policemen making arrangements to have it towed away. The Sunbeam still had its Norwegian number plates and a Norwegian flag flying from the radio mast, and this, together with some quick thinking, enabled John Bolster to save the situation. He remembered the lines of a Norwegian drinking song he had learned in

Monte Carlo, and repeated them over and over again to the two baffled London bobbies, until in the end they gave up and wandered away, muttering, 'Bloody foreigners, they are everywhere nowadays!'

Apart from the publicity Rootes got from the outright win, 1955 was the first time in the history of the Monte Carlo Rally that the two principal awards—the Prince Rainier Cup and the Coupe des Dames—were won outright by the same make of car. In addition to winning the Prince Rainier Cup as outright winners of the rally, Per Malling and Gunnar Fadum won the Viking Cup, for the highest-placed competitors starting from Oslo, the Norwegian Cup and the Unlimited Class award for cars of over 2,000 cc. Europe's champion woman driver, Sheila Van Damm, with her co-drivers Anne Hall and Françoise Clarke, won the Coupe des Dames for the top women's team—the first occasion that the prize had gone to Britain for 23 years. They also won the L'Officiel de la Couture Challenge Cup, and the L'Equipe Challenge Cup, awarded to the manufacturer whose three cars obtained the best results in the rally, went to Sunbeam as well. To cap it all, the Sunbeam works team, which had won the Charles Faroux team prize for the previous two years, was placed third that year.

Norman Garrad was always meticulous in planning every event, leaving nothing to chance. The cars were all carefully prepared, the rules and regulations were studied for any flaws, the route was reconnoitred and copious notes made of any potential problems and places where back-up vehicles and mechanics might be needed. His choice of drivers was always excellent, both for their ability and publicity potential, and he was the first competitions manager to persuade Britain's top racing drivers to be members of a company team and compete in international rallies on a regular basis. They did so, not only because of the cars and the way in which they were always prepared, but also because of Norman Garrad's true professionalism and knowledge of their requirements as a racing and rally driver himself.

Stirling Moss, Mike Hawthorn, Peter Collins, Tommy Sopwith, Les Leston, Peter Jopp, Leslie Johnson, Jack Fairman, Ken Wharton and Ivor Bueb all drove for him, along with Peter Harper, George Hartwell, Paddy Hopkirk, I. D. Lewis, John Waddington, Peter Bolton, W. R. 'Chips' Chipperton and Peter Elbra. His team of women drivers was second to none, led by the bouncy Sheila Van Damm, who was European champion on several occasions and whose father owned London's Windmill Theatre, famous for its nudes and the opportunities many famous comedians such as Tommy Trinder and Jimmy Edwards were given there. She had served in the Women's Royal Air Force during the war and was a qualified pilot. So was Mary Handley Page, another regular member of the works team and the daughter of Sir Frederick Handley Page of aircraft fame. Anne Hall, a Yorkshire housewife, was Sheila Van Damm's courageous co-driver when she won the Women's European Championship. Another Yorkshire housewife in the team was Yvonne Jackson, who started driving in rallies when she got fed up with navigating for her husband and swiftly won a reputation as a gifted driver. There were many others over the years, but these were some of the drivers who helped to make Sunbeam a name to conjure with in the post-war racing and rally world.

Norman Garrad's team of regular drivers could always be relied upon to lend their support to any sales drive or marketing initiative. Some even went further. Racing driver Peter Collins got almost as much pleasure out of driving a large truck as he did from being behind the wheel of a racing car. He frequently 'test drove' one of our new Commer trucks for a special feature in newspapers and magazines, bringing much wider publicity to the product than normal. It was usually only the commercial vehicle press which gave much space to truck announcements.

Just before his death, Rootes had arranged for him to open his own new truck dealership near his home in Worcestershire. He was retiring from Grand Prix motor racing and he and his lovely wife Louise, the American actress, wanted to settle down and build a new house near Kidderminster, which would be quite near to their new truck dealership. Peter and I had been at Bromsgrove School together and were good friends. My wife and I were spending some time on their yacht at Dartmouth when the call came through from Enzo Ferrari, pleading with him to do just one more race for their Grand Prix team. Louise had appealed to Peter not to go to Germany and to finish with racing altogether, but he insisted that he couldn't let 'Le Patron' down and would drive for Ferrari one more time even though he had already announced his retirement. We waved goodbye as he went ashore in his launch and that was the last Louise or we saw of him, as he was tragically killed at Nurburgring a few days later, in what would certainly have been his final Grand Prix. He left behind on the yacht the designs and plans for his new Rootes dealership which we had all been looking at and discussing before that fatal telephone call.

Apart from the calibre of the drivers, the reliability of the Sunbeam as a rally car was also quite remarkable. In 1954 Sheila Van Damm's car covered more than 8,500 miles when she took part in the Monte Carlo, Dutch Tulip, Lisbon, British RAC and Austrian Alpine rallies, winning major awards in each of them.

During the 1950s and '60s, rallies like the Monte Carlo received a tremendous amount of media coverage before and during the event. Every national morning and evening newspaper sent their motoring writers to cover the rally and so did the major provincial newspapers. Many of the journalists competed, using the rallies as a good test for new models as well as providing their papers with daily news reports. Those who were regular competitors included Basil Cardew of the *Daily Express*, one of the most outstanding motoring writers of the day. He covered every major motoring event over a period of some 40 years, including those early record-breaking attempts on Daytona Beach in the 1920s and '30s, and when he retired, his place was taken by David Benson, who had worked with him for many years. Basil Cardew's opposite number on the *Daily Mail* then was Courtenay Edwards, who was equally talented and was later succeeded by Michael Kemp. Tommy Wisdom, whose wife 'Bill' was also a well-known racing driver, combined racing with writing for the *Daily Herald*, and Harold Nockolds of *The Times* was the brother of Roy Nockolds, the well-known cartoonist. Dudley Noble went back to writing for *The Observer*, making full use of his wide motor industry experience. W. A. 'Bill' McKenzie and later John Langley of the *Daily Telegraph*, along with Charles Fothergill of the *News Chronicle* and Peter Cartwright and Sidney Henschel of the *Financial Times*, were others who gave good coverage to motoring. The former Brooklands racing driver Kay Petre also wrote regularly for the *Daily Sketch*.

Pat Mennem's coverage of motoring for the *Coventry Evening Telegraph* led to a lengthy period with the *Daily Mirror*, and Jack Hay of the *Birmingham Post*, Geoffrey Hancock of the *Birmingham Evening Mail*, Clive Birtwistle of the *Westminster Press* Group, Ross Giles of the *Wolverhampton Express and Star*, and Jack Jellen of *The Scotsman* were others whose papers wanted regular rally coverage. Even *The Sporting Life* covered important motoring events in those days and sent J. N. Bennett on reporting assignments to places like Monte Carlo.

The three London evening papers all had motoring correspondents who competed fiercely for information and early results. Robert Walling of the *Evening Standard* and Bill Paulson of the *Evening News* were mere youngsters compared with the *Star's* remarkable Laurie Cade, the doyen of them all who knew the Rootes brothers from their days in Maidstone.

The motoring magazines were also well represented by Christopher Jennings of *The Motor*, Maurice Smith of *Autocar*, Gregor Grant of *Autosport*, Bill Boddy of *Motor Sport* and Frank Page and Tony Salmon of the *Garage and Motor Agent*. Sammy Davis, who won fame with the Bentley team at Le Mans, Gordon Wilkins (who was also successful at Le Mans) and his wife Joyce, Douglas Armstrong, previously editor of *Motor Racing*, Eric Dymock, now with the *Sunday Times*, Lord Strathcarron, Frank Page, now with the *Mail on Sunday*, and Sue Baker of *The Observer* were leading motoring writers whose services were in great demand.

Thanks to Paul Fox (now Sir Paul, but then editor of the very popular BBC 'Sportsview' programme), Peter Dimmock, who became Head of BBC Outside Broadcasts, and Raymond Baxter, rallies like the Monte Carlo also got tremendous media coverage. Peter Dimmock and Ronnie Noble were always popular competitors with their BBC 'Sportsview' entry, and so was Raymond Baxter, the ex-Spitfire pilot who sometimes competed as a member of the Sunbeam team or in a spare works car.

We frequently lent the BBC a car for Peter Dimmock and his crew, but because of the amount of equipment they had to carry it was usually one of the large Humbers, and I had great admiration for Peter's professionalism and enthusiasm. Getting to Monte Carlo without mishap was a big enough challenge, but having to do so in a car that was not ideal for the job and at the same time take film of the rally and meet daily transmission schedules, required considerable skill and determination. Even so, they always reached Monte Carlo in time to ensure excellent television coverage and then join in the fun.

Foreign currency was severely rationed in those days but Ivor Bueb's Le Mans successes had left him with large quantities of francs which he was unable to take out of France. When he was in the Rootes team we never had any foreign currency worries and although the head barman at the Metropole Hotel in Monte Carlo was usually good for some extra francs, I managed to do a much better deal with Ivor. He settled all our bills in Monte Carlo and I gave him a cheque to cover the amount when we arrived back in England, so we were both happy.

Whenever the Rootes cars did well, Brian Rootes flew out to help us celebrate and the extra francs came in very handy, enabling us to enter-tain the British and foreign journalists who were finding the currency restrictions very difficult. Fortunately, our cars and drivers usually won enough pots to justify at least a mild celebration.

The casino was always a popular place to relax and everyone seemed to find enough francs to play the tables. Frank Grounds was a popular Ford driver who had realized a small fortune when his Birmingham transport business was nationalized. His lovely Spanish wife Lola was driving for us and, as Frank was unable to enter one year, he decided to have some fun at the tables before she arrived. After doing the usual deal with the head barman at the Metropole, he had enough francs to try his luck at one of the baccarat tables.

When I arrived at the casino his piles of chips were disappearing fast. 'Can you lend me some money, John?' he asked, running his last remaining chips through his fingers. 'This doesn't seem to be my evening! I've been trying to get to know that bird next door but she keeps giving me the cold shoulder and seems more interested in that dark-skinned bloke over there, the one with the flunkey standing behind him who keeps passing him more chips.'

'Come and have a drink, Frank. It's not going to be your night, either,' I replied. 'The bird is Rita Hayworth and the dark-skinned bloke is Aly Khan. I don't think that even the British Government paid you enough money to take him on!'

One year, a team of army officers took part in the event. They reached Monte Carlo and the three of them were the life and soul of every party. On the stroke of midnight on their last night their leader, Major Donald McCleod, slow-marched through the casino salon, immaculate in full dress uniform complete with kilt and bagpipes and playing 'Scotland the Brave'. Play stopped at all the tables and the Brits stood and clapped until the lone piper marched out of the room. As he left, he was handed his passport and told never to darken the casino's doors again. They were great times.

Stanley Schofield and his team made a film of every international rally. They managed to get some additional exciting coverage by accompanying the factory team during their pre-rally recce of the route. The drivers used spare cars fully kitted out with equipment and rally numbers so that they looked the same as the official rally cars, and during the recce there was plenty of time to take shots of the drivers taking corners at speed in the snow and ice in the mountains. Ronnie Clayton and his stills photographers also went along, so that we had some excellent photographs to give to the newspapers during the rally.

Wiring photographs was expensive and not very successful and so everyone was very pleased to have some good stills available. As most of the really exciting photographs were taken in mountain passes or way-out villages, there was little opportunity to wire photographs anyway. It was some time before other companies worked out how we got so many good photographs of Rootes cars published.

I always made sure that the BBC had copies of all our films, and they came in very handy on Saturday afternoons when the weather was bad and sporting events which going to be televised had to be cancelled. The wide television coverage we received then more than paid for the cost of the films and the additional copies we made. We were careful to make sure that the camera crews used in making the films were all accepted by the BBC unions, so that there were never any problems there. We did the same when John Mills of Formula One Films worked for us and some of the films he made are now classics. Many of the original Rootes films are now with the National Motor Museum at Beaulieu.

It wasn't only the races and rallies which got publicity and helped to promote the cars. The 1950s also produced a number of remarkable record-breaking performances and some outstanding journeys in ordinary family saloons which caught the imagination of the public.

The Sahara Desert was still a challenge to motorists, as it had been to Dudley Noble in 1933 when he towed a caravan behind a Humber from Algiers across the Sahara and back to establish the reliability of the new type of epicyclic gearbox which had been devised by Captain Edgar de Normanville. He was a clever engineer and former motoring writer who had impressed the Rootes brothers with his ideas. The de Normanville gearbox had a steering column lever working in a simple quadrant without a gate, and all the driver had to do was place the lever in whichever notch he wanted.

On this occasion Dudley Noble had with him Ernest Appleby of *Autocar*, a de Normanville mechanic and a young Arab youth, who attached himself to them at Bou-Saada oasis and insisted on acting as their interpreter and guide. The gearbox worked well but Humber later had to abandon it because of difficulties in manufacturing it efficiently. De Nomanville went on to design an overdrive unit which was used on Rootes cars for more than 30 years.

In 1952 it was George Hinchcliffe, a 43-year-old former bus conductor from Bradford, who took up the challenge of the desert, driving the 10,500 miles from London to Cape Town in a 10 hp Hillman Minx saloon in 21 days, 19 hours and 45 minutes. His companion was James Bulman, a 35-year-old ex-mechanic, and they broke the record set up by Ralph Sleigh and P. S. Jopling in 1949 with their Austin A70 by 2 days, 7 hours and 5 minutes. Hinchcliffe and Bulman crossed the Sahara, with its 2,399-mile stretch of sand, in 4 days, 23 hours and 50 minutes—the fastest crossing ever.

Billy Rootes was probably less impressed than he should have been because both men had beards. He disliked people who wore beards and never employed anybody with one. When my colleague Liam Hunter was forced to grow a beard after a car crash, having fallen asleep at the wheel on his way back from the Ryton-on-Dunsmore factory one evening after a particularly tiring week, Billy became very concerned that it might become a more permanent fixture on a young executive he liked and was very relieved when Liam was eventually able to shave it off.

On another occasion, when we were leaving Devonshire House together one evening, Billy noticed a tall man with a beard standing doing nothing while other people were busy getting the showroom ready for a new model announcement the following day. 'Tell Bill Elsey to get rid of him. He is obviously a slacker and not pulling his weight,' he told me as we reached the door. 'Go and do so now and I will wait for you.'

Bill Elsey winced when I told him. 'If I did that we would be in trouble,' he explained. 'the man with the beard he wants to get rid of is the managing director of the company which has designed all our special display units and he has only called in this evening to see that everything is alright.' When I gave Billy the news he just grunted, then said, 'In that case, tell Elsey to check his bill carefully.' What he would have done about the present craze for designer stubble is difficult to imagine!

Still wearing a beard, George Hinchcliffe set off again for Cape Town 10 months after setting the new record in his Hillman Minx. This time he was driving the company's latest Humber Super Snipe and had with him Robert Walshaw, a 38-year-old car salesman, and Charles Longman, a 39-year-old mechanic. The 4 litre Super Snipe established the fastest-ever time for the overland run from London to Cape Town, covering the journey across the desert, over mountains and through scrub and swampland in the amazing time of 13 days, 9 hours and 6 minutes, knocking 8 days, 10 hours and 39 minutes off Hinchcliffe's previous record with the Minx. On that occasion we provided Hinchcliffe and his crew with a cine camera which they used on their journey and we then made the results into an exciting film. This time all three men returned with beards. No doubt Billy was relieved to get the car back!

In May 1955 Geoff Aldridge, a 25-year-old New Zealander, and John Cameron, a 23-year-old Tasmanian, set out from London in their little Hillman Husky to drive the 9,000 miles over land to Calcutta. They travelled through France, Switzerland, Italy, Yugoslavia, Greece, Turkey, Syria, Lebanon, Jordan, Iraq, Iran, Afghanistan, Pakistan and into India in seven weeks, and the only mark on the car when they got there was a scratch on the rear wing which had happened in Trafalgar Square before they left London.

Australia's best-selling travel author, Fred Thwaites, also did a remarkable journey from London to his home in Australia in a Hillman Husky, accompanied by his fashion model wife and their 14-year-old son Gary. His book *Husky Be My Guide*, which told the story of their journey, turned out to be another bestseller. The most unbelievable part of the story to me, however, was his address in Australia, which he assured me was Bucking Bong, Bong Bong Hill, Bong Bong. With an address like that to remember, findings one's way across a few continents with a Husky must have seemed relatively simple.

Soon afterwards, ex-RAF flier, author and world traveller Richard Pape and his co-driver David Roat set up a new record for the treacherous 5,000-mile round trip from Vancouver to Fairbanks in Alaska and back in 4 days, 22 hours, driving a Hillman Minx saloon. According to Pape, 4,000 miles of the trip was over gravel roads, through floods and electrical storms and entailed numerous detours. He already held the record for the time taken to drive from the northern most tip of the European continent to the Cape of Good Hope in South Africa in another standard 1,390 cc Hillman Minx saloon.

Perhaps the most remarkable journey, however, was the 15,000-mile trip from Colombo to London done in 1955 by Annette Massey, an American nurse, in her three-year-old Hillman Minx coupé, after only a few hours' tuition in car maintenance. Her adventures and narrow escapes from death during her journey through India, Pakistan, Iran, Iraq, Jordan, Lebanon, Syria, Turkey, Greece, Yugoslavia, Italy, Switzerland and France were almost unbelievable.

They seemed even more so when she arrived out of the blue at Devonshire House, parked her battered old Hillman convertible outside in Piccadilly and came in to see whether I could arrange to have the car serviced before she took it back to America with her. I sent for a driver to take the car to our main service station at Ladbroke Hall while I took her off to lunch at the Caprice.

When we got back, the traffic in Piccadilly was being held up to allow the little Hillman to be loaded onto a car transporter. It appeared that the driver had only driven a few yards in the Minx before he had a close encounter with a bus and another with a taxi and decided that he was not going any further in a car that was devoid of any brakes, steered violently to the right even when the steering wheel was being turned to the left, and which had a badly slipping clutch. 'I knew the little Minx had a few problems, but after 15,000 miles I must have got used to them,' was all that Annette said when I told her that her car was completely unroadworthy.

Chapter 24

Some you win and some you lose

ALTHOUGH ROOTES'S ANNUAL profits were never high by modern standards, the future of the Group was never in any doubt while Billy Rootes was alive and the brothers' partnership remained intact. Indeed, during the 1950s there were a number of occasions when it was the brothers who were on the takeover trail. Not all their plans came to fruition, but some certainly did. During the early part of the 1950s Reggie Rootes's close friend Reggie Hanks was one of the senior directors at Morris Motors. Serious discussions took place about some form of co-operation between the two companies over a period of many months. It was eventually decided that Morris and Rootes should amalgamate, but this idea was dropped before details were agreed. This was before Austin and Morris got together to form the British Motor Corporation.

Discussions between Billy Rootes and Leonard Lord some time later were also unsuccessful, mainly due to the fact that both men had very strong personalities and neither was prepared to give ground to the other. In the end any idea of an amalgamation, or even any form of close co-operation, was dropped and nothing came of their talks. It is interesting to speculate about what would have happened if they had managed to agree and instead of Austin and Morris it had been Rootes and Morris or Rootes and Austin that had amalgamated, and on the effect that would have had on the British motor industry.

By the autumn of 1955, the Singer Motor Company was in desperate trouble. Since the war it had never regained the reputation and glory it had achieved in the days when Billy Rootes was an apprentice there. Quality and craftsmanship had been the ideals that had inspired George Singer when he started making bicycles at Coventry in 1876, and the success of his policy, and the reputation of his products at the time, can be judged by the fact that his customers included the Queen of Portugal, two princesses, two grand duchesses, two duchesses, a marchioness, 13 countesses and 31 other peeresses of varying rank. Singer motor cycles gained a similar reputation for quality, and the first Singer car produced in 1904 firmly established the company as a successful motor manufacturer. An attractive two-seater, it was offered for sale complete with pneumatic tyres, spare wheel and all-weather equipment. By 1909 four versions were available, ranging from a 7.9 hp twin-cylinder model to one of 24.8 hp. During 1911, soon after Billy Rootes joined the company, Singer cars achieved a remarkable series of record-breaking successes at Brooklands and elsewhere.

The Singer name had already become famous when in 1912 the firm introduced the revolutionary new Singer 10, which was the country's first real light car and brought motoring within reach of the masses with its low price of £195, easy maintenance, and petrol consumption of more than 40 mpg. It was the model which helped Billy Rootes to start on his own career in the motor industry and was the first really small horsepower model which was not in some way an adaptation of a motorcycle.

Singer designers had again brilliantly anticipated the trend of public taste and by 1914 the Singer 10 had taken up the bulk of the company's production capacity. Its popularity remained undiminished and it was not until 1922—10 years after its introduction—that the company dared to modernize it or make any radical changes. By then Singer designers were again looking ahead and anticipating demand for another cheap family car, and in 1923 the Singer 10 four-seater was introduced. Costing only £250, it was about half the price of other cars offering comparable accommodation.

Throughout the inter-war years the Singer designers and engineers maintained this tradition of technical progress. In 1934 Singer became the first British manufacturers to fit independent front suspension and to produce a car with a clutchless gear change. They also brought out the world's first streamlined car, the Singer Airstream, although this was never a real success.

The quality and performance of Singer cars were still being proved on the race tracks and in 1933 a Singer 9 was the first unsupercharged car under 1,000 cc to qualify for the Rudge Whitworth Biennial Cup at Le Mans. Its successes provided the name for one of the firm's most famous ranges—the Singer 9 and $1\frac{1}{2}$ litre Le Mans models. During 1934 and 1935 more than 1,000 Singer cars were entered for races and 75 per cent of them were successful. It is not surprising that the company was so confident about its cars that they were the only manufacturers in the world to guarantee all their models against cylinder bore wear.

After the war, the SM roadster and the SM 1500 saloon, which was later developed into the Singer Hunter, maintained the tradition of craftsmanship and quality, but economic conditions in post-war Britain were unfavourable to smaller manufacturers, however good their products, and singer was one of those companies unable to achieve its export quota.

On 29 December 1955, Singer shareholders decided to accept an offer to become part of the Rootes Group, with the assurance that the Singer name and reputation would be kept alive, and at 9 a.m. the following morning Rootes and Singer executives met. Within three hours they handed their designers the brief for a new 80 mph (129 km/h) car which was to set new standards of luxury and quality in its price range. It was to be called the Singer Gazelle.

Billy Rootes took over as the new chairman and visited the Singer factories for the first time since his apprenticeship days. He promised the workforce: 'We plan to inject new life into the arteries of this old and distinguished company.' He was surprised to find that the lathe he had worked on as a young apprentice was still in use and immediately had it removed and placed in the Rootes museum.

The battle for control of Singer had been a tough one and not without a certain amount of intrigue. It took all the Rootes brothers' negotiating skills and Rupert Hammond's brilliant financial brain to hammer out a deal which eventually swung the decision their way, and sank the rival offers made by those representing the interests of the George Cohen 600 Group. For some weeks Julian Hodge, acting on behalf of a substantial body of stockholders, had been a thorn in their side, demanding more money for the shares and insisting that Rootes guaranteed the Preference Dividend for at least five years. Hodge was certainly a hard nut to crack and it was only after several late-night meetings at Devonshire House that he was eventually won over and gave his support to the Rootes offer.

On 15 December 1955 Billy Rootes invited the city editors to a press conference and told them:

'I must confess some degree of sentiment in our offer to buy Singer Motors, because I was there as an apprentice, raced motor cycles for the company, and then became its biggest distributor. I consequently know something about the Singer Company. It is clear from the statements issued by the company's Chairman and Managing Director, Mr A. E. Hunt, that unfortunately Singer can no longer continue unaided.

While in no way underestimating the task ahead we believe that we can, in association with the resources of our Group, revive the old company and let it see prosperous days again. In opposition to ourselves, however, is another interested party acting on behalf of an organization whose name has not been disclosed and who have not revealed their intentions in the event of their bid being successful. My main object of meeting you today is to make the Rootes position clear and to put our cards on the table. As you know, we have always been frank with the press and they have, through their motoring writers and city editors, always given us a fair hearing.

As matters stand I believe there is every prospect of our offer being accepted by the shareholders, but if the margin is insufficient, then a position of stalemate will arise. I consider the position of the company to be so critical that unless urgent action is taken, the process of

disintegration will be rapid. In these circumstances we have decided
to increase our offer substantially so as to ensure that a decision is
made on December 29th at the Annual General Meeting. Unless
there is, we will no longer be interested. I would be grateful if you
would make this quite clear to Singer shareholders'.

It was a masterly move which swayed the shareholders who could see
the company, and their own investment, disappearing unless something
was done quickly, and the Rootes offer was the only real option open to
them under the circumstances. If Rootes kept to their threat and pulled
out of the deal then they and the company would be in very serious
trouble.

The city editors, without exception, backed the Rootes offer, and
even though the Annual General Meeting and the subsequent meetings
of Preference and Ordinary Shareholders at the Extraordinary General
Meeting were lengthy, and at times vitriolic, Rootes eventually won the
day. A telephone call to Devonshire House late that afternoon told the
Rootes brothers that the Singer Motor Company was theirs and that
Billy was now the boss of the company that he had joined more than 44
years before as a young penny-an-hour apprentice.

The situation had developed into an involved public relations battle
which Rootes won through careful planning, and a series of skilful
financial calculations on the part of Rupert Hammond. When Rootes
won, the press had a field day writing about the penny-an-hour motor
apprentice who later 'bought the company'.

My own visits to the Singer factory were initially met with a mixture
of resentment and disdain, which I found disconcerting. People seemed
to be particularly interested in the health of my father, and the news
that he had died several years earlier seemed to have an almost cheering
effect. This surprised me, because he had never been involved with the
Singer Company or the motor industry.

When I mentioned this to Billy Rootes he solved the problem during
our next visit. He made it clear that I was no relation to William
Bullock, who had run the Singer Company before the war with a tyran-
nical rule which was still remembered with considerable ill feeling by
some of the older executives.

From then onwards I had everyone's full co-operation and there were
no further problems.

Singer was Rootes's second acquisition in 1955. Earlier in the year
they had purchased Hills Precision, a Coventry-based company which
specialized in zinc castings used in the production of door handles and
badges and other car accessories.

Both were shrewd purchases. The Singer deal was not just a matter of
sentiment. It was the large number of Singer dealers, many of them
strategically placed in areas where there was a high sales potential for
Rootes cars, that interested them most. By eventually amalgamating the

two sales forces, they would end up with a stronger and much more effective dealer network.

The Singer models themselves were outdated and there was little new in the pipeline, except a prototype steam car which was still in the early design stages. The six-storey Singer factory in Coventry Road, Birmingham, which had originally been built by BSA during the First World War for small arms manufacture, had what must have been the only vertical assembly line in the motor industry. The famous Singer Junior had been built there, but at the time of the Rootes takeover the SM1500 saloon and the Roadster were the only two models being made.

Production started on the fourth floor, body trim and paint were on the fifth and final assembly on the sixth. Cars sometimes had to be swung out of the building, turned round manually and then brought in again on the next floor for the assembly to continue. Little wonder that the rate of production was never much more than a steady trickle, and when production was eventually moved to Ryton-on-Dunsmore the old Singer factory was transformed into a modern spare parts depot for the whole Group.

Rootes's next attempt to enlarge their empire, however, was not so successful. When Sir John Black left the Standard Motor Company in 1956, Alick Dick, the managing director, had to consider the company's future very carefully because of several problems which had to be dealt with. Standard also owned Triumph, but the Standard–Triumph Company wasn't formed until 1960. One of the first telephone calls Alick Dick received was from Spen Wilks, the head of the Rover Company and John Black's brother-in-law through his marriage to one of the Hillman girls. Alick Dick's uncle, Major T. S. Dick, had also married into the Hillman family and he was under family pressure to give serious consideration to Spen Wilks' proposal that Standard and Rover should join forces.

According to Alick Dick, he wasn't very keen on the suggestion because he wanted to sell the Standard Company rather than become involved with Rover, due to the situation which had developed over the company's tractor interests after Massey Harris had bought Ferguson. Earlier in the year Massey Ferguson had purchased 25 per cent of Standard shares and was also a major customer. This had only led to more problems.

Alick Dick was a great admirer of Billy Rootes, who had given him a lot of support and advice while he was still a young executive making his way up the motor industry ladder. He had also picked up a number of useful ideas from watching the way in which Billy dealt with the press and tried to emulate him as much as possible. He noticed that whenever they both spoke at a motor industry function, it was always Billy's speech which got the most editorial coverage. Billy suggested that he should have typed copies of his speeches available to give to the press whenever he wanted good editorial coverage, even though by doing so he was giving the younger man advice which could reduce the amount of space available for his own speeches.

A trust built up between them, and Alick Dick told Billy Rootes about the situation with Spen Wilks. Billy liked the idea of becoming involved with Standard and Triumph, and the two of them discussed ways in which they could outmanoeuvre the two brothers-in-law. He remembered the ill feeling there had been when Rootes bought Hillman and the action taken by both Spen Wilks and John Black.

Rover was also in trouble at the time that Rootes bought Hillman, and a young accountant called George Farmer was brought in as receiver. Spen Wilks took over Rover and his brother-in-law John Black went to Standard, which was also in a mess. Their new model was being held up waiting for components from Fisher & Ludlow and the company was rapidly running out of cash. Major T. S. Dick, another former Hillman director, had left the company to take over Auto Machinery, a company making ball-bearings for the motor industry, and which was also eventually bought by Rootes.

The idea of again putting one over on Spen Wilks and John Black gave Billy's plans some additional appeal, quite apart from the business advantages which could result from a close association between Rootes, Standard and Triumph. At Alick Dick's suggestion he had discussions with Ed Taylor and Eric Phillips when he was next in Canada. Both were Canadian directors of Massey Harris and each owned 25 per cent of Argus Trust, which in turn owned 25 per cent of Massey Harris which owned 25 per cent of the Standard Motor Company. They wanted Massey Harris to buy Standard and then sell the car side of the business to Rootes, or Rootes to buy Standard and then sell the tractor business to them.

Lord Tedder had taken over from Sir John Black as chairman of Standard and Triumph. It was an unusual appointment for such a distinguished airman, but few people wanted to be chairman of Standard at the time. Billy Rootes had a house in Nassau and invited Lord Tedder and Alick Dick to come to the Bahamas so that they could discuss the possibility of a deal in comparative secrecy and under convivial conditions.

Before going to Nassau, Alick Dick asked for a further meeting with Billy Rootes and this took place in Billy's bedroom at the old Berkeley Hotel. He sat on the bed with his legs dangling over the side while they discussed the possibility of Lord Tedder becoming chairman of a joint company with Billy Rootes as president and Geoffrey Rootes and Alick Dick as joint managing directors. When they all met again in Nassau, however, Eric Phillips put forward a scheme which he said was acceptable to the Massey Harris board and would only need the acceptance of the Standard board if Rootes agreed as well. The suggestion was that a joint company should have Billy Rootes as president, Lord Tedder as chairman, Reggie Rootes as deputy chairman and Geoffrey Rootes, Brian Rootes, Timothy Rootes and Alick Dick as joint managing directors. Eric Phillips's father was the biggest General Motors distributor in

Canada and lived in Toronto. He had a great deal of influence in the motor industry there, as well as with Massey Harris.

Reggie Rootes's son Timothy had been strengthening his position in the Rootes Group and was Director of Sales and Service of the Rootes manufacturing companies, a director of Rootes Motors Limited, the parent company, and of Humber Limited, the senior manufacturing company and its subsidiary companies. He was also on the board of Rootes Limited, the Group's merchandizing division, and its subsidiary companies.

After the meeting with Eric Phillips at Billy's house in Nassau, when the new proposals were discussed, Lord Tedder and Alick Dick went out to dinner together to mull over the situation, but from then onwards everything seemed to go wrong and Lord Tedder became more and more disgruntled. They tried to get a table at the luxury hotel opposite the casino, but they were refused admittance because Lord Tedder was wearing an ordinary lounge suit with a plain tie and the house rules insisted that in the evening men should wear bow ties at dinner. It didn't seem to matter that many of the men already dining there were wearing coloured shoes and pink or yellow ties. The important thing was that they had bow ties, which conformed with the evening dress rules in Nassau at the time.

The next meeting was to be held on a large and luxurious yacht which the Argus Trust had chartered from the president of General Electric Company of America. There were so many celebrities on board, including David Brown of Aston Martin and Lagonda fame, that there was little opportunity for Lord Tedder and Alick Dick to have the quiet meeting they were hoping for with Billy Rootes and Eric Phillips, unless they were prepared to wait until the other guests had gone. After they had been on board for about 45 minutes, Lord Tedder decided that he didn't want to wait any longer and, turning to Alick Dick, said, 'Do you know, I don't think that anyone would miss us if we left.' They slipped away and set off to walk the two miles or so to the Governor General's office. During the walk they agreed that the real reason why Rootes and Massey Harris were keen on the proposals was because they intended splitting up the car and tractor business, and Tedder didn't want to see that happen. From then on the deal was doomed and Tedder did his best to prevent it from going ahead.

By the time they arrived at the Governor General's office, they were both covered in dust from the very dusty track and when they walked up the steps and rang the bell their appearance must have been rather a shock to the Governor General's staff. As the Governor General was not there, Lord Tedder told his assistant, 'I want to telephone Ike.' Alick Dick had to convince the rather mystified young man that the Englishman in the crumpled suit and covered in dust really was Lord Tedder and a friend of General Eisenhower.

After a brief telephone conversation, Eisenhower agreed to send his personal aircraft to collect Lord Tedder and take him to Washington, while Alick Dick returned to London on a scheduled flight. On his way home Lord Tedder stopped off in New York and lost the pen he had used to sign the peace treaty on behalf of General Eisenhower. That was the final mishap during an abortive trip.

Although the deal between Standard and Rootes didn't materialize, Alick Dick later sold the tractor plant for cash to Massey Harris and Standard went to Henry Spurrier. He told me later that Henry Spurrier paid about four times as much as the company was really worth and that that was the real reason why he (Alick Dick) was forced to leave Standard about a year later.

Billy Rootes continued to help Alick Dick with his career and played a leading part in his election as president of the Society of Motor Manufacturers and Traders. There was no doubt that Billy still liked to encourage young executives, particularly when he felt that they had the necessary talent and ability to succeed. He remembered the time when he and his brother had been the young men of the motor industry and had had to overcome the attitudes and prejudice of those who looked upon them as young upstarts.

Chapter 25

Anniversaries, successes and adversities

THE REMARKABLE HILLMAN Minx came of age in 1952. It was 21 years since the first model had been unveiled at the Paris Salon de L'Automobile at the Grand Palais on the Champs Elysées in October 1931, to a blaze of publicity, as the first family car to be produced by the Rootes brothers since they had branched out as motor manufacturers, and the papers had been full of stories about the part which Billy had played in its testing. They had made great play then of his decision that the roads of the British Isles were not a tough enough test for a model aimed at the export markets. Most had published his own account of the weeks he and George Vallet had spent driving the Minx prototype 'over the paves of Belgium, the long straight roads of France, the twisting mountain tracks of Switzerland and Italy, and across the rocks and sand in the intense heat of the deserts of North Africa and the Near East, sometimes for days and nights on end'. Billy's prophecy then that the Minx would be a world-beater had proved correct and during the intervening years many thousands had been sold in 119 different countries. It was estimated that Minx owners had done more than 21 billion miles of motoring during those 21 years, and the model was still as popular as ever.

There was certainly no shortage of owners willing to verify that fact, and some of the early models were still giving good service in many parts of the world. A Mr L. R. Pearce wrote from New South Wales, to say that he had just used his 20-year-old Minx for a trip from Wagga Wagga along the Murray Valley to South Australia and back through central Victoria. The car had covered 2,024 miles, including about 400 miles of rough roads, and for two days they had travelled in temperatures of 112°F through sections of almost barren country, followed by steep winding roads through the Adelaide hills. The letter ended: 'I had no trouble of any kind and could not resist writing to let you know my appreciation for a really great little car.'

There was so much praise for the Minx that everyone got quite carried away. Basil Butler, the Rootes advertising agents, suggested that the anniversary should be looked upon as an achievement of national and international importance and put forward proposals under the heading 'Chorus of Praise' which included a rally to enable Hillman Minx owners from Britain and every country in the world to get together and publicly profess their faith in the car. 'Other people's praise appears genuine, generous and spontaneous', they emphasized, and there would be a real 'Chorus of Praise' for the Minx. They also proposed a '21 Club' for Hillman owners.

Delays in the production of the company's new 'Anniversary' model meant that many of the more ambitious plans had to be dropped, and the coming-of-age party was postponed until February 1953, when the new 1953 Anniversary Minx models were ready. A celebration party was held at Devonshire House, where all the new models were on display, and Billy Rootes was able to draw attention to the fact that more than 100 of the 250 people who had been employed in producing the first Minx in 1931 were still with the company.

It would have been evident to anyone who accompanied him on a walk through any of the Rootes factories that Billy still knew many of the older workers by name. He would frequently stop for a chat and to enquire after members of their family, or how a son or daughter was doing at school or university. He made them feel that they were important members of what he referred to as 'the Rootes team', and they were a steadying influence on the occasions when some of their younger colleagues were inclined to urge unofficial industrial action over some dispute with the management.

The friendly relationship between Billy and those employees always seemed very genuine, and there were many instances when he and his brother went out of their way to provide help when they heard that there were domestic problems. There was certainly a different atmosphere in the plants after his death. Perhaps that was the reason for many of the later union problems.

Although the Anniversary Minx was very similar mechanically to the model first announced in 1948, there were a number of styling changes, and the new cars were easily distinguished by their different front ends and their wide-mouth chromium grilles. Later versions also had a longer tail and a larger boot. Rootes announced the Minx Californian in 1953, which was a very attractive hard-top version of the convertible. The agreement with Raymond Loewy Associates to act as design consultants for the Rootes Group was renewed in March 1953, with a view to them providing a regular interchange of American ideas and design trends with the company's own design team in Coventry.

The brand-new overhead-valve, 1,390 cc engine introduced in October 1954 proved to be a remarkably versatile power unit. During the next 30 years it was improved or enlarged for use in a variety of new Hillman models, and even provided the basis of the power unit for the

Sunbeam Rapier when it was announced in 1955, as well as many other Sunbeam models, including the high-performance H120 in the late 1960s. The Hillman Husky, which was launched in 1954 with the old side-valve, 1,265 cc engine, used a shortened underframe of the Hillman-Minx estate car, and was a sturdy little load-carrier. In van form it was best known as the Commer Cob.

Rootes produced at least one genuine new model a year between 1952 and 1964, with probably the most outstanding being the Sunbeam Rapier, the Sunbeam Alpine, the Sunbeam Tiger, the Hillman Super Minx, the Humber Sceptre and, of course, the Imp. The Singer Gazelle and Singer Vogue provided Singer dealers with two competitive models in 1956 and 1961, but there was nothing particularly outstanding about them, because they were basically variations on existing Hillman and Humber models.

The Sunbeam Rapier had the unenviable task of having to take the place of the much-loved Sunbeam 90, which had given Rootes so many rally successes and was eventually discontinued in 1957. The Rapier started life in 1955 as a two-door, four-seater sports saloon which bore some resemblance to the Hillman Minx Californian, but with much more performance and panache. The first models used a modified over-head-valve Minx engine fitted with a downdraught Stromberg carburettor and a modified Humber Hawk gearbox and overdrive unit. It was soon realized that the car was not fast enough to be called a true Sunbeam and be an adequate successor to the Sunbeam 90 and the Mark III, and so from 1956 it was given the R67-type engine, which used twin Zenith carburettors and produced an additional 4.5 bhp, boosting the acceleration and top speed of the Rapier considerably.

The Sunbeam Rapier was a closely guarded secret prior to the launch, until someone on the staff of Silver City Airways took photographs of the prototype and sent them to the editors of every national newspaper in Fleet Street some three months before the announcement date. There was a company rule that a prototype going abroad for testing should not be accompanied by another car manufactured by Rootes, because that would reveal that the car under test was a new Rootes model. There were usually plenty of other makes of car in the engineering department which could be used for this purpose because, like every other manufacturer, Rootes bought other people's models to test and to see how they compared.

Two Rootes engineers set off for France one weekend to do some performance testing on a prototype Rapier, but because there wasn't any other car available that day, they took a Hillman Minx estate with them which contained their testing equipment and spares. When they arrived at Lydd Airport to board a Bristol freighter to cross the Channel, they had to hand the keys of the Rapier and the Hillman Minx estate over to the Silver City personnel responsible for the safe loading of the aircraft. It was while the Rootes engineers were in the airport building, having a cup of tea, that the photographs were taken by a bright young member of the Silver City ground staff, who was an amateur photographer and had a camera handy in his car. He thought that photographs of the mystery car would be a quick way of making some easy money and perhaps getting a job as a professional photographer.

His plan backfired on him, however, because when he captioned the photographs he referred to the car as a new Hillman Minx on its way to be tested secretly in France. He was misled by the fact that the support car was a Hillman, and assumed that they both must have been.

My telephone started ringing early on Monday morning as editor after editor wanted more information about the new Hillman, to publish with the photographs they had received from the Silver City opportunist. As far as they were concerned they had a scoop and our normally tight security measures had been breached. It was bad luck on Rootes but good luck for them. All's fair in love and news reporting, and this was the first occasion they had got hold of some good photographs of a new Rootes car before they were restricted by any official embargo date.

As soon as I saw the photographs I realized what had happened. My good luck was that nobody was expecting the replacement for the Sunbeam 90 to look like a Hillman and the car in the photographs was obviously too small to be a new Humber. As foul means had been used to get the photographs, I saw no reason why I shouldn't use a certain amount of guile myself. If the photographs were published, someone would no doubt recognize the car as being the new Sunbeam Rapier and the cat would be out of the bag. There were still three months to go before the Rapier was due to go into production and the cost to Rootes in lost Sunbeam sales in the meanwhile could have been considerable.

I pointed out to the editors that Rootes designers were always experimenting with different ideas and body shapes, many of which never got further than the prototype stage, and told them that the company was certainly not going to be launching a new Hillman that year. To emphasize the point, I told everyone that if the photographs they had in their possession proved to be of a new Hillman I would make sure that they each had a new Hillman Minx delivered to them free of charge.

When none of the photographs was published, I knew that the offer had worked and, apart from making sure that the engineers had a really good ticking-off when they got back to the factory, there was nothing more to do but hope that there would not be any more stupid clangers dropped before development work on the new Sunbeam Rapier was completed and it went into production.

The editors agreed that I had been quite truthful in insisting that they didn't have photographs of a new Hillman, although there were a few four-letter words used when they realized that they had been sitting on pictures of the new Sunbeam Rapier—an entirely new Rootes model—for nearly three months without being aware of the fact. I didn't have to give away any new Hillmans, although there were some rather expensive lunches. Billy thought the whole episode a great joke, but he made sure that there was stricter security for future models going abroad for testing.

The Sunbeam Rapier went on to be a great success and certainly upheld the Sunbeam tradition. Many of us mourned the demise of the popular Sunbeam 90, but production costs for that type of car were getting far too high, and there was no real option but to design models which could be mass-produced in much larger numbers and take advantage of the Group's rationalization policy. The situation was rather similar to the problems which the manufacturers of hand-built cars faced in the 1920s and '30s, when they were unable to cope with the lower-priced, mass-produced models on the market.

A factory-entered Sunbeam Rapier, driven by Sheila Van Damm and Peter Harper, won its class in the classic Italian Mille Miglia road race in 1957 at an average speed of more than 65 mph (105 km/h) for the 1,000 miles, with a privately entered Rapier in second place. The winning cars had been prepared in the Rootes Group's Competitions Department under the experienced eye of Norman Garrad, who had achieved considerably more power from the engine and made several other important modifications. These included 10-in diameter brakes with finned drums and wider linings, a remote control, floor-positioned gear lever, an oil cooler and 20-gal (76 litre) fuel tank with a duplicate fuel system, and a quick-action filler pipe on each side of the car. A Laycock de Normanville overdrive was also fitted and used in conjunction with a rear axle ratio of 4.7 : 1. There was an air scoop arrangement fitted beneath the car, to duct air directly onto the rear shock absorbers to ensure adequate cooling.

In 1957 it was decided to enter a team of four similar cars for the Alpine Rally. Afterwards, I managed to obtain one of them for my own use; the other three went to Stirling Moss, Peter Collins and Peter Garnier, the sports editor of *Autocar* magazine. I don't know what happened to them eventually, but I certainly had a lot of fun with mine until it was sold on to another Sunbeam enthusiast.

The problems our designers and engineers faced in trying to ensure that there was adequate security for the new models being tested abroad were brought home to me before the first Sunbeam Alpine two-seater sports car was launched in 1959. Bernard Winter suggested that I would learn much more about the car, and be able to write and talk about it more knowledgeably, if I was able to drive it on the Continent. My wife Jean and I were planning a holiday in Le Lavendou and the drive to the south of France seemed to provide an ideal opportunity. There were no distinguishing badges on the pre-production models and it was the first real two-seater sports car that Rootes had produced, so it seemed unlikely that anyone on the Continent would relate it to the company. We would also be well away from the prying eyes of the motoring press and it didn't seem that security would be a problem.

There was no doubt that Bernard Winter and his team were very enthusiastic about the car, and he arranged to have the one I was to test drive delivered to my home in Surrey on the evening before we were due to leave. We flew across the Channel with the car to Le Touquet and made our way to Rouen. The weather was fine and we had the hood down as we drove south. The centre of Rouen was unusually crowded and we were held up for some time at the traffic lights. While we wait-ed, three young men in their early 20s crossed the road and began admiring the car. One of them then said, 'I thought it was one of the new Sunbeam Alpines and I told my friends it was. Make the Frenchies sit up a bit, won't it?' It turned out that he worked at the old Armstrong Siddeley factory in Coventry where the Alpines were going to be assem-bled and painted.

Somewhat crestfallen that the car had already been recognized and we'd only been in France for an hour or so, we pressed on towards the coast. When we came to a long stretch of open road I put my foot down and was pleased to see how quickly the speedometer needle approached the magic 100 mph (161 km/h) mark. Suddenly there was a loud bang as one of the rear tyres went. I managed to slow down sufficiently to pull into a garage and filling station about half a mile down the road. By that time the tyre was too hot to handle and I decided to let the garage mechanics change the wheel and fill the car up with petrol while Jean and I had a welcome aperitif in the café and bar alongside. The garage proprietor came across to join us and started asking all sorts of questions about the car, its make, horsepower and performance, but I told him quite truthfully that it wasn't a production model, just one that had been lent to me for a few days, and I didn't know any of the technical details.

As he turned to go, he asked if they could checked the oil but, as I presumed that it had been checked before the car left the factory, I told him not to bother as we wanted to get away as quickly as possible. When I went to pay the bill he handed me his card and, to my horror, written on it were the words 'Correspondent pour L'Auto Journal', the French motoring magazine notorious for publishing details of new cars before they had been launched. Had I agreed to the oil being checked, he would have seen the name 'Sunbeam' written in large letters on the top of the engine. It was the second time that day that we'd had security problems and I couldn't wait to get to Le Lavendou, which in those days was just a small village with few tourists and no inquisitive garage pro-prietors.

When we reached the coast I stopped to get a newspaper, and on my return to the car was surprised to see that, despite our decision not to talk to anyone, Jean was deep in conversation with a tall young man wearing an English-type raincoat. As I opened the car door he held out his hand and said, 'Hello, Mr Bullock. You probably don't remember me but I was a waiter at the Leofric Hotel in Coventry and when I saw you pull up in the new Sunbeam Alpine I thought I must come and speak to you and find out how the car is doing. When I lived in Coventry I used to see the Alpines going out on test.' Three times in two days couldn't be just coincidence. I began to wonder if Bernard Winter was getting his own back for the times I had complained about the lack of security shown by some of his engineers.

Although the Alpine was aimed at the North American market, where British sports cars like the MG, Triumph TR3 and Austin Healey were selling well, it sold well in Britain and in many other overseas markets. It was available in hard-top form and from 1962, when the contract with Bristol Siddeley Engines came to an end, the Alpine had its own assembly line at Ryton-on-Dunsmore. Armstrong Siddeley's parent company, Hawker Siddeley, had merged with the Bristol Aeroplane Company in 1959 and became known as Bristol Siddeley Engines.

The first Sunbeam car to bear the name Alpine, which appeared in 1953, was derived from the Sunbeam Talbot 90 in respect of its frontal features, bonnet and wings. It was, however, an open two-seater with a folding hood and a falling, flowing back which merged very well with the front end.

Sheila Van Damm drove a Sunbeam Alpine on the Jabbeke highway in Belgium at the sensational speed of 120.13 mph (193 km/h) in June 1954, setting up a new women's speed record for the $2\frac{1}{4}$ litre class over the flying kilometre. She then went on to the racing circuit at Montlhéry, near Paris, and lapped the track there at a speed of 114 mph (183 km/h).

In 1959 the Alpine bore no resemblance to the 1953 model which had been dropped in 1955, and the two-seater sports car we took to France made use of the Hillman Husky wheelbase and shared some parts of the Husky underframe. Although it was basically an open two-seater, there was room for one or two children behind the front seats. There was also the option of an all-metal hard-top. It had very pleasing lines, a swept-down bonnet with low cooling intake, and individual wings containing the headlamps. In its Series I form there was also a marked rise to the rear wing-tips.

Ken Howes was working for Ted White when the car was originally styled and was responsible for many of the design features which gave the Alpine its appeal. There was some criticism of the rising rear wing feature which led to a change to a more conventional horizontal line and form later, with the lamps common to some Hillman models.

The Alpine sports car was ultimately marketed with several specifications, including a GT version, and also as the Sunbeam Tiger with a 4.2 litre Ford V8 engine, to make it more attractive to the American market. This proved rather an embarrassment when Rootes became involved with Chrysler in 1964, but there wasn't a suitable Chrysler power unit available.

Rosemary Smith, the Irish driver, went to America in 1966 and, with Smokey Drolet as her co-driver, won the ladies' award with a Sunbeam

Alpine in the Daytona 24-hour race, a performance which gave a considerable boost for the car in the dollar markets.

When it was decided to fit the Sunbeam Rapier with fuel injection, the experimental car did many thousands of miles on the Continent. As there was nothing externally to indicate that the car was any different from any standard model, the test engineers no doubt felt they were safe. They were, until two of them stopped one evening in a small town in Holland and decided to have dinner and spend the night at a local hotel. Because the hotel didn't have any undercover garage accommodation, they parked the car at a nearby garage, but left it open so that it could be pushed out of the way in the morning if it was found to be blocking the entrance for other customers.

They didn't know, however, that the owner of the garage was having dinner at the same hotel and overheard them talking in the bar. While the two Rootes engineers were asleep, he pushed the Sunbeam out of the garage, wired up the ignition and did several test runs on a fast stretch of road outside the town, noting all the performance figures and taking photographs of the engine layout. When he had finished he turned back the speedometer and put the Sunbeam back in the garage.

We were none the wiser until a few weeks later, when Holland's leading motoring magazine published a full set of photographs and performance figures of the 'hush hush' Rootes fuel injection Sunbeam. I felt sorry for the engineers, but there was nothing we could do about it, and taking the garage proprietor to court would only have made matters worse.

Although the full-width Humber Hawk had been launched in 1948, it was not until 1952 that the long-awaited new Humber Super Snipe appeared, which was much larger and had the latest overhead-valve, straight six-cylinder engine that had already been used in some of the Commer commercial vehicles. It was a very powerful 4,139 cc power unit which gave the car an excellent performance to go with its undoubted luxury and comfort. In the years that followed, there were a number of new Hawk and Super Snipe models, but the Hawk relied on the very reliable and less thirsty four-cylinder 2,267 cc engine throughout its long and successful life. There were estate car versions of both models.

By the start of 1961 the Rootes management was in a quandary. They knew that the company badly needed a new range of cars, but money was very short and expensive strikes had left little opportunity for the development programme to be maintained. They were planning a Hillman Super Minx, Singer Vogue and Humber Sceptre series and at the last minute decided to create the new models by making major face-lifts to the original Audax model, which had been the basis for the Hillman Minx-based range of the 1950s.

According to Ted White, the chief Rootes stylist at the time, this range of models was the least satisfying of his career and much better results would have been achieved if the management had agreed to completely new designs from the outset. As it turned out, they started with the mock-up of the original Minx and tried to create a new style with major facelifts, but as time went on they were forced to change every section of the mock-up until a completely new car emerged, despite the original intention.

The roof of the Hillman Super Minx was modified several times during the styling period and the car was reviewed by Billy and members of the family with several roof forms, and as both a four-light and six-light car. Finally, a rounded roof and four-light formula was adopted. By the time the Super Minx design had been finalized, the car was much larger and more expensive than intended, and so Billy decided to retain the existing Minx model as well.

The original intention was for the Hillman Super Minx, Singer Vogue and Humber Sceptre all to have four headlamp systems, with the lamps dictating the width of the front wing form which was beginning to look very heavy. Rather late in the styling programme a decision was taken to specify two 7-in headlamps on the Super Minx, which meant styling a new bonnet and wings. In order to give an individual, wider look, the headlamps were lowered into the radiator grille area, but as the wing line in elevation had to be retained, small 'half moon' parking and turn single lights were mounted above the headlamps which, although the subject of some criticism, were at least original.

Due to the pressures being placed on the styling department by the constant changes, the Singer Vogue front received some attention from an outside consultant in addition to the Rootes staff, and the final result can only be described as very disappointing. It did, however, give the Singer dealers a much-needed additional model to go with the new Singer Gazelle which, like the Super Minx, had a 1,592 cc engine, whereas the Vogue and the Humber Sceptre had larger, 1,725 cc power units.

The stylists were at least given greater scope with the Humber Sceptre, and the rear seats were lowered, allowing a new, more sporting roof line. A new rear wing treatment was also adopted. The front end sported a vertical grille and four headlamps, and was probably the most distinctive of the three makes. Whereas the Super Minx and Vogue had horizontal facia treatments, being walnut-veneered, the Sceptre had a completely new facia and instrument panel with centre console, which gave an individual cockpit feeling that turned out to be a major selling feature on this model.

During the lifetime of this range of cars the squarer 'box form' style became generally fashionable and the Super Minx and Vogue were restyled with squared-up roofs. The Sceptre, however, was maintained in its original form with its individual falling roof line.

The series II, III and IV Hillman Minx saloons were given detailed face-lifts, with each series having a new radiator grille, rear wing and interior changes, but in 1963 the Minx V was given a major change. Starting at the front, there was a new bonnet sloping down to the front, a new, wider radiator grille, and new signalling and parking lights. The new squared-up look involved new rear doors, added to which were the new rear wings and tail-lamps. The overall effect was to give the car a completely new look and the rise in sales confirmed the success of the new design.

Car manufacturers always used to compete with each other to find the most attractive or exotic place to hold their new car launches, which usually took place a week or so before the official announcement date. As everything was embargoed until the day of the announcement, the motoring journalists were able to test the new model thoroughly and discuss it with the technical staff at their leisure, and still have plenty of time to write their reports. We usually favoured the south of France, where the weather was very good and there was always a mixture of mountain roads, fast stretches and town driving to enable everyone to get a fair impression of the cars. There were also plenty of good hotels and usually a casino. Everyone was, of course, given the opportunity of a longer road test later, after the car had been announced. It was always money well spent as far as we were concerned, because the exotic atmosphere did wonders for everyone's good spirits and driving along the Mediterranean coast was far more pleasant than enduring the rainy, blustery conditions likely to be found in Britain, even in the summer months, and we all looked forward to getting away to the sun for a while.

There was one occasion when we had a new Sunbeam to announce and all the papers had special features on the new model ready for publication the morning after our usual press reception at Devonshire House. I had taken some of the motoring writers off to lunch at the Wellington Club in Knightsbridge and we were part-way through the meal when Basil Cardew of the *Daily Express* left the table to take a call which had been transferred from my office.

He came back ashen-faced. 'I don't think you will be getting much publicity for the car tomorrow, John,' he said as he sat down. 'The news desk has just told me that there has been a serious plane crash at Munich and nearly all the Manchester United football players have been killed. All the news and feature pages are being redone to carry details of the crash and the team.' It was a terrible disaster for the country, the club and everyone else involved, and we no longer felt like celebrating what we hoped had been the successful launch of a new model. As far as the company was concerned, I was certainly relieved when all the papers carried features on the new car a day later. They knew how much the publicity meant to us and in those days their readers were genuinely interested in getting details of new models.

The Suez crisis in 1956 also wrecked our new model launch plans, but on that occasion it was the new Hillman Minx that suffered. With severe petrol rationing, all road tests had to be cancelled, and there was little enthusiasm for writing or reading about new cars at such an austere time. Our photographer, Ronnie Clayton, and I were having a drink at the Ritz one evening, regretting the fact that much of our efforts had been wasted, when we hit on an idea which we thought would at least cheer up some of our motoring friends, including the motoring writers, who were feeling very down in the dumps with little cheerful to write about.

We decided that instead of having literature containing photographs of the new Minx car we would produce a sales brochure unveiling a different, but more exciting, type of Minx. A visit to one of the top model agencies provided us with a very beautiful young model who was prepared to enter into the spirit of our plans, and we photographed her illustrating all the salient points of the new car, such as independent front suspension, stylish rear, and the ability to turn on a sixpence and park neatly. We took the usual sales brochure format and as far as possible used the same wording. In the studio we even managed to place a white dust sheet over our Minx in such a way that we produced an outline that looked like the side view of a car, and we made this our cover picture.

The result was quite stunning and I'm glad to say that it also led to a lot of extra work for our delightful young model. Everything was done, in the words of Kenny Everett, 'in the best possible taste', and there was nothing in the brochure which could have caused offence to anyone, or damaged the company's reputation. Even so, I thought it best to restrict the internal distribution to Brian Rootes and a few close colleagues who I knew would appreciate its subtlety. He had an extra large version which he kept in his desk and showed to dealers who were complaining that there was little to be cheerful about in austere Britain.

Our press friends thought it a great laugh, appreciating the joke and our efforts to make some joy out of what was a rather miserable situation for us all. We only printed a few dozen copies to begin with, but were soon inundated with requests for more. One Yorkshire dealer said that he had been promised an order for 50 new Hillmans by one of his largest fleet customers if I would let him have a dozen copies. I'd never been so popular.

My secretary also thought it a huge joke and had a great time dealing with enquiries from people who didn't know how to ask for the Minx model version instead of the usual new model Minx brochure. She always pretended that she didn't know what they were talking about, unless they were close friends. She had a number of Members of Parliament and several members of the House of Lords on the telephone, who insisted that they had been Rootes customers for many years and wanted one of the company's special new brochures. If Billy and Reggie got to hear about our special sales literature they never mentioned it, but I have a feeling that the Minx model brochure probably sold more of the new Hillman Minx cars than the standard brochure ever did, and kept customers' goodwill—except perhaps in the case of those who couldn't get a copy.

Nearly every morning, evening and Sunday newspaper used to publish road tests on new cars within a few months of their announcement, and we had a fleet of road test vehicles controlled by our technical press manager, John Rowe, who was well qualified to deal with the technical details of each model, and did a remarkably good job of making sure that everyone had their fair allocation of new Rootes products to test drive. The cars were kept at Ladbroke Hall, our main London service station, in the charge of Cyril Bowness, who ensured that they were all kept in perfect order.

Some of the motoring writers, like Robert Glenton of the *Sunday Express*, made a special feature of the road tests each week and developed a style of writing which gained them a considerable following. Robert was, I think, the first journalist to try and make car tests more interesting to the average man or woman in the street, and he succeeded well.

Autocar and *The Motor* magazines were then in keen competition with each other, and to ensure that there wasn't any favouritism, we arranged for them to take it in turns to be the first to road test a new model. If we were announcing a saloon and a convertible at the same time, they usually tossed a coin to decide which one they each had. Both magazines went to great lengths to ensure that their road tests were very thorough and we relied on the performance figures they achieved for use in our sales literature. Because the figures were achieved independently of the factory, the public were more inclined to accept them as being fair and honest. Their fifth-wheel equipment was more accurate than any of the facilities other journalists had at their disposal, and so the *Autocar* and *Motor* figures were widely quoted in newspapers as well.

We did run into a few problems occasionally. When we were introducing a new Hillman Minx we arranged for *Autocar* to have the saloon and *The Motor* to have the convertible. Both magazines had the cars about six weeks before the official announcement, to give them time to do all their testing and obtain their findings and performance figures. They observed strict security measures while the cars were in their possession, so that neither photographs nor information were ever published before the official launch date, and because of this we never had any problem in releasing cars to them early.

The new Motor Industry Research testing ground had just been opened in the Midlands and *The Motor* decided to take the Hillman convertible there for some of the testing and make use of the excellent new facilities. Unfortunately, one of their test drivers mistook the very deep water test used for tanks as the water splash used to check the underbody sealer on cars. The tank test was several feet deep, but the water splash was only a few inches. He approached the tank test at speed, expecting to drive through and come out safely the other side, but the inevitable happened. The Minx sank to the bottom and the driver was lucky to escape injury, particularly as he couldn't swim and the water came over the top of the car.

I could hardly believe my ears when the editor, Christopher Jennings, telephoned to let me know what had happened. I could see the funny side, although the sight of a lovely new white convertible with all its red upholstery hanging off in a ghastly soggy mess when they returned the car to us was sad, to say the least. I had just got over the shock when Maurice Smith, the editor of *Autocar*, rang to tell me that one of their drivers had taken the saloon to Wales to test its roadholding in the mountains, and had misjudged his speed and the camber of the road on one particularly tight corner. The Hillman had left the road and ended up in the front garden of a cottage, straddling a wide stone wall. They were making arrangements to have it removed as quickly as possible, but some amateur photographers from the nearby village were already having a field-day and the old couple who owned the cottage were understandably concerned about getting in and out of their home.

These were the only two instances we had of damage to any of the scores of cars which *Autocar* and *The Motor* magazines had from us for road test, which says a great deal for the skill and care of their road test teams. Both magazines also bought different new models which were then driven by various members of their staff over a period of one or two years. They reported every few months on the cars' performance, servicing record, and the general impressions gained of their day-to-day performance. It was a very good idea, because they were able to write about each model from the point of view of an ordinary customer.

Autocar purchased a Hillman Husky soon after it was announced and were quite generous in their praise, except that there was an infuriating rattle which neither their local dealer nor our service station was able to cure. In the end I arranged to have the car returned to the factory and stripped down to try and get to the bottom of the trouble. When this was done, our mechanics found a milk bottle, still half full, inside the body of the car. The men in the spray booths used to drink a lot of milk each day, and one of them must have put his bottle down on a section of the body frame, and the body shell was put over the top and secured in place before he realized what had happened. The milk was very sour, but it was quite remarkable that the bottle was still intact, despite rattling around inside the car for so long.

Chapter 26

Little Jim and the Imp

THE ROOTES BROTHERS first started thinking about producing a small car before the start of the Second World War, and the project was given the code-name 'Little Jim'. Although various suggestions were put forward, the likelihood of war with Germany and the company's involvement in the shadow factory scheme meant that their plans had to be postponed. It was not until the late 1950s that positive action was taken and the Rootes Group decided to enter that highly competitive segment of the market.

Ted White and the Rootes styling team were not initially involved and the first designs were produced in a small development area of the engineering department. Everything was very 'hush hush' and those working on the project had been carefully selected to ensure the utmost secrecy. The mock-ups produced by this development team were of a very rounded form, with headlamps mounted in the wings, but after some months the mock-ups were taken to the styling studio and Ted White and his team of stylists were asked to put up counter-proposals.

Bob Saward, who had earlier joined Rootes from Ford, was put in overall charge of the project and an entirely different styling approach was immediately embarked upon. This took the form of a more angular look, with notched back, no separately identified wing forms, a strong horizontal accent, and head and tail-lamps mounted as far out as possible, in order to give the maximum feeling of width. A strong roll form was given from front to back, with a flute immediately below it. Sculptured forms surrounded the tail-lamps and a flat-opening back window was considered to be essential, to allow easy access to the parcels area behind the seat squab. Various alterations to detail were tried during the styling programme and the final design was looked upon by the design team as being both attractive and fashionable, as the squarer look was gaining ground rapidly.

While this was going on, a decision had to be made about where the new Rootes small car was going to be built. The assembly lines at the

Ryton-on-Dunsmore plant were already working at full capacity and, without dropping some of the popular medium-range models, it would have been impossible to start producing a small car there, particularly one that needed to be built in quite high numbers.

A new factory was needed. The Rootes board wanted to utilize the land on the other side of the road to their existing assembly plant at Coventry, which they had already set aside for development. The Government refused to allow planning permission, however, claiming that the land was now going to form part of the new Green Belt scheme. It was a rather lame excuse, the real reason being that, at the time, they were determined to force manufacturers to move into development areas where unemployment was running at a high level.

This policy might have been more successful if they had used a carrot instead of a big stick and had provided sufficiently attractive inducements to persuade industry to go to those areas. As it was, the inducements, by way of loans and grants, were not high enough to encourage companies to go there on their own initiative. That being the case, the Government decided that they would present any company wishing to develop with no other alternative but to do so in one of their designated development areas, by refusing to grant them Industrial Development Certificates anywhere else.

Apart from the spare land at Coventry, Rootes also had some available for development alongside their large factory complex at Dunstable, where the Group's commercial vehicles were produced. Although this site would not have been as satisfactory as the Coventry one, which would have been close to their accessory manufacturers and with plenty of skilled labour available, it was not as bad as the other two alternatives, which were to build their new factory near Liverpool, or in Scotland, somewhere in the Glasgow area.

When the Government turned down the Dunstable proposal by again refusing Rootes the necessary Industrial Development Certificate, the situation began to get desperate. To survive in the present climate when international competition in the motor industry worldwide was becoming even more fierce, a volume-produced small car seemed essential and time was running out. The Mini was gaining an increasing following of new owners, particularly among the younger element, and there was serious concern that it was getting too great a start in the small car market. It would in any case take some years to build and equip a large new factory and train a labour force, particularly if Rootes were forced to move into a development area which was new to car production. Coventry had been the centre of car production for nearly 80 years and there were generations of skilled men and women there ready to become involved in any new project, with a very good chance of making it a success in a comparatively short time. A company setting out to produce a revolutionary new design of car, in a completely new factory, in a development area with an almost totally unskilled labour force, needed all the luck it could get, and luck was something the Rootes brothers seemed finally to be running out of.

The Liverpool area was turned down because there wasn't really one good reason for going there, although Ford did later build their new assembly plant there. Linwood, near Glasgow, did have the advantage that the Pressed Steel Company, which had supplied Rootes with Hillman Minx bodies for many years, already had what was a former shadow factory on an adjoining site. They were prepared to supply the bodies for the new small car from that body plant and this would at least help to reduce the capital expenditure. The other reason for choosing Linwood was more sentimental: Billy, along with other members of the Rootes family, loved Scotland and in 1946 he had bought a large estate at Glenalmond in Perthshire.

Although the deal with Pressed Steel did help with the capital expenditure situation, that was not a large enough benefit to counteract the more serious problems presented by the considerable duplication of overheads, an unsuitable labour force, the lack of any proper industrial infrastructure in the area, and the distance between Linwood, the company's major suppliers and every other Rootes factory. Their hands were tied, however, and work went ahead on building a new factory across the road from the modern Pressed Steel body-building plant. The two factories were joined by a covered bridge straddling the main road, which had a conveyer belt system to take the bodies directly from Pressed Steel into the new Rootes assembly plant.

The plan to build the new Rootes baby car in Linwood was announced in the autumn of 1960. The factory area would cover 54,000 sq ft (5,016 sq m) and there would be a workforce of some 5,500, who would aim to produce 150,000 cars a year, more than 50 per cent of which would be earmarked for export. The whole project would cost £22 million and a £10 million assistance package, to be advanced by the Board of Trade in 1962, was to be paid back at the rate of £376,000 a year, starting in 1964.

While the factory at Linwood was being built, Rootes entered into an agreement with Carrozzeria Touring Superleggera of Italy, for them to assemble Sunbeam Alpine sports cars and Hillman Super Minx saloons at their new factory at Nova Milanese. Production went ahead there in 1962 from kits delivered to them from Coventry, with local content being increased as production began to build up. In 1963, however, they decided to build the ill-fated new Sunbeam Venezia coupé, which was based on the Humber Sceptre floorplan and running gear. The Venezia was not a success and the Humber Super Minx was also beginning to look rather outdated in a country famed for the beauty of its car styling. Sales fell and in 1964 the Italian company ran into serious financial difficulties, until it was forced to close down completely in 1966.

In the meantime, Peter Ware had joined Rootes as the new chief executive engineer and was to play a leading role in the overall concept of the Imp from then on. The design and development of the car was very much a team effort and took place over a period of nearly five years. The overall shape was functional, although aesthetically pleasing, but it was the mechanical features of the Imp which were so remarkable, for a number of reasons.

Perhaps the most fundamental problem was the siting of the engine. The team's studies indicated quite clearly that a compact engine-cum-transmission unit was the correct solution for that type of car if they were to achieve the roomiest and least complicated design within the given overall size. It would also incorporate modern trends and help them meet the tightly targeted selling price.

Having considered these implications, Peter Ware and his team decided to put the engine at the rear. Doing so gave them several advantages: the car had a nearly ideal weight distribution; there was good traction on slippery roads and gradients; and the engine position gave a more even distribution of braking power between the front and rear wheels, resulting in a better tyre wear balance than any of the more conventional front engine, front-wheel-drive models, where the front wheels took all the power and nearly all the braking.

The engine at the rear also led to increased manoeuvrability, because the absence of excessive weight at the front, made light, precise steering possible, giving quick car response. There were no driveshaft problems when taking power through the steering wheel and less noise for the driver and front passenger, who would obviously be the people most likely to spend most time in the car. There were two other important advantages: the remoteness of the petrol tank from the exhaust system certainly reduced the fire hazard, and the superior aerodynamics resulted in low wind noise and better fuel consumption. This was because the rear engine made for cleaner lines at the front, and the absence of any radiator duct there lowered the drag because air was not being forced into a forward engine compartment.

The design team was very preoccupied with the safety factor and, due to the suspension design and the way in which the major weight masses were distributed, they were able to give the Imp superb road-holding and ride. Safe cornering characteristics, with mild understeer, were the result of a careful study of the relationship between the front and rear suspensions. At the front the suspension consisted of a large, rubber-bushed, pressed steel, wishbone-type swing axle system and at the back there were rubber-bushed, pressed steel trailing arms with fully articulated driveshafts. This design gave both lightness and basic simplicity. The application of the swing axle to the front suspension led to a relatively high roll centre at the front and helped produce the stable handling characteristics they wanted for the car. The way the Imp was able to go round corners quickly, with ease and safety, was quite remarkable and became very evident later when the car was successfully raced.

With so much careful attention to detail and such wise thinking, the question which must be asked is, 'What went wrong and why wasn't the Imp the world-beater it should have been?' There were several reasons, but the first major problem was the very advanced power unit. Aluminium cylinder blocks had been used on the larger and more expensive American engines with considerable success for some years, but the Imp was the first large-scale production British car to have an all-aluminium engine, which had been chosen because it was half the weight of a comparable cast-iron unit. The lighter engine meant greater economy and it was also much easier to remove for major overhauls.

The overhead camshaft design, of the type usually only seen on more expensive cars, also had many advantages. It allowed the use of a compact and positive valve gear and a high compression ratio which contributed to the car's outstanding fuel economy. The car was fitted with a pneumatic accelerator, to give a more positive and direct throttle control, and the simple and compact design of the clutch, used in conjunction with a gearbox with powerful synchronizers on all four forward speeds, was a substantial advance in the technique of manual gear-shifting. The 875 cc engine was produced in close collaboration with Coventry Climax, whose successes with single and double overhead camshaft aluminium engines in the racing world had already spoken volumes for their knowledge in that field.

Because the aluminium engine lent itself to high productivity foundry techniques, the new die-casting plant at Linwood was completely different to any seen before in the motor industry. Die-casting can perhaps best be described as the shortest route from raw materials to finished product, and yet such a close association of metal-casting with car production was at that time unusual. It was a more common practice in the motor industry for companies to buy finished or partly finished parts from sub-contractors, and then confine the actual production of the cars within their own factories to assembly processes.

Perhaps Rootes should have realized that, with so many entirely new features in the design and production of the Imp, they were biting off more than they could chew and were being far too ambitious in their overall plans. Certainly that proved to be the case, but had they succeeded in bringing it off, the Imp might well have turned out to be the world-beater they were hoping for, and it would have been produced in one of the most modern and best-equipped factories to be found in the motor industry on either side of the Atlantic. The car and the factory would have been the envy of every motor manufacturer.

It should also be appreciated that the Mini, which was the Imp's nearest competitor, was unique in its design and already had a substantial lead in the highly competitive small car market. If the new Rootes model was to make sufficient inroads into Mini sales and break fresh ground in the market, particularly among younger car owners, it needed to have enough new features and a special appeal of its own. This would not have been possible if Rootes had gone for a more orthodox type of design and produced a car which lacked any special sales appeal. A more orthodox model with a cast-iron engine would probably not have suffered many of the reliability and production line problems the company had to cope with, but it is doubtful whether it would have caught the imagination of the public in a way which would have sold the numbers needed to make the car really profitable, and to repay the large expenditure on plant and machinery.

Rootes was faced with a timetable at Linwood which gave them no room for manoeuvre. The Duke of Edinburgh had agreed to open the new factory and the date had been set for May 1963. It was consequently essential that everyone worked to that target date and the whole project was completed on time. The company's problems began when not everything was ready for the opening day. The car looked fine and was performing well but there were still serious reliability problems, mainly concerning the water pump, which took a long time to solve. There were also difficulties with the new die-casting plant, as one might have expected in view of its advanced design and the lack of sufficient experienced staff to cope with the difficulties. This was even more disconcerting because the plan was to produce castings at Linwood for other Rootes models and provide batch production for other industries.

The labour force throughout the plant at Linwood presented a major problem, and one which was never really overcome. Because the Imp was the first car to be produced in any volume in Scotland for more than 30 years, there were not enough skilled workers available who had sufficient knowledge of assembly-line production. Many of the workers had been recruited from the local shipyards and they brought with them a dockyard mentality which they never lost, despite every attempt to impress upon them that factory life was different and that they wouldn't be working themselves out of a job if they hit production targets each week. They were also receiving more pay at Rootes than they had been used to in the shipyards and by mid-week had usually earned enough money to cover their needs for that week. The Rangers and Celtic football matches, or some other form of entertainment, then became much more important to them than any desire to go back to the factory. Absenteeism became higher as the week progressed, so that the relatively modest early production targets were never met and quality also became a problem.

Some hundreds of skilled Rootes workers had been sent to Linwood from Coventry to help train local labour and solve some of the more complex production problems, but they naturally wanted to return home as soon as possible and, when they did, they left a vacuum of really skilled and experienced staff who were capable of dealing satisfactorily with emergencies. Many of the shop stewards at the factory had been union officials in the shipyards. They were more used to confrontation than negotiation and provided a hard core of trouble-makers who felt that their main task was to fight any move by management to

improve productivity or output. Their total lack of motor industry experience proved an additional handicap during their almost daily discussions with the management.

Rootes's advertising and sales promotion for the new car was first class
and Bill Elsey and his team did their job well. Perhaps even more successful was the press and public relations campaign which was skilfully
handled by John Wilcox and his colleagues. The news that the influential and remarkably successful Rootes brothers were at last moving into
the small car market was bound to receive worldwide publicity, and it
was not surprising that the news of the problems when they became
known also received more attention than would otherwise have been
the case. The fact that Rootes's potential world-beater, which was being
made in their magnificent new Scottish factory, wasn't living up to
expectations became an even better story in some sections of the media
than news of its success would have been and it was a story which,
unlike many of the new Imps, just ran and ran.

The Scottish press, however, always remained faithful to the car and
the Linwood project. As far as they were concerned, the Imp was
Scotland's one and only car and they were prepared to defend it, Rootes
and the Linwood workforce against any amount of 'Sassenach' criticism.
Reliability did improve and the launch of the Imp saloon was followed
by a series of derivatives which were produced in abundance, including
a Singer Chamois and the Sunbeam Sport. The Hillman Californian
and Sunbeam Stiletto were also variations and had faster and lower roof
lines, the Sunbeam having four headlamps, an exclusive facia and
instrumentation, and different seating, front panel and exterior trim
changes. The opening back window was a feature on both models.

Bill Garner was sent from Coventry to take charge of production. He
was the company's most experienced manufacturing director with an
excellent track record, who had dealt successfully with the difficult
union situation at the Coventry factories. In doing so he had built a fine
reputation for fairmindedness and had a clear understanding of the
problems created by assembly-line work. It was said that he knew how
to do every process himself. He was always at the plant when the day
shift arrived in the morning, held regular meetings with his shop
stewards, often in the bar of the Rootes sports club after work, and had
succeeded in changing the working atmosphere at Coventry from one of
aggression into one of co-operation. There seemed a genuine liking for
him throughout the plant, even among some of the more left-wing
trouble-makers.

It was hoped that he would be able to do the same at Linwood, and
he very nearly succeeded. Soon after Bill Garner's move to Scotland I
persuaded Bill Morris to leave the *Daily Record* at Glasgow and join
Rootes as Head of Public Relations in Scotland. He was a former
bomber pilot who was also an experienced journalist with a good understanding of the motor industry. He would, I knew, get on well with

everyone at the plant, including the shop stewards, as well as his management colleagues. He was also very well liked by all his newspaper colleagues and, as it turned out, there couldn't have been a better choice.

He did nearly blow it on his first day, however, when he unwittingly caused problems for some of the workers which could have jeopardized the goodwill he needed to create on the factory floor as well as with management. Bill Garner had suggested on the day he arrived that he might like to spend the morning wandering around the plant to get a feel of the atmosphere and see what was being produced there, and then join him and some of the other senior staff for lunch. Bill Morris did so and reported back to Bill Garner's office in time for a pre-lunch drink.

'Well, what do you think of the place? Were you surprised at how much there is going on?' Bill Garner asked him.

'I certainly was impressed, Bill', he replied, 'and there is obviously a lot I have to learn. I didn't realize, for example, that we were making golf clubs'.

'What!' Bill Garner exclaimed. 'Golf clubs! Put down your drink and come and show me at once'.

Poor Bill Morris didn't know what to do, but Bill Garner was wise enough to realize that he would place the new public relations manager in a very invidious position if he took serious action. Instead, he told the golf-mad foreman in the die-casting department that he had better forget about his new sideline and develop any other extramural business initiatives he might have elsewhere and in his own time.

The arrival of Bill Morris at Linwood forged an even closer link between Rootes and the media. Rootes Scotland had the second-best brass band in Scotland, second only to the police, and the company's pipe major was in constant demand at local functions. He was the shortest pipe major in Scotland, being not much over 5 ft (1.5 m) tall, but that didn't affect his skill with the pipes. His height even proved a great advantage on some occasions, particularly on Burns nights at functions held on the *Garrick*, a delightful old ship moored at Glasgow which was hired out for dinners and receptions. There was so little headroom below decks that he was the only piper short enough to be able to pipe in the haggis while still remaining upright. The Scottish Guild of Motoring Writers regularly held their dinners there and Bill Morris always arranged for the company's pipe major to be in attendance.

Bill's talent for addressing the haggis meant that he was also in demand on Burns nights and, as he never liked letting people down, that sometimes entailed attending two or three different functions during the evening, with the usual dram or two of whisky at each. The *Garrick* was moored in tidal waters and the gangplank could become very steep and difficult to negotiate even when one was sober. Burns nights presented an even greater challenge to one's ability to stay upright until dry land was reached but, apart from a broken arm one year, Bill Morris always coped with those difficulties remarkably well.

The parties held on the *Garrick* by the Scottish motoring writers were notorious for their friendship and the generosity of the Guild members, particularly when characters like Bill Amos, Alistair Cameron, Jim Bowman, Jim McLaren, Jimmy Scott, Graham Gauld and Frank Walker were there. An invitation to be a guest was rarely turned down, certainly never by me, and Scottish motoring personalities like Jim Clark, Jackie Stewart and Alan Fraser were frequently among the guests.

The Imp did become a successful competition car and Alan Fraser ran a team of Imps for a number of years which raced with distinction at Brands Hatch, Goodwood, Silverstone, Snetterton, Castle Coomb, Oulton Park, Crystal Palace, Lydden and Mallory Park, usually driven by Ray Calcutt, Pete Brown and Nick Brittan. The engine size was increased and Alan Fraser Engineering, which was based at Hildenborough, did a lot of the development work. They produced a prototype GT model with a 1,100 cc engine which they code-named the K9, and they also purchased from Rootes the company's prototype Imp-based sports car which had been code-named 'The Asp'.

The Rootes Group also gave support to Roger Nathan and Paul Emery, who drove Imps to a series of victories in saloon car races. In 1965, however, Rootes entered into a three-year agreement with Alan Fraser Engineering for the development of further racing versions of the Hillman Imp and for them to take part in a comprehensive saloon car racing programme for Imps and other Rootes models in Britain and overseas. Alan Fraser was given the full official backing of the Rootes Group's engineering and competition departments. During the previous season, Fraser Imps had competed in 25 events in Britain, gaining nine overall victories and three class victories, and creating new class lap records at Brands Hatch, Lydden and Silverstone.

The Rootes Group's own competitions department was concentrating mainly on rallies with Sunbeam Rapiers and Alpines, though Rosemary Smith, the Irish driver, did win the Tulip Rally outright in her Hillman Rallye Imp in 1965. The Rallye Imps had enlarged and more powerful engines of 998 cc which produced more than 100 bhp, and the model was very successful in circuit races until it was succeeded by the Sunbeam Imp Sport.

It is interesting to speculate on what might have happened if the early Imps had been more reliable and had enjoyed the same success and reputation gained by some of the later models.

Chapter 27

The end of an era

ALTHOUGH THE PROBLEMS at Linwood and the unreliability of the early Imp models were a great disappointment, they couldn't be blamed for the weakened state of the Rootes Group during the early 1960s which led to the Rootes family's decision to become involved with the Chrysler Corporation in 1964. The real damage had been caused three years earlier, in September 1961, when a dispute which started at the company's British Steel Pressings plant at Acton developed into one of the most crippling strikes any company in the British motor industry had ever faced.

It couldn't have come at a worse time. There was a nationwide slump in new car sales and every manufacturer was finding it difficult to remain profitable. Faced with such a large drop in sales in the home market, any interference with deliveries in the export markets only made matters worse. The shop stewards at British Light Steel Pressings, no doubt concerned about possible redundancies, had demanded a 'no redundancy' agreement, refusing to discuss the alteration to production schedules necessary to cope with the drop in sales. Ignoring the instructions of their national leaders, they called all their members out on an unofficial strike which lasted for 13 weeks.

Their action had an immediate knock-on effect on production at other Rootes locations where the pressings were needed for car and truck production, and thousands were thrown out of work in the company's own factories and those of their major suppliers. A number of unauthorized stoppages at the Acton plant had already taken place that year and Billy was convinced, probably with good reason, that the disruptions were communist-inspired. Labour relations generally within the group had been good, but Acton had been the exception. The shop stewards there had been particularly aggressive, with walk-outs taking place without warning.

A note of weariness and pessimism began to appear in even Billy Rootes's normally buoyant nature after the strike had been going on for more than two months, and towards the end of November he sacked all the strikers and opened a recruiting office in Acton to take on replacements. In a statement issued to the strikers and the press he said: 'The challenge to industrial law and order is such that the directors have no alternative but to oppose it'.

He was sure that they were dealing with industrial anarchy and that if they gave in to the shop stewards' demands at Acton repercussions might be seen in other factories. Some of the shop stewards there were also disgruntled because of the action which had been necessary to deal with the national situation, and which was being taken throughout the motor industry. Although the shop stewards at the other plants had been flexing their industrial muscle, the workers had so far refused to take unofficial action.

It was a courageous stand for the Rootes board to take, but also a very expensive one. It eventually cost the company more than 50,000 cars and £3 million in lost profits. From making a pre-tax profit during the financial year to 31 July 1961, despite the heavy outlay at Linwood, the Group made a substantial loss in the 12-month period to 31 July 1962 and a further loss of £200,000 in the next year. The lack of profits to finance new models put the company's whole future in jeopardy.

The tragedy was that the British Light Steel Pressings strike was a disaster for everyone, except of course the Group's competitors. Rootes lost the money it badly needed to help finance its essential new small car project as well as other new models; the strikers achieved no benefit for themselves; and few of the shop stewards who were sacked got their jobs back when the strike ended at the end of November. It was the first of many unofficial strikes which brought the British motor industry to its knees, called at the whim of the shop stewards without any thought to the permanent damage their action could inflict on their companies and the long-term future of their members.

Media attention often seemed to give the shop stewards delusions of grandeur to which they were not entitled. It gave them the impression that they could ignore the wishes of their national union leaders and disregard any union agreement if they felt they could get away with their actions. Stoppages over such minor complaints as cracked cups were not uncommon during the 1960s and '70s.

The other car manufacturers in Britain admired the stand which Rootes took against the Acton shop stewards and were grateful that the company had won such a crucial battle, because it helped them with their own problems at a time of volatile labour relations within the industry. When the strike ended, the many hundreds of letters of congratulations which Billy Rootes received included messages of thanks from other company chairmen. When I suggested to him that the letters showed their solidarity with him he just smiled, shook his head and said, 'They know I had no option, but it was nice of them to write,' then added, 'but it would have been nicer if they had included a cheque'. His feelings were understandable. Everyone in the industry would benefit from the stand he had just made, but it was Rootes who had paid the price, even though they could least afford to do so, with their heavy commitments in Scotland and elsewhere.

Just how high a price became evident later. The market for cars declined during the early 1960s and international competition became increasingly fierce, particularly from the Japanese. The financial pressures involved in competing on a world basis for a family-controlled manufacturing company like Rootes became so great that it was difficult to see how they could survive.

In the spring of 1964, when Rootes was approached by Chrysler International in Geneva with a view to some form of amalgamation, both Geoffrey and Brian recommended to their father and uncle and other members of the board that they should enter into negotiations with the American company. It was, perhaps, the fact that the suggestion had come from the younger members of the family that persuaded Billy and Reggie to treat the invitation seriously. The future of the Group would eventually be in their hands and their feelings needed to be considered if the family was going to dilute its shareholding for the first time.

The original Chrysler car had made its appearance in 1924 and created a sensation on both sides of the Atlantic because of its remarkable performance, which was way ahead of any other make of car at anywhere near the same price. Walter P. Chrysler conjured $50 million out of the Chase Securities Corporation and his Chrysler Corporation came into existence in 1925.

He took over the Maxwell Company, which had hit difficult times during the post-war depression of the early 1920s, and also bought Dodge, whose two brothers, John and Horace, had both unfortunately died a few years earlier. By doing so, Walter P. Chrysler put his company firmly alongside the other two big-time car manufacturers, Ford and General Motors. He had been friendly with Billy Rootes during the 1930s until the time of his death and Rootes and Chrysler had continued to liaise on various projects during the post-war period.

During May 1964 Henry Ford II also came to Britain and had meetings with Billy Rootes, but the discussions were over the provision of American Ford V8 engines for Rootes's Sunbeam Tiger sports car, and not about any form of amalgamation. Even so, the meetings did provoke a considerable amount of speculation which was increased when Billy visited Detroit the following month. A long period of negotiations with Chrysler did follow, however, with discussions being held in both Detroit and London. Rootes were advised during these discussions by Lazards as their merchant bankers, Casenoves as their stockbrokers and Linklater & Payne as their lawyers.

Heads of Agreement were eventually finalized and Billy and Reggie Rootes flew to New York, accompanied by Rupert Hammond, to conclude the necessary formal details, while Geoffrey remained behind in

London to keep contact with the banks, stockbrokers and lawyers, as well as the financial press and the rest of the media.

The broad outline of the agreement was that the Rootes family would sell to Chrysler Corporation a considerable block of their equity shares, but not enough to give the American company control. To prevent this, the family retained a sufficient number of voting shares, which was made possible because the equity capital had been divided into voting and non-voting shares. Chrysler had the right to nominate a number of directors to the Rootes board and in return would provide the British company with advice, particularly in the important field of manufacturing engineering.

Billy Rootes was determined that the Rootes family should retain control and he refused to sell any further shares, even though by doing so he and the rest of the family would have been better off by several million pounds. Rupert Hammond told me later that Billy was far from happy about the deal even so, and had telephoned him late at night on the day they had signed the agreement to tell him so and to ask if there was any way in which they could rescind the deal. Rupert Hammond recalled that when he told Billy there was no way of going back on the agreement, he sighed and said,'I just hope we have done the right thing, but I feel we may all live to regret the involvement with Chrysler. I wish we could do something about it, but I suppose you are right and there is nothing we can do now'.

It would certainly not have been a bad deal had the working arrangement with Chrysler operated satisfactorily. This unfortunately did not happen, and animosity began building up between the two companies within a few months of the signing. Members of the Rootes family got on well with George Love, the Chrysler chairman, but the chief executive and effective head of the corporation was Lyn Townsend, and their relationship with him was far from happy. At the time, Townsend had a high reputation within the American motor industry, but events did prove that Billy and Reggie's judgement of him was correct, and the Chrysler Corporation went through very difficult times under his chairmanship.

When he returned to England in July with his brother and Rupert Hammond, Billy Rootes still appeared to be in good health, although he was only a month away from his 70th birthday. He decided to take a well-earned holiday with his wife and chartered a yacht in the Mediterranean from Onassis, called *The Sister Ann*, for a cruise in the more peaceful waters off the French coast. What should have been a happy holiday turned to tragedy when in September he slipped and fell down a companionway, striking his head on a beam and badly cutting his forehead. He was taken to hospital and, although the fall had given him a very considerable shock, initially he appeared to recover. He was host at a new model reception at Devonshire House before leaving for the Paris Motor Show in October, but he was obviously extremely unwell during the show, and on returning to London was taken to the

London Clinic, where his illness was diagnosed as cancer of the liver. The accident on the yacht was thought to have contributed to the speed with which the cancer developed, and he went downhill rapidly.

He was moved from the London Clinic to his London home in Shepherd's Close and died there on 12 December 1964. It was, perhaps, ironic that a man who had always disliked taking holidays should have met his untimely death partly as a result of one. While he was on holiday he also received the sad news that his first wife, Nora, who was Geoffrey and Brian's mother, had died in London.

The shock of Billy Rootes's death extended far beyond the motoring world. The Bishop of Coventry spoke of him as being 'a shining example of someone who loved life and all that is in it'. Sir Patrick Hennessy, chairman of the Ford Motor Company in Britain, said: 'He did his stint for his country in war and gave more of his time to the motor industry in peace than anyone else I knew.' The newspapers referred to him as 'the greatest salesman in the history of the motor industry', and frequently used the word 'genius'. Sir Miles Thomas wrote:

'The death of Lord Rootes is an inestimable loss, not only to the British motor industry, but the whole British trading and diplomatic world as well. He was always spontaneously chosen to lead business delegations and to be the chairman at serious business discussions involving the whole question of trade. To the legion of us to whom he was a friend and colleague, his death leaves a gap that can never be filled. He was a businessman who radiated sheer energy, yet he always made it plain that, while acknowledging the importance of mechanisation, he knew instinctively that men were more important than machines'.

Sir William Lyons, the chairman of Jaguar, referred to him as 'a dynamic worker, not only for the British motor industry but for the country as a whole, and people in many walks of life would be the poorer for his passing'. George Harriman, the head of the British Motor Corporation, said: 'We all admired him as a first-class competitor and one of the best salesmen in the motor industry, but the country ought also to be grateful for all his efforts to increase exports, particularly to the dollar areas.' The president of the Society of Motor Manufacturers and Traders, William Swallow, chairman of Vauxhall Motors, added: 'Everyone was always impressed by his dynamic energy and infectious enthusiasm, and he never allowed us to become complacent.'

His death was also felt deeply in many other areas away from business life. In the early 1960s he had held a series of lunches and dinners in London, mostly at Devonshire House, which were attended by a number of distinguished contemporary figures, including Sir Oliver Franks, Bill Williams, then Warden of All Souls, Oliver Littleton, Aiden Crawley and Sir Archibald Forbes. A fund-raising campaign was organized which eventually resulted in the foundation of Warwick University. Jack Butterworth, then Bursar and Fellow of New College, Oxford, and who later became Lord Butterworth, was chosen as the first Vice-Chancellor. In the January before his death Billy Rootes became Chancellor elect, and accepted the stiff challenge of making sure there was enough money available for the university to be finished on time and for the right staff to be appointed.

Like his brother, he also never lost touch with Cranbrook School, where they were both educated, and always gave the school his active support. During visits there he would urge the boys to 'work and think hard and never take no for an answer'.

Throughout his life Billy never lost his keen interest in the land. Not only was he a successful farmer, but the Hampshire Down sheep and Aberdeen Angus cattle which he bred on his estates at Hungerford and Glenalmond were exported to countries throughout the world. For many years he was president of the Aberdeen Angus Society and of the Smithfield Show, and he attended the reception held at the Dorchester Hotel in London on the eve of the Royal Dairy Show only a few weeks before he died. His farms were always models of efficiency and were frequently visited by members of Young Farmers Clubs and students from agricultural colleges who were keen to learn from the methods he used so successfully. His dairy herd topped Britain's national milk record on three occasions and his Hampshire Down sheep also established a new record by winning the Supreme Championship at the Smithfield Show for four successive years. It was a bull from his Aberdeen Angus herd that probably gave him most pleasure, when it set a new price record for any animal of any breed when it was sold at Perth Sales in 1955.

The bull and Billy received some less welcome publicity several months later, however, when the Scottish farmer who had bought the beast announced that he was going to sue Billy, because the bull had been put to five heifers without result, and was obviously impotent. Paddy Ryan, an Irishman with a wonderful sense of humour who worked in the Rootes public relations department, brought in a copy of the paper containing the story and said: 'Billy isn't going to like that, is he? You know what he is going to say? "There you are! If I don't do the job myself it never gets done properly." '

I dined out on the joke afterwards on numerous occasions, particularly among Billy's farming friends, but it was not until some years later, when the two of us were dining alone one evening at his London home, that I plucked up enough courage to tell him. We'd had several glasses of his best port and he seemed in the right frame of mind to enjoy the joke. Billy listened in silence and then to my relief got up from the table and stomped round the room, guffawing loudly. Then he suddenly stopped. 'You tell them the rest of the story, don't you, John?' I was puzzled and started to explain that as far as I knew there wasn't any more to tell, when he began to look annoyed. 'You must tell people the end of the story or you will ruin my reputation as a breeder,' he insisted. 'Tell them that the bull was cured and has already bred three champions.' I promised that I would and he looked relieved. 'Don't forget, will you, John?' he said as I got up to go. 'That's an important part of the story, don't you agree?'

Reggie Rootes was also a successful farmer with a pedigree Jersey herd at his estate in Kent.

Billy Rootes was cremated at Golders Green on Saturday 15 December, at a service attended only by members of his family. A memorial service was held later in London and was attended by industrialists and business leaders from all over the world. Ramsbury Manor, his 'perfect Charles II house' at Hungerford, together with its 460 acres in the heart of the Kennet Valley which he had bought from the Earl of Wilton in 1964, was sold to Harry Hyams, the London property dealer. At nearly £300,000 it was the most expensive English country house to change hands since the war, almost £100,000 more than Paul Getty had paid for Sutton Place in 1959.

Geoffrey and Brian arranged to share Glenalmond, his magnificent country estate in Scotland. Geoffrey took Glenalmond House and the portion of the estate to the east of the Crieff–Amulree road, while Brian took the portion of the estate to the west, which contained the two best grouse shoots and a delightful secondary house called Dallick. The two brothers continued to operate the estate in that way until Brian's death in 1971, after which Geoffrey kept Glenalmond House and his share of the estate until 1981, when it too was sold.

Woods Mews, Billy's London house, was also divided up into two apartments. Geoffrey and Marian had the ground floor and Brian and his wife Bet occupied the first floor. The roof garden above was also divided into two.

A major reconstruction of the top management of the Rootes Group was announced in January 1965 and Reggie Rootes took over as chairman. Geoffrey, who had succeeded to the title, took his seat in the House of Lords and became deputy chairman as well as managing director, and Peter Catchpole became company secretary on the retirement of Bill Rankine

The major reorganization, however, affected the administrative structure, for it was decided that from then on the Group would be administered in three operating divisions. The Overseas Operations and Home Distributing Division would have Brian Rootes as managing director; the Passenger Car Division was under the control of Timothy Rootes; and the Commercial Vehicle Division was headed up by Rex Watson Lee, the managing director of Commer cars and an old friend of Geoffrey's from army days. Watson Lee had commanded a tank transporter column in the Western desert and was one of the youngest lieutenant colonels in the British Army. He had been Geoffrey's personal assistant in Coventry when he had become managing director of Humber and the head of the Group's Manufacturing Division. The strengthening of the top management was intended to bring the Group more into line with modern concepts of industrial administration, instead of relying on what had been called the semi-feudal approach to which Billy Rootes, a rugged individualist, had insisted on clinging very firmly.

John Panks was brought back from America to run the Overseas Operations and Home Distributing Companies and was replaced in New York by Malcolm Freshney. His place as managing director of Rootes Canada was taken by E. J. B. Mackie, an executive of Rootes Motors Inc., and George Hartwell became managing director of the Home Division, with Geoffrey Rossiter as administrative director. In Scotland Bill Garner took over as director and general manager from George Cattell, who returned to Coventry as managing director of Humber Limited.

Without Billy's presence, the directors' floor in Devonshire House, still referred to by everyone as 'The Green Belt' because of its sage carpeting, seemed strangely quiet. John Wilcox once referred to him stomping round the building like some 'gouty tiger' who never walked, but bounded about the place. The moment he came into a room he created an atmosphere of optimism, and it was this feeling of optimism which was now lacking. Everybody knew that the flair with which he had overcome problems was no longer there, and there was no-one to take his place.

He had always had a remarkable knack of dealing with people. During the talk of a slump in 1960, his immediate reaction was, 'They should get on their feet and fight as I am fighting. I am sick and tired of the moans that the British motor industry is dead. We are very much alive and kicking.' He also dealt with disgruntled customers in his own inimitable style and would no doubt have coped much better with the growing number of complaints about the Imp. On many occasions I heard him ask Charles Morris to bring in the complaints file he kept in the top drawer of his desk. It was usually early evening, when people were at home having dinner. Billy would insist on dialling the call himself and, when they answered, he apologized for telephoning them at that hour, explaining that as he was still in his office he wanted to deal with their complaint personally. Within a few minutes he usually had the customer agreeing to see a salesman the following day with a view to doing a deal on a new car. As one customer said in a letter to the *Sunday Times*: 'It seemed to us remarkable that Lord Rootes should have found time to make the telephone call himself, ignoring the usual medium of secretary or assistant, to a complete stranger whose name could have meant nothing to him.'

As Billy had predicted, the deal with Chrysler did turn sour, and the hoped-for advantages did not materialize. It was no real surprise to anyone when in 1967 Chrysler Corporation bought another tranche of shares and obtained control of Rootes.

Chapter 28

Farewell to Rootes and Chrysler

THE TAKEOVER OF the Rootes Group by the Chrysler Corporation led to the retirement of Sir Reginald Rootes from the company which he and his brother had started nearly 50 years earlier. His retirement was not unexpected. He had already passed his 70th birthday and wasn't willing to remain at the head of an organization which would now be controlled from Detroit. He had always been at the centre of the decision making and the passive role of a figure-head did not appeal to him.

Sir Reginald had understandably had enough of the cut and thrust of business life and wanted more time to relax and enjoy his new hobby. He was a keen amateur photographer and photographic equipment had been among the retirement gifts he received during the farewell party at the Ritz arranged by some of the people who had worked with him over the years. It was a nostalgic occasion: many knew that they too would soon be leaving the company and they recognized that his departure marked the end of an era for Rootes and the motor industry.

Three of those who left were his own son Timothy, Billy's younger son Brian and his son Bill, who had become the fourth generation of the family to work for the company. The Chrysler influence was evident in the make-up of the new Rootes board, which now included Angus Murray of The Prudential, Lord Inchyra, who as Sir Frederick Hoyer Millar had been head of the Diplomatic Service, Daniel Meinertzhagen of Lazards, Sir Eric Roll, who later became Lord Roll of Ipsden, and Rupert Hammond, who had been the Rootes financial director for nearly 40 years. There were also several overseas directors, including Louis Warren, a prominent New York lawyer, Irv Minette, who co-ordinated Chrysler's international activities, Tom Morrow, another Chrysler director, and Georges Hereil, who was managing director of Simca in France and had previously been head of Sud Aviation. The company still had a Lord Rootes as chairman, but this time it was Billy's eldest son Geoffrey, who had been persuaded by the family to stay and look after the interests of the minority shareholders.

The presence on the Rootes board of so many influential personalities gave the impression that Chrysler was trying to appease critics in the government who had been vociferous in their claim that a fine old British company like Rootes should not have been allowed to fall into foreign hands. Ford and Vauxhall were American-owned and the critics were concerned that a third motor manufacturing company was now going the same way.

Much of the criticism came from union and left-wing sources, who feared that the Americans might prove tougher adversaries when it came to shop-floor bargaining and would try to inflict their own form of productivity agreements on the Rootes plants. There was a lot of huffing and puffing, but few grounds for preventing the deal from going through. Approaches had been made to Sir Donald Stokes to see whether the Leyland–Triumph–Rover combine might take a stake in Rootes, but he already had plans for the British Motor Corporation and Jaguar, and the Linwood project remained a daunting challenge to any motor manufacturer. The problems inflicted on Rootes by strikes, many of them unofficial, during the previous six years had been enough to frighten off any British buyers and it was only because Chrysler already had a large investment in the company, and had been trying to get the same sort of foothold in Britain and Europe that their main competitors Ford and General Motors already enjoyed, that the Rootes deal was attractive to them.

With so many eminent people on the company's new board, and with a member of the Rootes family as chairman, Chrysler hoped that the company would still have the semblance of being British. However, they needed a good professional managing director with the strength and personality to carry through the considerable changes they planned to make in almost every aspect of the company. The man they chose was Gilbert Hunt, the managing director of Massey Ferguson in Coventry, who knew the motor industry, had a good knowledge of American business methods and had the reputation of being an efficient administrator. He also spoke good French and Spanish.

Few Chrysler executives spoke a foreign language and most would have had difficulty in ordering a meal in any language other than English. Georges Hereil was a very astute businessman who spoke good English, and Chrysler wanted the managing director of Rootes to sit on the board of their French company, Simca, and help to create a closer working relationship between the two companies. Their company in Spain was still being run by a Spanish entrepreneur who resembled Billy Rootes in some ways, although Billy would never have gone to the lengths of having a telescope installed on the verandah outside his dining room at the factory, so that he could see whether the men were late arriving back for work while he was at lunch. Bill Brownell, the Spanish company's head of public relations, was an American who spoke the language fluently and was able to deal with visiting Chrysler executives.

The appointment of Georges Hereil to the Rootes board did pose some problems for the British company because, quite understandably, the French wanted to play the leading Chrysler role in Europe. Because of this they were not averse to turning the problems of Rootes to their own advantage in the media, including the British press, at a time when Rootes was trying to keep a low profile. Simca's public relations chief, Joe Ris, had also spent time in America and spoke good English. This made it easier for British television and news media to send people to Paris when they wanted to find out about Rootes. When Georges Hereil was interviewed about the European motoring scene, he could usually be persuaded to talk freely about Chrysler's new British company.

It was some time before we were able to stop him doing this, but in fairness to the French, the executives of Simca and the Spanish company were very fed up with the continuing industrial relations problems and the frequent strikes taking place at Rootes which affected the overall profits of Chrysler in Europe. Simca was almost strike-free and the situation was the same in Spain. It was only in Britain that strikes occurred and the media were already beginning to refer to strikes as 'the British disease'. Simca executives also resented the decision to move the headquarters of Chrysler International from Geneva to London.

I met Gilbert Hunt on a number of occasions while attempts were being made to persuade him to join Rootes. I usually drove to Massey Ferguson in a different make of car so that people there wouldn't realize I was from Rootes and put two and two together. I was pleased when he finally accepted the job and looked forward to working closely with him. Gilbert Hunt was appointed managing director and chief executive officer, which rather pointedly confirmed that he was in full command. When the news was announced, he invited me to join the new eight-man Executive Committee he was going to form, which would be responsible for the day-to-day running of the company.

The formation of the Executive Committee was a shrewd move, because it not only gave Gilbert Hunt immediate access to information, it also ensured that the people in charge of all the main activities of the company, including sales and marketing, manufacturing, personnel, industrial relations, engineering, finance, purchasing and public relations, knew exactly what was going on and what was expected of them.

Decisions made at Executive Committee meetings had to be adhered to and attendance was always obligatory. Deputies were never allowed to attend on behalf of their superiors and strict confidentiality had to be observed. The plan worked very well and all executives knew they had access to the decision-makers, which in turn led to better internal relations and a feeling that the company was not being run by people they rarely saw and probably didn't know, who only met occasionally for board meetings.

Executive Committee meetings could be called at short notice to deal with pressing problems and to pass information quickly down the line.

Gilbert Hunt proved to be a very able administrator and created a very good impression both within the company and with Chrysler in Detroit. He also got on well with Geoffrey Rootes. Any feeling of animosity between them would have made life difficult for many of us. I had enjoyed Geoffrey's friendship for many years and would not have wanted to jeopardize that relationship by having to take sides in any issue between the two of them.

Gilbert Hunt knew this, and that he also had my full support and loyalty. I was never called upon to take sides and, to my knowledge, neither were any of the other Rootes executives. Most of us admired Geoffrey for the way in which he had accepted what must have been a difficult situation. Passing the control of the company over to a relative stranger and giving him full support took courage, particularly as it was the first time in more than 50 years that Rootes was being run by someone who was not a member of the Rootes family.

It was unfortunate that the calibre of some of the Chrysler executives who were sent to Britain during the late 1960s was not so high. Too many of them looked upon the posting as a means of educating their children free of charge and being able to live in a style which was considerably higher than they would have enjoyed in Detroit. Many of them had no experience of living outside America and refused to adapt to the British way of life and methods of working. Their flamboyant lifestyles, at a time when their British colleagues were being asked to cut back and accept tighter budgets and further redundancies for their staff, showed a lack of understanding which led to an anti-American feeling in some quarters which could have been avoided.

Everyone dreaded the annual PIP, or Profit Improvement Programme, which was decided in Detroit with little or no consultation. Every department had to accept a percentage cut in personnel each year, even if that department had been given additional responsibilities and was already understaffed.

The easy answer seemed to be to get rid of junior and secretarial staff because the reductions were usually based on head-counts rather than cost. Departments consequently tended to become less efficient each year, because there were not enough secretaries or clerical staff to deal effectively with correspondence and requests for information. It was a weakness in the system which led to many problems. I had been forewarned, and overcame the situation by getting agreement for additional staff before the annual cuts were announced. Instead of making the appointments, I struck their job titles off the department head-count when the time came to show the required percentage cut in manpower. It worked like a charm and everyone seemed satisfied. Certainly members of my staff didn't have the awful feeling that they might be the ones to be made redundant when the next PIP arrived from Detroit. Some departments got to the point where the staff used to ask, 'What will they want this time—an arm or a leg?'

I was also fortunate that John Ford, who was Chrysler Corporations' vice-president in charge of public relations, made very infrequent trips to Europe, and the executive responsible for co-ordinating the corporation's international public relations was John Guenther, who liked Europe and knew it well, having been to university at Tuebingen in Germany. He was one of the few senior Chrysler executives who could speak a foreign language fluently. He was also a very experienced and capable public relations executive with considerable charm and good-natured humour. John Guenther was liked by all the members of my staff and we became close friends. Apart from appreciating the problems we were facing at Rootes, I knew he could also be relied upon to look after our interests in Detroit.

Bill Elsey, the Rootes advertising director, found a novel way of solving his annual PIP problem. He did a deal with the company's London advertising agency and they took 60 per cent of his advertising staff onto their own books. He then had his advertising budget increased to cover the cost of their salaries and overheads. It cost the company much more, but Chrysler was delighted to see an advertising department down to only a handful of permanent staff. Those who moved over to the advertising agency were also very pleased with the deal, because most of them ended up with higher salaries, bigger cars and larger pensions. Bill Elsey spent all his working life at Rootes, apart from the war when he flew bombers, and was one of the most able and well-liked executives in the company. He had many friends worldwide and his death at a comparatively early age came as a great shock. I doubt that he ever made an enemy and he was certainly very highly regarded by Billy and Reggie Rootes, not least for his remarkable capacity for hard work.

Chrysler seemed to want to remove all traces of Rootes as it had been in the days of Billy and Reggie. All the company's fine antique furniture was replaced by modern steel equipment, even Billy's famous desk without drawers. He always insisted that drawers in a desk invited people to hide work which they hadn't had time to deal with, or which presented too much of a problem. He was right, of course, but he was always prepared to work late at night to ensure that that didn't happen. That was probably why he needed three secretaries.

The portraits in the boardroom at Devonshire House of Mr Hillman, Mr Humber, Mr Singer and Mr Thrupp, which had been looking down on the company's directors for nearly 40 years, disappeared, and within a while the headquarters of the company was also moved from Devonshire House to Bowater House in Knightsbridge. Perhaps they were trying to lay a ghost, but to many people it was all done too suddenly and brought to an early end the loyalty which the name of Rootes still conjured up in Britain and elsewhere among customers and Rootes dealers throughout the world. Many of those dealers had been selling Rootes cars and trucks since the 1920s and '30s, and their support was needed as much in 1967 as at any time in the company's history.

The Chrysler influence became apparent in the Rootes styling department at Coventry as early as September 1965, when it was decided to display the corporation's own corporate identity, a five-pointed 'pentastar' symbol, on all the cars and in the sales and advertising literature. A major corporate identity programme then followed in 1967 when pentastars began appearing everywhere, including on dealer premises. Executives were expected to wear pentastar badges, a request treated as a joke by many members of staff, who insisted that they hadn't worn badges in their lapels since they were children. There were stock answers to the question 'Where's your pentastar?', two of which were 'I must have left it on my pyjamas' and 'I have a plastic one and it must have dropped off in the bath'. In some quarters the pentastar was also referred to rather irreverently as 'the puckered arse', but it was surprising how many of them appeared in lapels when the Chrysler president paid a visit. There were obviously times when promotion took priority over protest.

The pentastar campaign was well planned and orchestrated throughout all the Chrysler companies in Europe and did make a lot of sense. The Chrysler name didn't mean much in Europe at that time and there were very few Chrysler cars or Dodge trucks being sold there. Putting a Chrysler badge or insignia on dealers' premises and on all the vehicles produced by Chrysler's European companies did help to get the name more widely known. It was, however, difficult for Chrysler executives to accept that a company and cars which were so well known in America and Canada should still mean so little in Europe, compared with names like Humber, Hillman, Sunbeam, Singer, Simca, Commer, Karrier and, of course, Rootes. The fact that the popularity of those names had been built up over a period spanning more than half a century, creating a considerable amount of brand loyalty in the process, didn't seem to matter to them. Neither did the knowledge that General Motors had wisely decided to build on the reputation gained by Vauxhall cars, and even Ford took some time to become established in Europe.

When the British Motor Corporation took over Pressed Steel, Rootes bought the company's pressings plant alongside their car assembly plant at Linwood and turned the two factories into one integrated unit. As a result, a new company called Rootes Pressings (Scotland) Limited came into being on 1 January 1966, about a year before Chrysler bought control of the Rootes Group. The British Light Steel Pressings factory at Acton was closed down and sold off when the production of the large Humber Hawk and Super Snipe models came to an end in 1967. There was little regret about the decision on the Rootes board, as the place had continued to be a hive of discontent, with the shop stewards refusing to accept coloured workers, among other problems. By the end of 1968, bodies for the new Arrow range of cars, which included the Hillman Hunter, Minx, Humber Sceptre, Singer Vogue and Sunbeam Rapier, were being made at Linwood and shipped by special freight trains to the siding at Gosford Green, close to the Humber factory at

Coventry, for assembly at the Ryton-on-Dunsmore plant. Engines and transmissions for the Imp models were then sent on the 300-mile (483-km) return trip to Linwood.

In August 1967 the famous old Thrupp & Maberly plant at Cricklewood had been closed down, and this streamlining process continued throughout the late 1960s until the 30 or so separate operating companies had been replaced by just two—Rootes Motors Limited and Rootes Pressings (Scotland) Limited.

The deal which Rootes had done with the National Industrial Manufacturing Company in Iran, to allow the assembly of Rootes cars there, was extended in October 1968, when the Shah decreed that only three sizes of car should be made in the country—large, medium and small. Rootes was awarded the medium contract for Hillman Hunters to be assembled from kits shipped there from Coventry and sold as Paykans. At one stage the Shah also agreed that 30,000 fully assembled cars could also be shipped to Teheran to deal with additional demand. The Hunters were landed at the wrong port, which meant that they had to be driven over the mountains to reach their destination. There weren't enough experienced drivers available, however, and many hundreds of them and their cars ended up at the bottom of ravines. John Guenther and I had had experience of the standard of driving in Teheran when we were driven by company chauffeurs each day between the Hilton Hotel and the factory during the week when new extensions at the plant were being opened by the Shah, so the fate of the Hunters and their over-exuberant drivers came as no surprise. The agreement continued after the Shah had been deposed and earned Rootes and Chrysler a considerable amount of valuable foreign currency until the mid-1980s.

Roy Axe, who styled the new Sunbeam Rapier which was launched in 1967, was one of the few Englishmen to make it to Detroit, when his undoubted talents were quickly recognized by Chrysler Corporation. Peter Ware, who had so much to do with the design of the Imp, was replaced as technical director by Cyril Weighell, and Harry Sheron, who was made head of design, later succeeded Cyril Weighell.

Hillman sales got a big boost in 1968 when a Hunter driven by Andrew Cowan and Colin Malkin won the first London–Sydney marathon. The victory came as a complete surprise as the company only had a single entry. Rootes had not intended to take part at all, but had been persuaded to do so by the *Daily Express*, who were sponsoring the 11,500-mile (18,503-km) event. Bill Elsey and I were having a drink in the Wellington Club in Knightsbridge on the evening that news of the victory was announced on the radio. We dashed back to the office to prepare press releases and arrange for advertisements to be set for the following day's papers. Bill Elsey, like everyone else, had thought our chances of winning with a single entry were so slim that he hadn't arranged for any space to be reserved in the national morning and evening papers.

We were so unprepared for the Hunter's success that the marathon was the only International event for nearly thirty years that we hadn't filmed when our cars were taking part! Fortunately Ford had a strong entry, being hot favourites to win, and had filmed every section of the route. Barrie Gill, their Marketing Manager, came to our rescue and provided us with enough footage to make up into a good promotional film. Before joining Ford Barrie had been a successful Fleet Street journalist. He pioneered the company's first comprehensive sponsorship programme and it was typical of his thorough approach to every event that all aspects of the London to Sydney had been so well covered for promotional purposes. He went on to become Chairman and Chief Executive of the CSS Group, one of the top corporate sponsorship service organisations in Europe, who handle the World Championship winning Formula 1 racing team of Frank Williams and also successfully introduced truck racing into Britain.

The London–Sydney was certainly a brilliant victory for Hillman and Andrew Cowan agreed to drive the same car 25 years later when he took part in the anniversary event. The winning Hunter had spent the intervening years on loan to the Royal Scottish Automobile Club. The event director of the 1993 Lombard-sponsored London–Sydney marathon was Nick Brittan, who had been one of Alan Fraser's team of drivers that raced Hillman Imps with such success for many years.

The last model to be styled while Rootes was still under the control of the Rootes family was the Hillman Avenger. Rex Fleming was the stylist and the car was completely new from nose to tail. The Ryton-on-Dunsmore plant was modernized specially for the Avenger and a completely new assembly line was installed. Chrysler had virtually nothing to do with the original design and, unlike the Imp, the Avenger proved to be almost trouble-free from the day it was launched in February 1970. It was a very conventional car, which probably accounted for its reliability, and it had a 1,496 cc or a more powerful 1,725 cc engine. Both were new from top to bottom. We launched the Avenger in Malta, flying in groups of motoring writers and dealers and their wives every 48 hours over a period of three weeks. Ted Ray, John Le Mesurier, Ami MacDonald and Lionel Blair provided the entertainment each evening and the presentation and launch was acknowledged to be one of the most successful of all the new models that year. Film of the presentation was flown back to England to be prepared for use at special dealer presentations throughout Europe.

The Avenger had several derivatives and was sold as a two-door or four-door saloon and as a five-door estate car. During the next 11 years more than a million of them were made. More than 50,000 were built between February and August 1970 and a total of nearly 650,000 were sold in seven years. It was marketed in America as the Cricket during the early 1970s and as a Sunbeam in some of the other overseas markets. The car was rebadged as a Chrysler in 1976 and then rebadged again as a Talbot in 1979. There was also a hatchback version produced in 1977. Billy and Reggie Rootes deserved a considerable amount of credit for the success of the Avenger in its various forms. It was the last model they planned together, and was known at the time as the 'B Car Project'.

Geoffrey Rootes remained with the company until 1973, when he was succeeded as chairman by Gilbert Hunt. For seven years he had ensured that the interests of the British shareholders were protected, but when Chrysler Corporation bought out the minority shareholders by means of a Scheme of Arrangement in 1973, he felt that he had fulfilled his obligations to the shareholders and resigned. He joined the board of Lucas Industries and Rank Hovis McDougall soon afterwards, eventually resigning both directorships in the mid-1980s. Like his father, he was also very involved with dollar exports and had become chairman of the American Committee of the British National Export Council in 1969, paying several visits to America in that capacity. He eventually resigned the chairmanship in 1972 when the BNEC was disbanded and a new body called the British Overseas Trade Board was formed.

Following the Rootes tradition, he had also served as president of the Society of Motor Manufacturers and Traders in 1960 and 1961 and played a leading role in many of the Society's activities. In 1976 he suffered a stroke while on holiday at Tignes, when skiing at too high an altitude for his age. He made a good recovery, however, and within a few months was able to resume a normal life.

When he died in January 1992 at the age of 74, his son Nicholas succeeded to the title. Brian Rootes had died of a heart attack at his Scottish home on New Year's Eve in 1971. He was only 52. Sir Reginald Rootes spent several happy years in retirement and was 86 when he died in December 1977.

The Rootes name disappeared in 1970 when it was dropped from the title of both companies, which then became known as Chrysler United Kingdom Limited and Chrysler Linwood Limited. The names of all the famous Rootes cars and commercial vehicles were also dropped in 1977, and from then onwards only Chrysler cars and Dodge trucks were marketed.

Chrysler was unable to prevent a serious series of strikes in Coventry and Linwood which continued to cripple production. This caused heavy financial losses and prevented the company from taking full advantage of the increase in demand for all their products. It was not surprising that, after getting into deep financial difficulties in America in 1978, Chrysler Corporation decided to dispose of its European organization and Chrysler United Kingdom Limited was then sold to the French Peugeot company. The Linwood complex never succeeded in becoming really profitable and was finally closed down in 1981.

The large commercial vehicle plant at Dunstable was bought by Renault, who produced their medium range truck models there until

1993 when all production at the factory ceased.

The assembly lines at Ryton-on-Dunsmore in Coventry, where the Rootes brothers produced their Humber, Hillman, Sunbeam and Singer models, are now turning out French Peugeot cars and the old Humber Road factory is producing parts for them. It is perhaps ironic that one of the first cars William Rootes sold more than 90 years ago when he started his motor business was a French de Dion Bouton.

Index

THE ROOTES BROTHERS